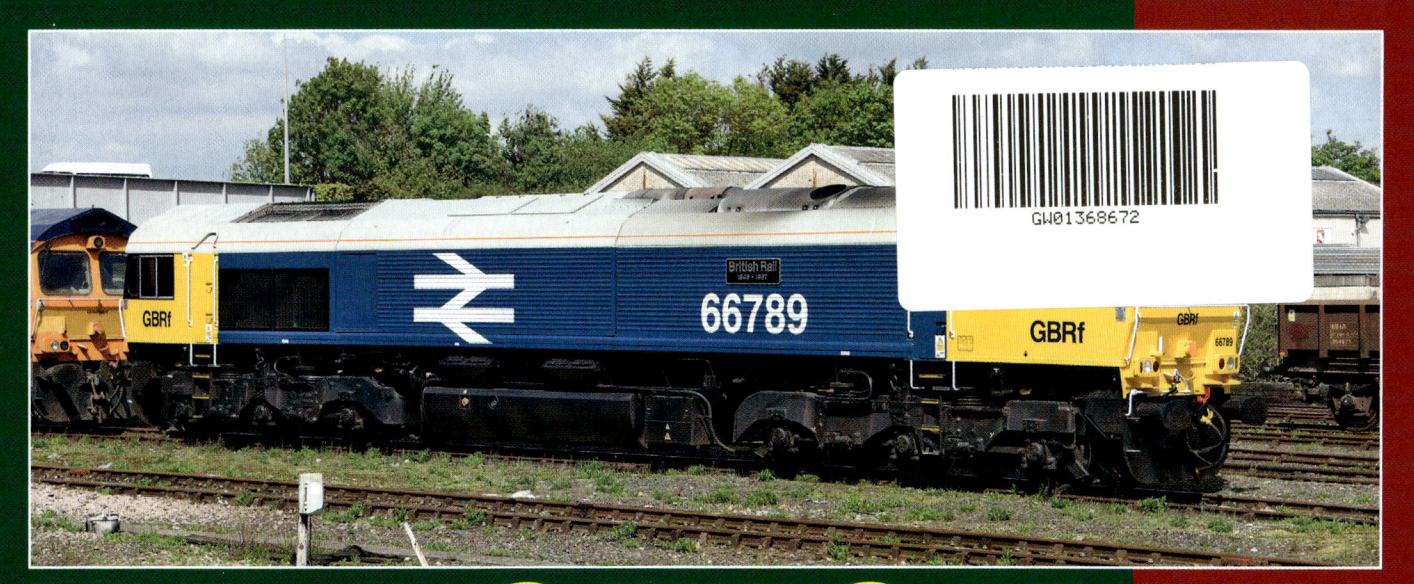

TRACTION TRANSITION

The story of General Motors / EMD power in the UK and Ireland

From The Editor

A very warm welcome to *Traction Transition - The Story of General Motors / EMD power in the UK and Ireland*. It was not until 1961 that locos from the main US loco builder General Motors (GM), started to operate in Ireland. It was another 20 years before we saw the first GM loco operate in England, with a yard 'switcher' for Foster Yeoman.

The start of the major traction transition in the UK came in 1995 after Foster Yeoman purchased GM main line locos to power their aggregate trains, as BR could not provide power which was reliable and suitable. No UK locos could meet the high-availability sought by Foster Yeoman and no UK builder was prepared to underwrite such a commitment if new British locos were ordered. Thus, Foster Yeoman turned to General Motors to fill their traction requirement.

After UK privatisation in 1996, the new main freight operator, US-based Wisconsin Central, trading in the UK as EWS sought new power to replace a fleet of near wrecks they inherited. EWS immediately turned to GM and thus the Class 66 soon entered the UK traction scene, together with the Class 67 passenger version, these classes transformed UK traction.

Many other operators followed EWS down the Class 66 path and eventually the design was added to the GM European catalogue, with a sizeable fleet now operating throughout mainland Europe.

In Ireland, further orders were made, culminating in the 201 Class in the mid-1990s.

Back in England, Porterbrook Leasing in partnership with Brush Traction developed a Class 47-57 rebuild project, using GM/EMD power units in a Class 47 body.

The General Motors/EMD traction story is one of the most interesting; and I sincerely hope you enjoy reading and browsing the pages of this special.   **Colin J. Marsden, Editor**

Editor:
Colin J. Marsden
Group Editor (Transport):
Roger Mortimer
Design:
TRC Productions
Advertising:
Sam Clark
CEO & Publisher:
Adrian Cox
Commercial Director:
Ann Saundry
Marketing Manager:
Martin Steele
Production Manager:
Janet Watkins

Contact
Key Publishing Ltd, PO Box 100, Stamford, Lincolnshire, PE9 1XQ.
Telephone +44 (0) 1780 755131
Fax: +44 (0)1780 757261
E-mail: enquiries@keypublishing.com
www.keypublishing.com

Printing and Origination:
Printed in Great Britain by Warners (Midlands) plc, Bourne and produced by The Railway Centre, Dawlish, Devon

All rights reserved. No part of this magazine may be reproduced or transmitted in any form or by any means electronic or mechanical, including photocopying, recording or by any information storage and retrieval system, without prior permission in writing from the publisher or copyright owner. Multiple copying of contents of this magazine without prior written approval is not permitted.

© Key Publishing Ltd 2019

Cover: *Freightliner Class 66/5 No. 66526 passes Newton St Cyres on 8 June 2005 with a ballast train from Meldon Quarry.* **CJM**

Top: *GB Railfreight Class 66/7 No. 66789 British Rail 1948-1997 painted Rail Blue is seen at Eastleigh.* **CJM**

Left: *Irish Rail 201 Class No. 217 poses at Dublin Heuston on 18 August 2015.* **CJM**

Contents

GM/EMD - A Brief History 4	Class 57 Re-engineering 54
General Motors in Ireland 10	GM/EMD offer the Class 66 66
Mendip 'Switchers' 32	EMD-Alstom Class 67 96
The Class 59 Fleet 34	The 'Euro 66s' 110

Traction Transition - GM/EMD power in the UK and Ireland

GM/EMD - A Brief History

One of the most recognisable names in diesel locomotive construction today is General Motors, or more specifically Electro Motive Division (EMD) Today, the company has more products working in more countries than any other railway supplier.

The business started in mid 1922, when the Electro Motive Engineering Corporation was founded by H. L. Hamilton and P. Turner in Cleveland, Ohio, USA. Their first product was a M300 rail motor of just 175hp, this small beginning has led to around 60,000 traction units built in its almost 100 year history.

After building a handful of small 'switch' locos in the mid-1920s, in 1924 the company were allowed to demonstrate their M300 rail motor on the main line in Chicago over the Chicago Great Western Railroad. A further demonstrator was tested on the Northern Pacific and eventually the railways purchased the vehicles. Both railways stipulated availability and operating conditions on their new traction and many thought this would not be met and would be the end of the company. However, both were a huge success and paved the way for the developing company. New offices were built in New York and a partnership with the Winton Engine Co commenced. Soon a demonstration train of EMD products toured the Eastern US. In 1929 the company was selected to provide power for the Chicago and North Western 'Bluebird' project, the forerunner to the 1930s 'streamliner era'.

In 1930 Electro Motive merged with General Motors and thus the business then traded as General Motors Electro Motive Division, a name which remained until the early 2000s. Winton Diesels also became part of the General Motors group.

The major investment made by GM, saw major advances in the design of diesel engines, in 1933 a prototype 2-stroke unit emerged which was the forerunner for the 567, 645 and 710 series engines we see in the majority of products in UK and Ireland.

Rail traction developed in the US quickly and by 1934 GM/EMD locos were ordered to power new lightweight diesel trains to operate the streamlined Burlington Zephyr service. When introduced this became the USA's first diesel-powered main line passenger service covering the 1,105.4 miles between Denver and Chicago in just 13hrs and 4mins, an average of over 77mph. This was a huge success and within days became world news, as a result GM/EMD were the envy of the railway world.

With this success, the company purchased land on the western side of Chicago, Illinois and built the La Grange factory. The first product emerged from La Grange in 1935, when a 600hp 'switcher' was delivered to Santa Fe, powered by a Winton 201A engine.

It was quickly agreed that mass dieselisation was the only way forward for US railroads. The famous semi-streamlined 'E' units started to appear in the late 1930s and in 1939 the famous bulbous nose-end made its debut when a A-B-B-A 'FT' prototype No. 103 emerged, this set operated an 83,700 mile US tour demonstrating the state-of-the-art diesel loco.

Just five years after the La Grange plant opened over 600 GM-EMD locos were in daily use, production peaked in 1940-41 when over 500 locos emerged from the plant.

With World War 2, the La Grange plant put rail traction on hold in 1942 for a short time, turning attention to building marine engines, however the following year the US Government forced the company to re-commence rail production, to build freight power. Even while under war time conditions, development of locos kept going including the production of F3 locos.

After hostilities ceased in the mid 1940s, huge demand existed for new diesel locos, with the company developing the 2,000hp E7 and 2,250hp E8 locos.

Until this time GM-EMD had only produced locos for the home market, but in 1946 the first export order was completed to supply F2 locos to Nacionales de Mexico.

In the 25th year of trading in 1947, the business soared with on average a staggering five locos per day being built. Concurrent with this came major expansion and development of the La Grange plant, which by now had a workforce of around 12,000.

During 1948 GM looked to the future of rail travel and produced the 'GM Train of Tomorrow', a four coach set powered by a 2,000hp loco, to showcase the possibilities, including piped music, air conditioning, radio telephones and a dome car for route observation.

In 1949 GM-EMD produced the first of their GP (General Purpose) four axle loco range, the dozens of derivatives of this design became the most popular diesel-electric in the world. With this in mind, by December 1949, the La Grange factory was building more that seven locos every day.

In 1950 one of the most significant events in company history took place when a major new construction site was built in London, Ontario, Canada. This was to take some of the pressure off the La Grange site and be in a good position to build loco's for the Canadian market, being close to both Canadian National and Canadian Pacific Railroads.

Originally the London plant was used to assemble kit parts supplied from La Grange. When opened in 1950 the site was known as General ⇨

Below: *The iconic style of the General Motors/EMD 'F' unit. This early F7 example was constructed in 1949, the launch year for the design, it was built for the Atchison, Topeka and Santa Fe Railway Company. It was fitted with a 16 cylinder 567B prime mover powering an EMD D12 alternator powering four EMD D27B traction motors. The loco was on the Santa Fe roster until 1986 when it was gifted to the California State Railway Museum in Sacramento where it is currently on display. A total of 2366 "A" cab and 1483 'B' non-driving locos were built.* **CJM**

Above: *Built in November 1954 as an FP9Au for Canadian National fitted with a 567 engine, this loco was later rebuilt by VIA with a 645 engine to increase output and renumbered 6305. Withdrawn in 1997, No. 6305 is now operated by the Ontario Southland Railway and is still in front line service working in the Salford, Ingersoll, Woodstock and St Thomas area. It is seen at St Thomas on 6 February 2017, carrying its original number.* **CJM**

Right: *Built at the GM Diesel plant in London, Ontario in 1959 for Canadian National Railway, No. 1059 is an A1A-A1A road switcher fitted with a 12 cylinder 567C engine set at 1,200hp. The loco is seen carrying CN black livery with a red solebar. A handful of this design, now rebuilt are still in operation.* **CJM**

Motors Diesels Ltd, which changed in 1969 to General Motors of Canada - Diesel Division. The first loco to emerge from the London plant was a GP7 No. 71 for the Toronto, Hamilton and Buffalo Railway (TH&B). In the first year 131 locos were constructed, by 1954 the annual figure was over 500 per year and by 1966 the figure was in excess of 2000.

By mid-1951, the GM-EMD operation delivered their 10,000th diesel loco and it was at that point it was realised that mass dieselisation of the US and world railways was the only way forward. Development of diesel traction progressed and in 1953 the company announced its Special Duty or SD product range of six-axle locos, allowing much heavier and more powerful locos to operate with no increase to axle loads.

Diesel loco production continued at both La Grange and London. In 1962 the company celebrated the assembly of their 25,000 loco, a GP30 No. 1014 for the Louisville and Nashville Railroad.

GM-EMD helped the Union Pacific Railroad mark its 100th birthday in 1969 with the design and contract for 47 DDA40X 'Centennial' twin engine locos measuring a staggering 98ft in length and mounted on two four wheel trucks. The locos housed two 645 prime movers and were delivered between 1969-71

Ongoing development in the 1960s saw the 567 series engine give way to the larger 645, later chosen to be fitted to the Class 59s. Development continued through the 1970s, culminating in the release of the 710 prime mover range in 1984, the engine adopted for use in the Class 66 and 67 locos.

As well as development of loco power units and hardware, modern diesel locos were increasingly dependent on electronics and GM-EMD were in the forefront in this area. Together with traction electronics came the development of wheelslip and creep control technology, this was largely developed by Bruce Myre and emerged as 'super series' traction control. This revolutionised the laws of adhesion and allowed greater tonnages to be shifted and improved wheel/rail interaction.

Since its expansion from the pure US market, GM-EMD had been keen to enter the European and especially the UK loco market, but until the mid-1980s this was a no go area, with all UK locos built in the home country. However, things started to change in the mid-1970s when the first 30 of the BR-Brush design of Class 56 were built in Romania. However it was not until November 1984 that GM-EMD entered the UK market. Following a long period of dispute between Mendip aggregate company Foster Yeoman and BR over reliability of locos provided for its services, Foster Yeoman decided to move on and purchase non-UK motive power in the form of initially four Class 59s. Following their experience with a General Motors 'switcher' compounded by close ties between the Yeoman family and the US loco industry. Details of this and follow on orders can be found in other sections of this title.

Back in the US, starting in 1987, GM-EMD ventured into new agreements with rail operators, when in place of the previous direct purchase of locos, it offered the market lease or 'power-by-the-hour' options. Whereby major operators could deploy state-of-the-art locos and pay for just the hours used. Over the years this type of business has considerably expanded.

In the 1980s, the previous direct current ⇨

Right: *Installed with the same prime mover as the UK Class 59s - the 16 cylinder 645E, the Canadian National fleet of GP 38-2s were originally numbered in the 55xx series and renumbered in 1988 to the present 47xx series. These road locos with a top speed of 65mph are today mainly confined to yard working and local 'trip' freight operations. No. 4707 is seen in the CN yard in London, Ontario on 24 January 2013. On the right is an example of the other huge US loco builder, General Electric, with one of their Dash9-44CW 4,400hp locos No. 2520 introduced in December 1994.* **CJM**

Traction Transition - GM/EMD power in the UK and Ireland

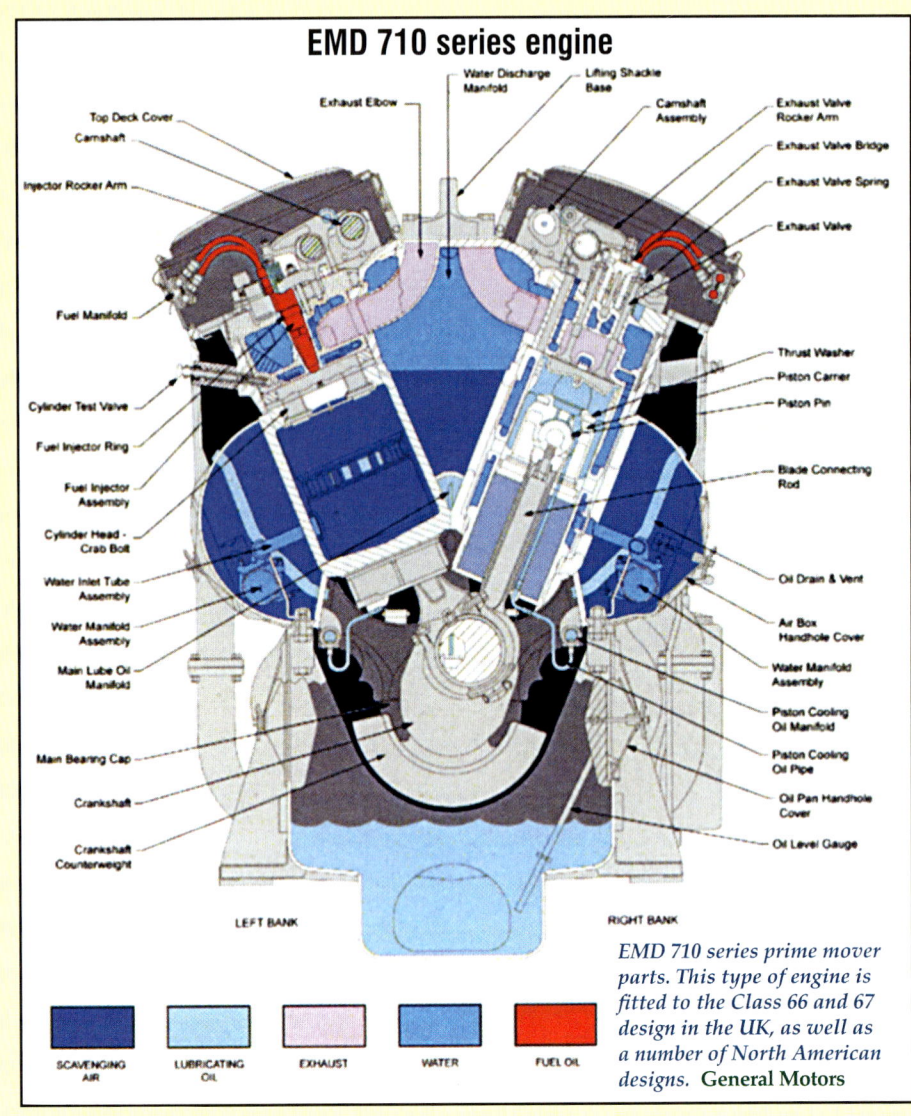

EMD 710 series engine

EMD 710 series prime mover parts. This type of engine is fitted to the Class 66 and 67 design in the UK, as well as a number of North American designs. **General Motors**

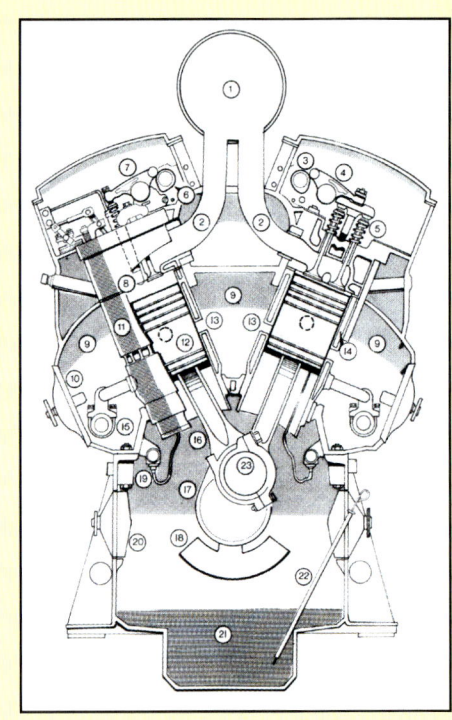

Above: *The UK Class 59 uses the US standard Electro Motive Division (EMD) 645 series power unit designated 645E3C, a two-stroke V-16 engine, set to deliver 3,300hp.*
Main components: 1 - Exhaust manifold, 2 - Exhaust elbow, 3 - Exhaust cam, 4 - Exhaust valve rocker arm, 5 - Exhaust valves, 6 - Fuel injector cam, 7 - Fuel rocker arm, 8 - Fuel injector, 9 - air box, 10 - air box lid, 11 - cylinder liner, 12 - Piston, 13 - Air inlet port, 14 - Cooling water jacket, 15 - Cooling water inlet manifold, 16 - Connecting rods, 17 - Crankshaft, 18 - Crankshaft counterweight, 19 - Piston cooling oil manifold, 20 - Oil sump cover, 21 - Oil sump, 22 - Oil dipstick, 23 - Crankpin. **General Motors**

traction systems were considered 'old hat' and new alternating current technology was being introduced and offered as part of the standard product range. The first examples taking to the Burlington Northern Railroad in 1992-93. Following on from the major ac traction development, huge orders for ac traction following from most of the Class 1 railroads

In addition to heavy duty freight power GM-EMD also refined their passenger offerings with a state-of-the-art F59 semi-streamlined passenger loco, installed with technically advanced traction control equipment. This model and its derivatives were taken up my many railroads.

Another innovation of the company was the 'whisper cab'. which using rubber isolation gave new levels of crew comfort and drastically reduced in cab noise, sadly this was not installed on the UK models. Another major development was the GM 'Radial Truck', which through complex mechanical connections 'slightly' steered the trailing axle of a bogie reducing huge strain on wheel-sets during curving. This advance allowed some railroads to deploy six axle bogies on routes previously restricted to four axle units. The radial track was incorporated on the Class 66s for the UK.

Looking at power units the two-stroke 567, 645 and 710 units started to give way to 16-cylinder four-stroke H series units in the 1980s, which combined with on board electronics and advanced control systems, soon became the norm.

GM-EMD's North American market share dropped below that of its main competitor General Electric in 1987. Following a Canada-USA Free Trade Agreement in 1989, the company decided to consolidate all loco production at the Diesel Division in London, Ontario, a development which ended loco production at the La Grange facility in 1991, although the plant continued to produce engines and generators.

In 1999, Union Pacific Railroad placed the largest single order for diesel locomotives in North American railroad history when they ordered 1,000 SD70Ms. The order then expanded by a ⇨

GM/EMD UK Production

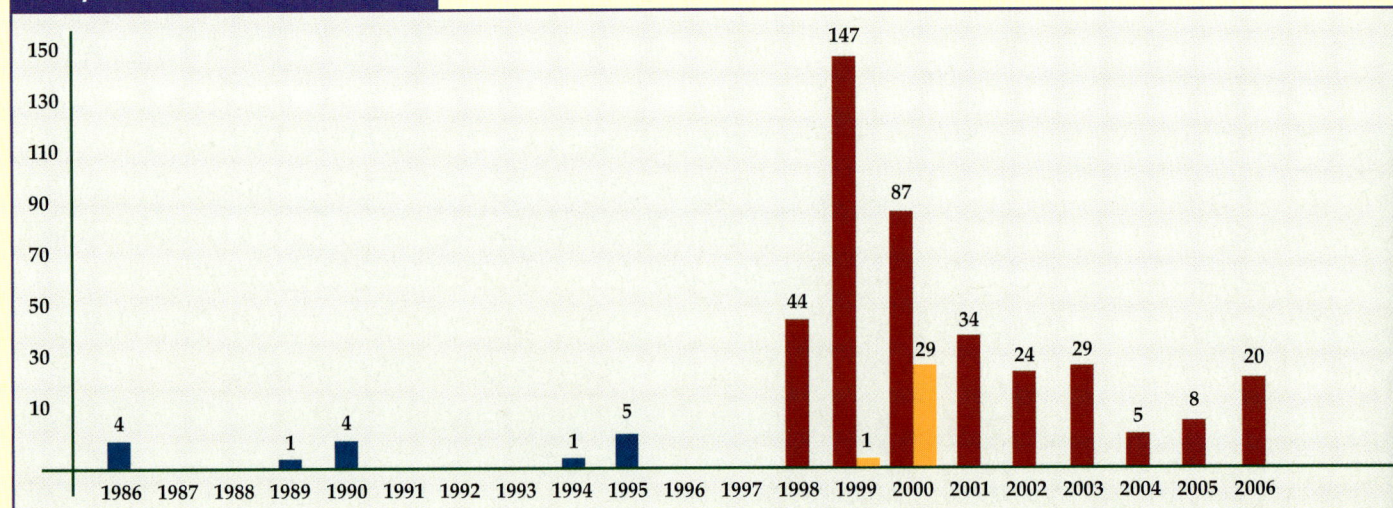

Year	Units
1986	4
1989	1
1990	4
1994	1
1995	5
1998	44
1999	147
2000	29 / 1
2001	34
2002	24
2003	29
2004	5
2005	8
2006	20

Traction Transition - GM/EMD power in the UK and Ireland

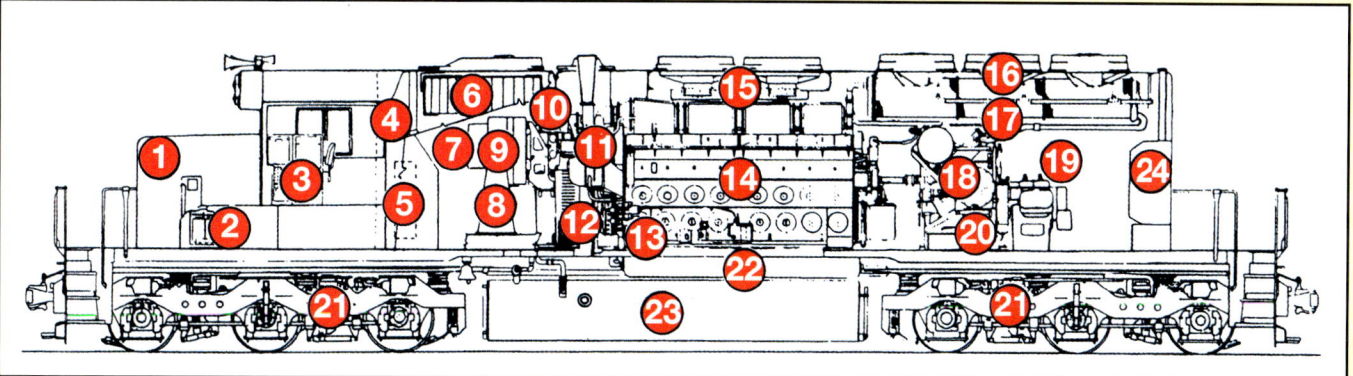

Above: *General equipment layout of General Motors EMD SD (Special Duty) 40-2 loco, the core design which was refined and fitted with a double cab configuration for the Class 59. 1: Nose end incorporating sand filler. 2: Battery box, 3: Driving control stand, 4: Electric cabinet, 5: Electric air filter, 6: Inertia filter, 7: Engine air filter, 8: Traction motor blower, 9: Generator blower, 10: Auxiliary generator, 11: Turbocharger, 12: Main generator, 13: Engine cranking (starting) motors, 14: EMD 16-645E3 prime mover, 15: Dynamic brake blowers, 16: Radiator cooling fan, 17: Radiators, 18: Equipment rack, 19: Air compressor, 20: AC power equipment rack, 21: six axle bogie (truck), 22: Air reservoir, 23: Fuel tank.* **General Motors**

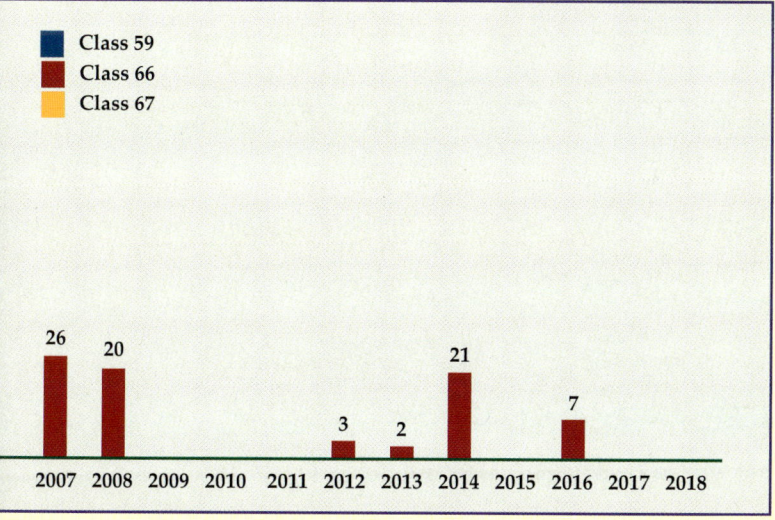

Top: *Between 1965-1971, GM/EMD produced 1260 SD45s, very similar to the SD40, but fitted with a larger 20 cylinder 645E3 prime mover giving 3,600hp, an increase of 600hp from the SD40. The loco illustrated, Wisconsin Central (WC) 7506 was introduced in June 1971 on Burlington Northern (BN) as No. 6506, to works number 37114. It was withdrawn in mid 1986 and sold to WC who renumbered it as 7506. On 8 December 1998 No. 7506 leads sister SD45 No. 6521 through Oshkosh with a manifest freight from Neenah to North Fond Du Lac. This line and Wisconsin Central are now owned and operated by Canadian National.* **CJM**

Above: *In addition to building freight power, a number of passenger locos have been built by GM/EMD. Originally ordered by Amtrak for medium distance passenger work the F40 is one of the most common, working for a number of passenger operators. The loco illustrated is a F40PH-2 built in April 1985 at EMD La Grange, USA for CalTrain, the regional passenger operator in the San Francisco area, working between San Francisco and San Jose/Gilroy. On 12 December 2013 No. 908 Redwood City awaits to depart from San Francisco station bound for San Jose.* **CJM**

Traction Transition - GM/EMD power in the UK and Ireland

Above: *EMD refined its high-horsepower locos over many years and in 1995 produced a series of SD70M (microprocessor) locos. Originally these were lease locos operated by EMDX, but after a period were sold to CSX. As lease locos they turned up all over the USA, displaying their smart silver, grey and maroon livery. On 31 May 1999 No. EMDX7006 basks in the sun in Mojave Yard, California. This loco is now operating for CSX as No. 4681.* **CJM**

Left: *In 1994 EMD unveiled the streamlined passenger F59PHI design, of which 83 were constructed. Two locos of the build, constructed to works number 996187 were delivered to Coaster, the regional passenger operator in San Diego, California operating services between Oceanside and San Diego. Fitted with a 12 cylinder 710G3C-EC prime mover set to deliver 3,200hp, No. 3001 departs from Solana Beach bound for Oceanside on 15 August 2016.* **CJM**

In 1995 EMD launched the SD90MAC, designed for the new 6,000hp 16-cylinder 'H' series four-stroke engine. However, technical problems with the 6,000hp prime mover resulted in locos being shipped with 4300 hp 16-cylinder 710G engines. These locos were given the model designation of SD9043MAC. An option existed to re-engine them with 6,000hp engines when they were available. This upgrade program was never carried out due to ongoing reliability issues with the engine. UP No. 8106, more recently renumbered to 3600, is seen in Mojave Yard, California on 28 May 1999. **CJM**

further 450. By way of follow-on orders, over 500 SD70ACes were constructed. UK domestic orders gave a constant production flow. In 2004 CSX Transportation received their first SD70ACe. This model meet the EPA Tier 2 emission standards and still used the two-stroke 710 prime mover. In 2005 Norfolk Southern took delivery of new SD70M-2 locos, the successor to the SD70M.

In June 2004 it emerged from the markets that EMD was being put up for sale. On 11 January 2005, it was officially announced by General Motors, that it had agreed to sell EMD to a partnership led by Greenbriar Equity Group and Berkshire Partners, the new company was named Electro-Motive Diesel, Inc, thus retaining the famous "EMD" initials. The sale was finalised on 4 April 2005.

On 1 June 2010, Caterpillar Incorporated announced it had agreed to buy Electro-Motive Diesel from Greenbriar, Berkshire for $820 million. Caterpillar's wholly owned subsidiary, Progress Rail Corporation, completed the purchase on 2 August 2010, making Electro-Motive Diesel a wholly owned subsidiary of Progress Rail Services Corporation.

The US Environmental Protection Agency Tier-4 loco emissions regulations on new locomotives went into effect on 1 January 2015. As of that date EMDs 710-engined locos could only be built for use outside the United States, Canada, Alaska Mexico. EMD had originally thought the 710 engine could be modified to meet Tier-4 standards, but it was not able to meet those requirements while maintaining optimum performance and reliability. Development of a Tier-4 compliant loco shifted from its original focus on the two-stroke 710 to the four-stroke 1010J series engine, derived from the previous 265H engine.

The first (pre-production) loco using the 1010J engine, was a SD70ACe-T4, using a 4,600 horsepower 12 cylinder engine. Testing began in spring of 2016, with the first two units of a 65 unit order delivered to Union Pacific in December 2016.

EMD currently operates major facilities in McCook, Illinois, and Muncie, Indiana in the United States, Sete Lagoas in Brazil and San Luis Potosí in Mexico. The London, Ontario, Canada plant closed in 2012.

The administrative headquarters of EMD in La Grange still houses design, engineering, emissions testing, rebuild unit, and shops for the manufacturing of major components, such as prime movers, traction alternators, electrical cabinets, and turbochargers.

The EMD San Luis Potosí plant in Mexico opened on 14 April 2010, for the maintenance, rebuild, and overhaul of traction motors and electrical systems.

The EMD Muncie facility opened in October 2010, when Caterpillar invested US$50 million to purchase and rebuild an existing 740,000 sq ft building for construction of new locos and the commissioning of a loco test track. The plant was officially opened on 28 October 2011, with the first loco produced being, a Ferromex SD70ACe No. 4092. The final batch of UK Class 66s were assembled at the Muncie plant (see numeric table for details. ∎

Right: *General Motors managed to get into the European loco market in the 1950s with a licence agreement with NOHAB (Nydqvist & Holm AB) a rail manufacturing company based in the city of Trollhättan, Sweden, to build GM locos. Locos were built for the Norwegian State Railway and Hungarian Railway (MAV), only 20 locos for MAV being built due to the Iron Curtain restrictions which saw Russian designs ordered. In Hungary the stylish M61 design was introduced, with an adaptation of the North American bull-nose. The 20 locos were introduced using a 16-cylinder 567 power unit. From the 1980s the class had an almost cult following and many were used on railtours and charter trains. No. M61 002 is seen painted in MAV orange livery at Székesfehérvár on 25 April 1997 with a service from Budapest.* CJM

Below: *The latest loco from the EMD passenger stable is the F125 'Spirit' a four-axle loco built at the new EMD plant in Muncie, Indiana, with body shells supplied by Stadler/Vossloh from Spain. Power is provided by a Caterpillar C175-20 V20 engine rated at 4,700 hp. This design is EMD's first new domestic passenger locomotive in 15 years. Features of the F125 include EPA Tier 4 emissions using exhaust after-treatment, AC traction systems, dynamic brakes and HEP regeneration. Currently the only operator to use the design is Metrolink, the regional operator in Los Angeles, who have an order for 40 locos currently being assembled. No. 914 is illustrated at the Metrolink service facility in Los Angeles on 31 December 2018.* CJM

GM/EMD/PR Locos for UK by Factory

Factory	Locos
La Grange, Chicago, Illinois	5 x Class 59
London, Ontario, Canada	10 x Class 59; 452 x Class 66
Muncie, Indania, USA	28 x Class 66
Alstom, Valancia, Spain	30 x Class 67

Traction Transition - GM/EMD power in the UK and Ireland

Traction Transition - GM/EMD power in the UK and Ireland

General Motors in Ireland

Ireland, was the first European country to take delivery of General Motors (GM) locomotives in 1961. Prior to that, most Irish diesel locomotives were constructed in Great Britain. After that date GM became the sole supplier of locos to the CIÉ, later Irish Rail, this later extended to Northern Ireland Railways.

The first fleet delivered were the 121 class, built at La Grange between December 1960 to January 1961 and numbered B121 to B135. In the early 1970s the 'B' prefix was dropped as repainting took place. The fleet remained in traffic until May 2008 with Nos. 124 and 134 being the last withdrawn.

The design, GL8 in the GM catalogue of Class 121 on CIÉ, were based on the American-style single cab 'road switcher' design. The driving cab design was very different from earlier CIÉ diesel designs, with the controls to the side of the driver, and not in front, this caused a number of complaints when locos were required to operate with the cab trailing. Eventually it was agreed that the class should operate with the cab leading. AAR style multiple working was installed and allowed two Class 121s to operate 'hood-to-hood'.

When delivered the class was fitted with an EMD 8-567CR engine of 960hp (720kW), they were later fitted with 645 style equipment as part of standardisation, however they kept their 960hp output. Later in their lives Nos. B126-B129 were rebuilt with EMD 8-645E engines of 1,100hp (820kW).

The fleet were to be found operating all kinds of trains, including later working with the Inchicore-assembled, BR style Mk 3 stock in push-pull mode. Entering service in 1989, the Mk3 formations consisted of a single Class 121 and six carriages, were mainly used on the Dublin suburban service. These became the last passenger duties for the class. The Class 121s operated the 'Limerick shuttle' for many years before being replaced by DMU stock.

The Class 121s started to be withdrawn in 1986 after No. 125 was badly damaged in a fire.

After delivery of the Class 201s from GM, these replaced the '121s' on passenger duties, and by 2005 just two locos 124 and 134 were left in service. The fleet bowed out of regular passenger service on 9 July 2005 working on the Sligo line.

When delivered, the fleet were painted in a silver/grey colour. This was replaced quickly by a black and golden brown scheme with a deep white band. Later, the scheme changed to tan and black. After CIÉ Rail services became known as Irish Rail, the livery again changed with two white bands added, high-visibility panels were also applied on the front ends.

The first Córas Iompair Éireann (CIE) GM/EMD 'follow-on' order came in November-December 1962, when the first batch of a fleet of 37 JL8 designated twin-cab locos were delivered. Later classified as '141' the locos were originally numbered B141 to B177 they were very similar in technical terms to the earlier Class 121s.

The design was originally fitted with an EMD 8-567CR prime mover of 960hp (720 kW), later, EMD 645 'power packs' were installed.

As part of CIÉ standardisation, many locos were later rebuilt with a GM 8-645E engine of 1,100hp (820kW). The class was delivered in CIE livery of brown, black and white.

In early December 1962 the class entered revenue service on the Dublin to Cork main line. This design was fitted from new with multiple control and frequently double-headed Dublin to Cork services. The class was introduced in the same month to the Dublin–Belfast 'Enterprise' service. As time progressed, the Class 141 fleet saw use on passenger duties on most main routes, until replaced by multiple unit stock.

The Class 141 fleet were withdrawn from regular service in February 2010.

In 1965 Córas Iompair Éireann commissioned GM/EMD to construct a follow-on order of Bo-Bo locos, almost identical to the previously delivered Class 141s, classified as 181. The order consisted of 12 locomotives, assembled at the La Grange plant and shipped by sea to Dublin arriving in 1966. The locos were numbered B181 to B192.

These locomotives were virtually identical to the '141s', but were fitted with the more powerful EMD 8-645E engine set to deliver 1100 hp, (820kW), the locos weighed 67 tonnes, had a maximum design speed of 89mph (143km/h), but were restricted to 75mph (120 km/h) in service. The locos were introduced into service in autumn 1966.

During its life, loco No. 186 was fitted with an EMD 8-567CR engine delivering 960hp (720 kW), as installed in the Class 141 fleet.

The Class 181s started to be withdrawn from 1991 with the final operational member of the class No. 190 withdrawn in November 2009.

In the 1970s CIÉ returned to General Motors with another order for main line locos, this time a fleet of 18 six-axle locos, classified 071. These were ordered for mixed (passenger/freight) operation and became the main passenger loco for many years, they were delivered in July 1976. In many areas, they displaced older classes and were eventually replaced by yet another GM class, the 201 series locos.

In 1980 Northern Ireland Railways (NIR) ordered two identical locos, classified by NIR as Class 111. A follow on order for one loco was made in 1983 and delivered at the end of 1984. The NIR locos are numbered 111, 112, and 113.

In 2019 all the CIÉ locos remain in service, now being used on freight and permanent way trains, displaced from passenger work by newer Class 201s.

From November 2006, CIÉ began an overhaul programme of the fleet and locos received the new Irish Rail freight livery. A further overhaul project commenced in 2013 for all 18 Class 071s, which has included an engine rebuild, refurbished bogies, replacement body panels, upgraded cabs and a new slate grey livery, with many locos now carrying European numbering.

In 2016, to mark their 40 years of service, No. 071 was repainted into its original CIÉ 'Supertrain' livery of black and orange. In July 2017, No. 073 was overhauled and repainted in 1987 Irish Rail livery to celebrate the 30th anniversary of the company.

On the NIR front, in 2007, the three locos were converted for push-pull working, a project which never came to fruition.

The three locos remain in use for permanent way and engineering duties.

In 1994-95 General Motors Diesel Division in Canada produced the largest fleet yet delivered to Ireland, when an order for 34 Co-Co Class 201 locos was executed.

Class:	121
Number range:	B121-B135, 121-135
Built by:	General Motors, La Grange, Illinois USA
GM model:	GL8 [Single cab, road switcher]
Years introduced:	1960-1961
Wheel arrangement:	Bo-Bo
Gauge:	5ft 3in (1,600mm)
Maximum speed	75mph (120km/h)
Length:	39ft 10in (12.14m)
Weight:	64 tonnes
Wheel diameter (new):	3ft 4in (1,016mm)
Engine type:	EMD 8-567CR
	126-129 re-engined with EMD 8-645E
Engine output:	EMD 8-567CR 960hp (720kW)
	EMD 8-645E 1,100hp (820kW)
Power at rail:	710hp (530kW)
Maximum tractive effort:	35,000lb (156kN)
Continuous tractive effort:	30,400lb (135kN)
Cylinder bore:	8½ in (216mm)
Cylinder stroke:	10in (250mm)
Transmission type:	Electric
Traction generator:	GM-EMD D25
Traction motor type:	GM-EMD D47
No. of traction motors:	4
Brake type:	Vacuum and Air
Brake force:	51 tonnes
Bogie type:	EMD
Multiple coupling type:	AAR
Sanding equipment:	Pneumatic
Note:	First full American-built locos delivered to Europe

Class 121 Fleet List

Number	Works No.	Builder	Notes
121	26271	GM-EMD, La Grange	
122	26272	GM-EMD, La Grange	
123	26273	GM-EMD, La Grange	
124	26274	GM-EMD, La Grange	Preserved
125	26275	GM-EMD, La Grange	
126	26276	GM-EMD, La Grange	
127	26277	GM-EMD, La Grange	
128	26278	GM-EMD, La Grange	
129	26279	GM-EMD, La Grange	
130	26280	GM-EMD, La Grange	
131	26281	GM-EMD, La Grange	
132	26282	GM-EMD, La Grange	
133	26283	GM-EMD, La Grange	Cab preserved
134	26284	GM-EMD, La Grange	Preserved
135	26285	GM-EMD, La Grange	

The locos are classified by GM/EMD as JT42HCW, and are fitted with an EMD 12-710G3B engine set to deliver 3,200hp (2,400 kW), the design weighs 108 tonnes, with a maximum speed of 102mph (164 km/h). The design is directly related to the UK Class 66 design.

The massive order was placed, as by the early 1990s, the existing fleet operating passenger services in Ireland were becoming increasingly problematic. An economic boom ⇨

Above: *Powering a rake of Park Royal passenger stock, Class 121 No. B126 is seen in the countryside between Cork and Cobh on 26 April 1969. As built, these locos were vacuum brake fitted only.*
Gavin Morrison

Below: *Class 121 No. B131 is seen on Cork shed on 26 April 1969, helping with the re-railing of derailed 2-6-4T No. 4. At the time the fleet carried small marker/tail lights above the buffers mounted on the cab end, these were replaced with larger units.* **Gavin Morrison**

'121' Fact File

- Preservation - 124 preserved by Irish Traction Group, RPSI have preserved No. 134. The driving cab of No. 133 is preserved at the Cavan & Leitrim Railway.

- Originally fitted with vacuum brakes, later dual brakes fitted.

Traction Transition - GM/EMD power in the UK and Ireland

Above: Carrying the interim un-lined orange and black livery and after multiple working had been installed No. 134 and an unidentified class member departs from Dublin Heuston on 15 May 1983 with the 18.25 to Mallow. **John Whiteley**

Left: The Class 121s could frequently be found working in pairs on freight services. On 28 July 2006 Nos. 124 and 134 approach Portarlington with a container service from Dublin to Ballina. **Robin Ralston**

Below: Operating in 'push-pull' service with three Irish Rail Mk3s including a Cab Control Car on the rear, Class 121 No. 124 pulls into the bay platform at Limerick Junction with a service from Limerick on 6 September 2003. The locos AAR multiple control jumper socket can be seen to the right of the left side light cluster. **Gavin Morrison**

12 Traction Transition – GM/EMD power in the UK and Ireland

Above: *The container handling crane at Limerick forms the backdrop to this image of Class 121 No. 124 arriving at the terminal station with a push-pull Mk3 'InterCity' set from Limerick Junction on 8 September 2003. The Irish Rail Mk3s, some of which were built in Derby and the balance at Inchicore, Dublin differ from the UK Mk3s in having plug doors and opening hopper windows.* **John Whiteley**

Right: *With evidence of a prosperous freight operation and two locos in the station at the head of departing services, Class 121 No. 124 departs from Limerick station on 8 September 2003 powering the 14.35 'shuttle' to Limerick Junction. Today, all services from Limerick station are in the hands of DMU stock.* **John Whiteley**

in Ireland during the 1990s allowed Irish Rail (Iarnród Éireann) to make a significant investment in the railways, which began with an order for 32 express locos from GM-EMD. Northern Ireland Railways took advantage of the order and purchased two.

The first loco No. 201 was delivered (by air) in 1994, with deliveries continuing through 1995. In a publicity stunt and a way of getting the first loco to Ireland for testing and staff training, No. 201 was taken by road from the GM plant in London, Ontario, Canada to London Airport and loaded inside an Antonov An-124 heavy lift aircraft, arriving at Dublin Airport on 9 June 1994. It was commissioned and operated a test run from Inchicore works to Kildare on 14 June 1994.

After the fleet had been delivered and started to enter service a number of problems were identified. Problems were identified with bogie cracks and engine fires. However the locos were modified and settled down to operate both passenger and freight services.

A number of the locos were later fitted with push-pull equipment to operate with Mk3 passenger rakes which included a remote driving trailer.

With traffic downturns and the introduction of multiple unit stock, the non push-pull fitted locos (201–205 and 210–214) were withdrawn from service and stored.

Today, the InterCity operation using push-pull Class 201s form the only loco-hauled passenger services in the Republic of Ireland linking Dublin with Cork. They operate with Mk 4 stock which was introduced in 2006-2007. These locos (and stock) sport a green and silver livery, with full yellow warning ends.

The only other loco-hauled passenger service is 'The Enterprise', a cross-border service between Dublin and Belfast, this is operated jointly by Irish Rail (Iarnród Éireann) and Northern Ireland Railways. This service is operated push-pull, with a driving trailer at the remote end. These train sets and locos are painted in light grey with a purple and red stripe. Locos sport a full yellow end. As this service is a shared operation between IR and NIR, locos (8)208 and (8)209 are officially owned by Northern Ireland Railways. The coaching stock is unusual in that it is owned by Irish Rail (Iarnród Éireann) odd numbered vehicles; and NIR even numbered vehicles.

While operating the Enterprise service, power for the stock is provided by a generator van coupled between the loco and train, as in the past a number of issues have existed with the Class 201s providing electric train supply or head-end power.

The Class 201s are also available to operate some freight services, including container flows between Dublin Port and Ballina and Belview (Waterford) and Ballina and timber traffic between Waterford and Westport/Ballina.

A new lease of life for one Class 201 came in 2016 when a fleet of 10 Mk 3 coaches were sold to Belmond Grand Hibernian, a luxury charter train operator who rebuilt the stock to a stunning luxurious standard. Loco No. 216 being repainted in Belmond dark blue with train branding.

In late 2016, IR commenced research into a re-power of most of the existing 201 fleet as part of a mid-life refurbishment, in 2019 the project plans were still to be confirmed. ∎

Traction Transition - GM/EMD power in the UK and Ireland

Class:	141
Number range:	B141-B177 (141-177)
Built by:	General Motors, La Grange, Illinois USA
GM model:	JL8 [Twin cab, road loco]
Years introduced:	1962
Wheel arrangement:	Bo-Bo
Gauge:	5ft 3in (1,600mm)
Maximum speed:	75mph (120km/h)
Length:	44ft 0in (13.42m)
Weight:	67 tonnes
Wheel diameter (new):	3ft 4in (1,016mm)
Engine type:	Original: EMD 8-567CR
	Rebuilt: EMD 8-645E
Engine output:	EMD 8-567CR 960hp (720kW)
	EMD 8-645E 1,100hp (820kW)
Power at rail:	710hp (530kW)
Maximum tractive effort:	35,000lb (156kN)
Continuous tractive effort:	30,400lb (135kN)
Cylinder bore:	8½ in (216mm)
Cylinder stroke:	10in (250mm)
Transmission type:	Electric
Traction generator:	GM-EMD D25
Traction motor type:	GM-EMD D47
No. of traction motors:	4
Brake type:	Vacuum and Air
Brake force:	56 tonnes
Bogie type:	EMD
Multiple coupling type:	AAR
Sanding equipment:	Pneumatic

Class 141 Fleet List

Number	Works No.	Builder	Notes
141	27467	GM-EMD, La Grange	Preserved
142	27468	GM-EMD, La Grange	Preserved
143	27469	GM-EMD, La Grange	
144	27470	GM-EMD, La Grange	
145	27471	GM-EMD, La Grange	
146	27472	GM-EMD, La Grange	Preserved
147	27473	GM-EMD, La Grange	
148	27474	GM-EMD, La Grange	
149	27475	GM-EMD, La Grange	
150	27476	GM-EMD, La Grange	
151	27477	GM-EMD, La Grange	
152	27478	GM-EMD, La Grange	Preserved
153	27479	GM-EMD, La Grange	
154	27480	GM-EMD, La Grange	
155	27481	GM-EMD, La Grange	
156	27482	GM-EMD, La Grange	
157	27483	GM-EMD, La Grange	
158	27484	GM-EMD, La Grange	
159	27485	GM-EMD, La Grange	
160	27486	GM-EMD, La Grange	
161	27487	GM-EMD, La Grange	
162	27488	GM-EMD, La Grange	
163	27489	GM-EMD, La Grange	
164	27490	GM-EMD, La Grange	
165	27491	GM-EMD, La Grange	
166	27492	GM-EMD, La Grange	
167	27493	GM-EMD, La Grange	
168	27494	GM-EMD, La Grange	
169	27495	GM-EMD, La Grange	
170	27496	GM-EMD, La Grange	
171	27497	GM-EMD, La Grange	
172	27498	GM-EMD, La Grange	
173	27499	GM-EMD, La Grange	
174	27500	GM-EMD, La Grange	
175	27501	GM-EMD, La Grange	Preserved
176	27502	GM-EMD, La Grange	
177	27503	GM-EMD, La Grange	

Left: *With a rake of Irish Rail Mk2 stock, 1962-built Class 141 No. 175 is seen at Limerick on 27 July 2006. This loco is now preserved by the Railway Preservation Society of Ireland.* **Robin Ralston**

Built in La Grange, Chicago, USA in 1962 and classified by GM at JL8, the 37 members of Córas Iompair Éireann (CIE), later Irish Rail Class 141 were the mainstay of passenger and freight operations for many years. Painted in its as delivered black and tan livery, No. B176 is seen skirting the banks of the River Lee on 26 April 1968 with a Cork to Cobh local service. **Gavin Morrison**

'141' Fact File

- Preservation. Nos. 141, 142 and 175 are under the control of the Railway Preservation Society of Ireland, while Nos. 146 and 153 are in the hands of the Irish Traction Group.

- Originally fitted with small marker /tail light clusters, replaced with larger units.

Above: Complete with single line token collection apparatus fitted to the cab side, black and tan-liveried Nos. B177 and B161 are recorded at Limerick station on 27 April 1969. The white 'bib' front, surrounding the standard two unit GM/EMD headlight unit gave these locos a distinctive appearance. The same design two light assembly was later incorporated into the front end of the UK Class 59 and many other company products. **Gavin Morrison**

Below: A good image to illustrate how GM/EMD car body design changed over the years. On the right we see Irish Rail orange and lined black-liveried Class 141 No. 141 at Dublin Connolly on 3 May 2004 with an empty stock train. On the right is 'modern' GM London, Canada built Class 201 No. 207, painted in 'Enterprise' livery awaiting to depart with the 10.00 service to Belfast. It is interesting to record that even as late as the mid-1990s when the Class 201s were introduced, vacuum brake were still installed.
Gavin Morrison

Traction Transition - GM/EMD power in the UK and Ireland

Above: With a train heating coach coupled behind the loco, Class 141 No. 152 is seen at Cork on 5 September 2003 with a local service from Tralee. Until the large scale introduction of diesel multiple units, most services in Ireland were loco operated. At just 44ft in length, the Class 141s were quite short by main line loco standards, but long enough to house the power, cooler group and generator. When this illustration was recorded the loco looked in need of some care and attention. **John Whiteley**

Below: One of the pleasures of looking at Irish Railways even today with its reduced network, is the quaint country stations and relaxed atmosphere. On 6 September 2003, Class 141 No. 160 awaits departure from Tipperary, the first station outside Limerick Junction with the 09.35 Limerick to Waterford service. Due to the track configuration, this train would have had to do a reverse move to depart from Limerick Junction to gain the Waterford line. **Gavin Morrison**

Above: *The wonderful lower quadrant semaphore signals of Irish Railways (which have now gone) added attraction to many locations. On 7 September 2003, Class 141 No. 176 departs from Farranfore powering the 18.15 Tralee to Cork via Mallow service.* **John Whiteley**

Right: *With two Craven coaches and a generator coach on the rear, Class 141 No. 160 makes its call at Wellington Bridge on 2 September 2003 with the 17.05 from Waterford to Rosslare Europort. This section of line is currently mothballed.*
Gavin Morrison

Below: *For most of the diesel loco era on Irish Rail, the area around Limerick was always good to find locos of most classes. On 8 September 2003, Class 141 No. 172 propels stock into Limerick station from the yard. In the distance, on the right, was the then very busy container terminal.* **John Whiteley**

Traction Transition - GM/EMD power in the UK and Ireland

Class 181 Fleet List

Number	Works No.	Builder	Notes
181	31248	GM-EMD, La Grange	
182	31249	GM-EMD, La Grange	
183	31250	GM-EMD, La Grange	
184	31251	GM-EMD, La Grange	
185	31252	GM-EMD, La Grange	
186	31253	GM-EMD, La Grange	
187	31254	GM-EMD, La Grange	
188	31255	GM-EMD, La Grange	
189	31256	GM-EMD, La Grange	
190	31257	GM-EMD, La Grange	Preserved
191	31258	GM-EMD, La Grange	
192	31259	GM-EMD, La Grange	

Class:	181
Number range:	B181-B192 (181-192)
Built by:	General Motors, La Grange, Illinois USA
GM model:	JL18 [Twin cab, road loco]
Years introduced:	1966
Wheel arrangement:	Bo-Bo
Gauge:	5ft 3in (1,600mm)
Maximum speed:	75mph (120km/h)
Length:	44ft 0in (13.42m)
Weight:	67 tonnes
Wheel diameter (new):	3ft 4in (1,016mm)
Engine type:	EMD 8-645E
Engine output:	1,100hp (820kW)
Power at rail:	810hp (605kW)
Maximum tractive effort:	38,000lb (170kN)
Continuous tractive effort:	27,000lb (119kN)
Cylinder bore:	9$\frac{1}{8}$ in (230mm)
Cylinder stroke:	10in (250mm)
Transmission type:	Electric
Traction generator:	GM-EMD D25
Traction motor type:	GM-EMD D77
No. of traction motors:	4
Brake type:	Vacuum and Air
Brake force:	56 tonnes
Bogie type:	EMD
Multiple coupling type:	AAR
Sanding equipment:	Pneumatic

Left: *The follow-on order for 12 Class 181s incorporated the later design 8 645E prime mover, while retaining virtually the same body style as the previous Class 141s. Class 181 No. 189 is seen at Dublin Heuston on station pilot duties.*
Robin Ralston

'181 Fact File

- Preservation - Just one loco of this fleet, No. 191 is preserved. Now owned by the Irish Traction Group.

- Locos fitted with full Association of American Railroad (AAR) style multiple control system.

- Installed with dual vacuum/air brakes.

Below: *Seen just to the north of Thomastown on the line from Kilkenny to Waterford on 3 September 2003, Class 181 No. 192 powers a rail train, formed of a pair of three wagon flats loaded with dozens of short rail lengths. In common with all Irish Rail diesel locos, a single warning note horn trumpet was mounted centrally on the cab roof.* **Gavin Morrison**

Right: *On 2 September 2003, Class 181 No. 188 leads Class 141 No. 175 out of the sidings at Arklow with a ballast train. Arklow is located on the line between Dublin and Rosslare via Wicklow. While the sidings have now closed, Arklow station is still a passing point on the largely single line between Bray and Rosslare.* **Gavin Morrison**

Class 071/111 Fleet List

Number	Works No.	Builder	Notes
CIE Class 071			
071	713736	EMD-DD, Canada	
072	713737	EMD-DD, Canada	
073	713738	EMD-DD, Canada	
074	713739	EMD-DD, Canada	
075	713740	EMD-DD, Canada	
076	713741	EMD-DD, Canada	
077	713742	EMD-DD, Canada	
078	713743	EMD-DD, Canada	
079	713744	EMD-DD, Canada	
080	713745	EMD-DD, Canada	
081	713746	EMD-DD, Canada	
082	713747	EMD-DD, Canada	
083	713748	EMD-DD, Canada	
084	713749	EMD-DD, Canada	
085	713750	EMD-DD, Canada	
086	713751	EMD-DD, Canada	
087	713752	EMD-DD, Canada	
088	713753	EMD-DD, Canada	
NIR Class 111			
111	798072-1	EMD-DD, Canada	Introduced 10/80
112	798072-2	EMD-DD, Canada	Introduced 10/80
113	838084-1	EMD-DD, Canada	Introduced 12/84
JT22CW-2 ZS Class 666 (Serbian Railways)			
001		EMD-DD, Canada named *Dinara*	Built for Tito's 'Blue Train' in Yugosalvia
002		EMD-DD, Canada named *Kozara*	Built for Tito's 'Blue Train' in Yugosalvia
003		EMD-DD, Canada named *Sutjeska*	Built for Tito's 'Blue Train' in Yugosalvia
004		EMD-DD, Canada named *Neretva*	Built for Tito's 'Blue Train' in Yugosalvia

Class:	071
Number range:	CIE: 071-088
	NIR: 111-113
Built by:	General Motors, La Grange, USA
GM model:	JT22CW
Years introduced:	1976-1984
Wheel arrangement:	Co-Co
Gauge:	5ft 3in (1,600mm)
Maximum speed	90mph (145km/h)
Length:	57ft 0in (17.37m)
Height:	13ft 3in (4.04m)
Width:	9ft 5¾in (2.89m)
Weight:	100.6 tonnes
Wheel diameter (new):	3ft 4in (1,016mm)
Min curve negotiable:	164ft (50m)
Engine type:	EMD 12-645E3B or EMD 12-645E3C
Engine output:	2,450hp (1,830kW)
Power at rail:	1,700hp (1,300kW)
Maximum tractive effort:	65,000lb (289kN)
Continuous tractive effort:	43,000lb (192kN)
Cylinder bore:	9⅛ in (230mm)
Cylinder stroke:	10in (250mm)
Transmission type:	Electric
Traction generator:	GM-EMD AR10D3
Auxiliary alternator:	GM-EMD D14
Auxiliary generator:	GM-EMD A-814M1 of 24hp
Traction motor type:	GM-EMD D77B
No. of traction motors:	6
Brake type:	Vacuum and Air
Bogie type:	EMD 'Flexicoil'
Multiple coupling type:	AAR
Fuel tank capacity:	790gal (3,600lit)
Sanding equipment:	Pneumatic
Note:	NIR 111 and 112 modified to provide head end power (later isolated)

'071/111' Fact File

- This design on GM/EMD loco classified as JT22CW by GM are all still in traffic, 18 with Irish Rail and three with Northern Ireland Railways.

- Most locos have now been refurbished, all are fitted with dual brake equipment.

- Heritage liveries are applied to some locos.

Left: *The two platform station at Manulla Junction on the Athlone-Westport line where the branch to Ballina diverges, is a unique station, with no road or passenger access, purely an interchange point for rail passengers. Overlooking the station from a bridge, Class 071 No. 080, one of the 1972-built GM/EMD locos arrives at the interchange junction with the 13.15 from Ballina on 30 April 2004 where passengers can interchange with main line services on the Westport to Athlone and on to Dublin route.* **Gavin Morrison**

Traction Transition - GM/EMD power in the UK and Ireland 19

Above: *With a rake of six Mk2s and a generator van behind the loco, Class 071 No. 077 departs from Dublin Houston on 15 May 1983, painted in its as delivered tan and black livery.*
Gavin Morrison

Left: *Sporting the revised tan and black livery, with a white edge to the black and orange front warning panels, No. 079 is recorded near Greystones, skirting the Irish Sea on 12 June 2000 powering the InterCity Mk2 formed 14.45 Rosslare Europort to Dublin Connolly.* Gavin Morrison

Iarnród Éireann (IE) Irish Rail grey-liveried Class 071 No. 082 shows the latest standard colour scheme for the Co-Co fleet. To provide some form of frontal visibility a yellow panel has been applied. Refurbished and repainted locos are now carrying their European Vehicle Number (EVN) No. 082 with an EVN identity of 92 60 0117082-4, is seen passing Portarlington with a container train from Ballina to Dublin Wall on 5 July 2018. CJM

CELEBRATING ONE OF THE WORLD'S GREATEST MODEL MAKERS

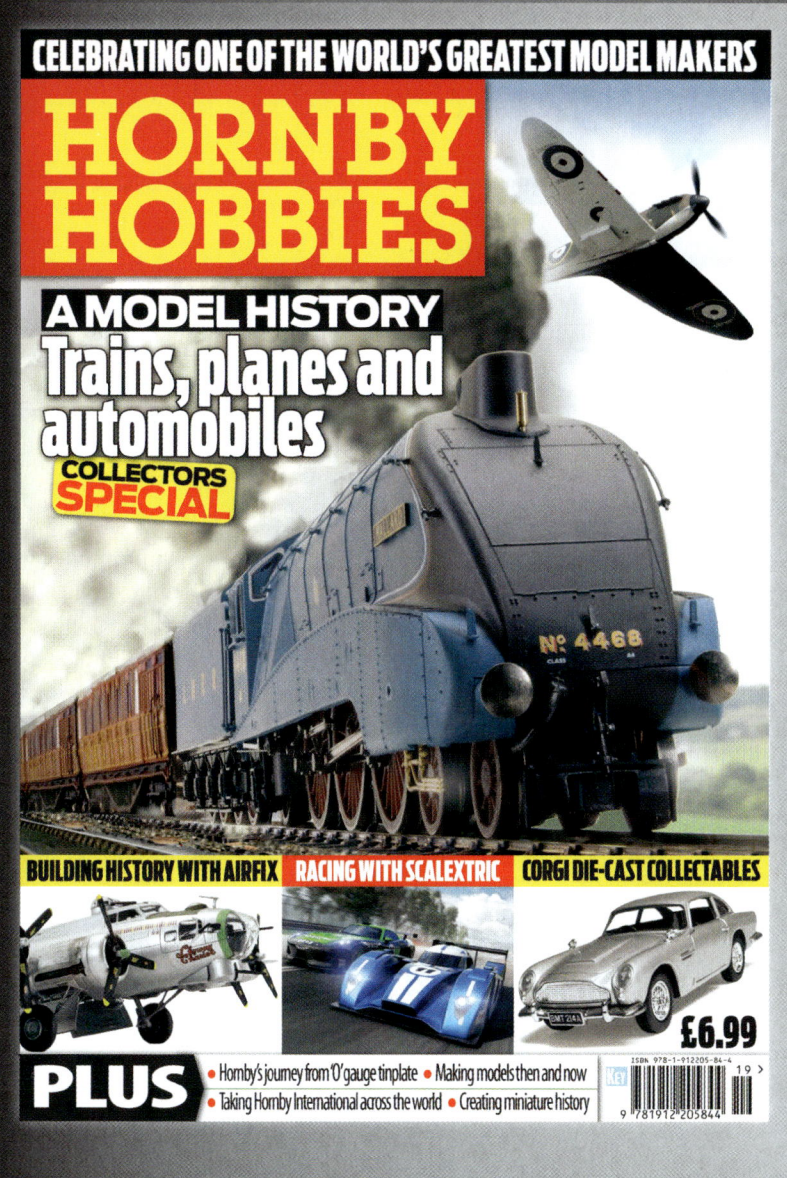

Today Hornby Hobbies comprises a diverse range of model brands creating stunning scale products across railway, aviation, road and military themes. The Hornby Hobbies portfolio has grown exponentially since the dawn of the millennium with the acquisition of European railway brands, Airfix, Humbrol and Corgi, all of which have joined Hornby and Scalextric to create one of the strongest hobby sector groups in the world.

In Hornby Hobbies – A Model History we will take you through Hornby's history and bring you right up to date with all its current activities.

It features:

HORNBY TIMELINE
With more than 100 years of history, Hornby has a rich past. We highlight its major achievements and changes since Frank Hornby introduced 'O' tinplate railways in 1901 across Hornby Hobbies' major brands

SCALEXTRIC
Slot car racing took the world by storm in the 1960s while today its models are more realistic and controllable than ever before. With stunning archive images dating back to the late 1950s we recount the story of Hornby's Scalextric brand - a brand that is still the first choice for electric slot car racing today.

THE AIRFIX STORY
Like many of the Hornby brands, Airfix has become a household name synonymous with plastic model kits. Spanning eight decades, this diverse business has made everything from plastic combs to scale model aircraft and ready-to-run model railway equipment.

POCHER CARS
These 1:8 and 1:4 scale kits are legendary for their detail and size. We recount the story of Pocher's unrivalled model cars.

And much more!

ORDER DIRECT

JUST £6.99 PLUS FREE P&P*

*Free 2nd class P&P on all UK & BFPO orders. Overseas charges apply.

Free P&P* when you order online at www.keypublishing.com/shop

OR

Call UK: 01780 480404
Overseas: +44 1780 480404
Monday to Friday 9am-5:30pm GMT

293/19

SUBSCRIBERS CALL FOR YOUR £1.00 DISCOUNT! SUBSCRIBERS CALL FOR YOUR £1.00 DISCOUNT!

Above: *Displaying the interim grey and silver livery, applied after the orange style was replaced, No. 072 is seen in the yard at Waterford on 18 August 2015 with a weed control train. Note the handbrake wheel half way up the body at the near end and the single access steps from track height, with cab access via the bodyside walkway.* **CJM**

Left: *Members of Class 071 can be regularly seen on the IR main line between Dublin Wall and Ballina, powering container trains. Passing through Portarlington station and about to take the junction towards Athlone, No. 079 heads for Ballina on 5 July 2018.* **CJM**

Below: *Approaching East Wall Junction and departing from Dublin Wall, No. 078 powers one of the regular Dublin to Tara Mines in Co Meath, trains. The Tara Mines freight only line branches off the main Dublin-Belfast line near Drogheda. This image was recorded on 27 April 2016.* **CJM**

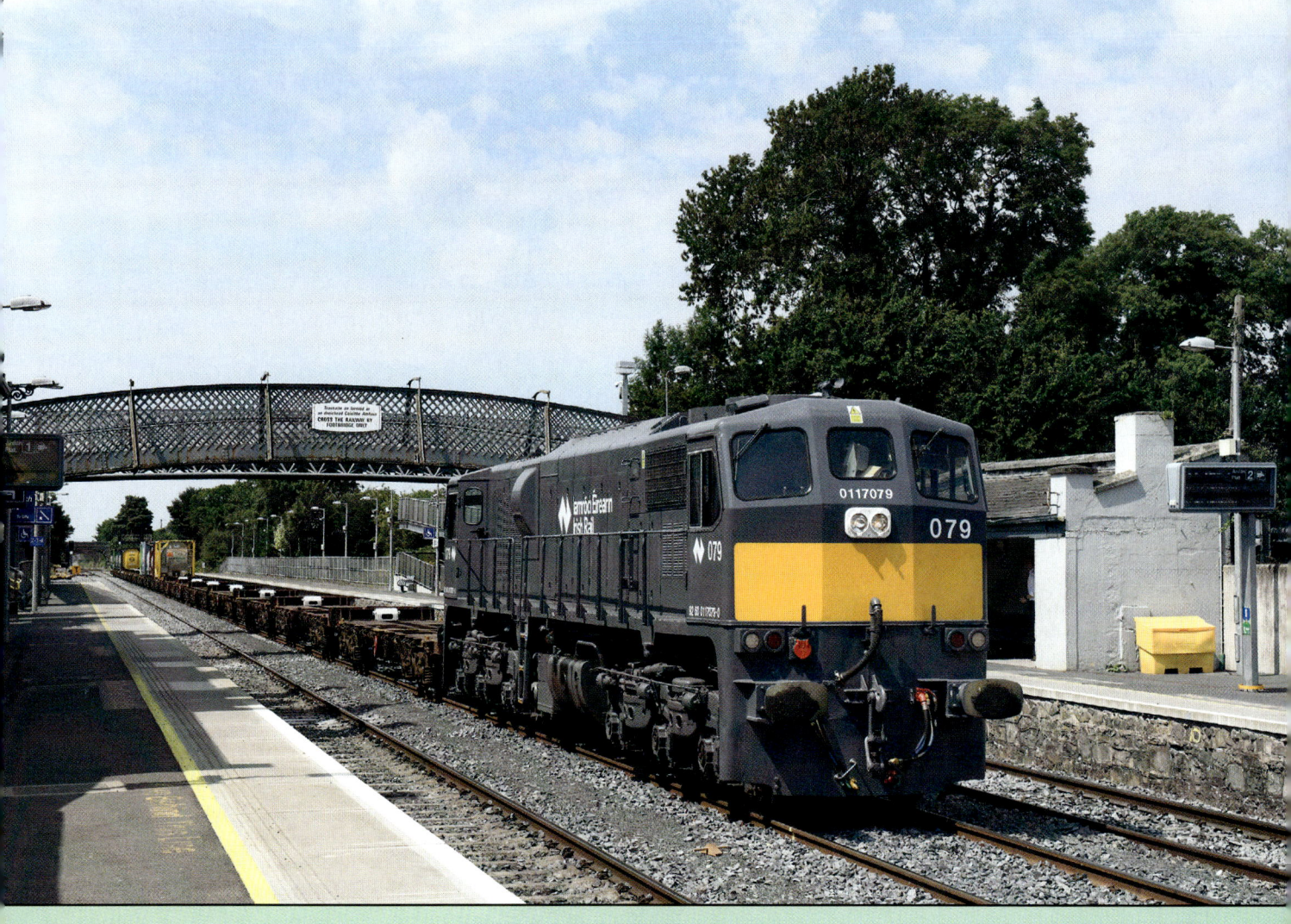

Above: *Taking the middle bi-directional track through Kildare on 4 July 2018, Class 071 No. 079 powers the Ballina to Dublin container terminal service. Business did not look to be too good on American Independence Day, with a string of empty flats at the head of the train.* **CJM**

Right: *The three Northern Ireland Railways locos of the 071 design, classified as 111 are based at Belfast York Road depot, located adjacent to Yorkgate station. The locos now see infrequent use, with no loco-hauled passenger services. The fleet only being used to power engineering trains. On 3 July 2018, No. 112 is seen passing Portadown, running light to Belfast York Road.* **CJM**

Tito's BlueTrain

Four similar EMD JT22CW-2 locos were purchased by Jugoslovenske Železnice (Yugoslavian Railways) designated class 666. They were intended for use by Yugoslav Railways to power Tito's Blue Train, and were thus finished in all blue livery. They differ from the Irish '071s' being standard gauge, and have a full width car-body. After the dissolution of Yugoslavia, the three locos have been used in general freight and passenger service. The fleet is now operated by Železnice Srbije (Serbia Railways). In this illustration loco No. 666-001 is seen powering a freight near Ruma.
Wikimedia Commons

Traction Transition - GM/EMD power in the UK and Ireland

Class:	201
Number range:	201-234
Built by:	General Motors, Diesel Division, Ontario, Canada
GM model:	JT42HCW
Years introduced:	1994-1995
Wheel arrangement:	Co-Co
Gauge:	5ft 3in (1,600mm)
Maximum speed:	100mph (160km/h)
Length:	68ft 9in (20.95m)
Height:	13ft 2in (4.02m)
Width:	8ft 8in (2.64m)
Weight:	109 -112 tonnes
Wheel diameter (new):	3ft 4in (1,016mm)
Min curve negotiable:	262ft (00m)
Engine type:	EMD 12-710G3B
Engine output:	3,200hp (2,400kW)
Power at rail:	2,970hp (2,210kW)
Maximum tractive effort:	43,700lb (194kN)
Cylinder bore:	9⅛ in (230mm)
Cylinder stroke:	11in (280mm)
Transmission type:	Electric
Traction generator:	GM-EMD AR8PHEA/CA6
Auxiliary generator:	GM-EMD5A-8147
Traction motor type:	GM-EMD D43
No. of traction motors:	6
Heating:	Head end power (HEP) Dayton-Phoenix E7145 of 220-380V three-phase
Brake type:	Vacuum and Air
Brake force:	72 tonnes
Bogie type:	EMD GC
Multiple coupling type:	AAR
Fuel tank capacity:	990gal (4,500lit)
Sanding equipment:	Pneumatic

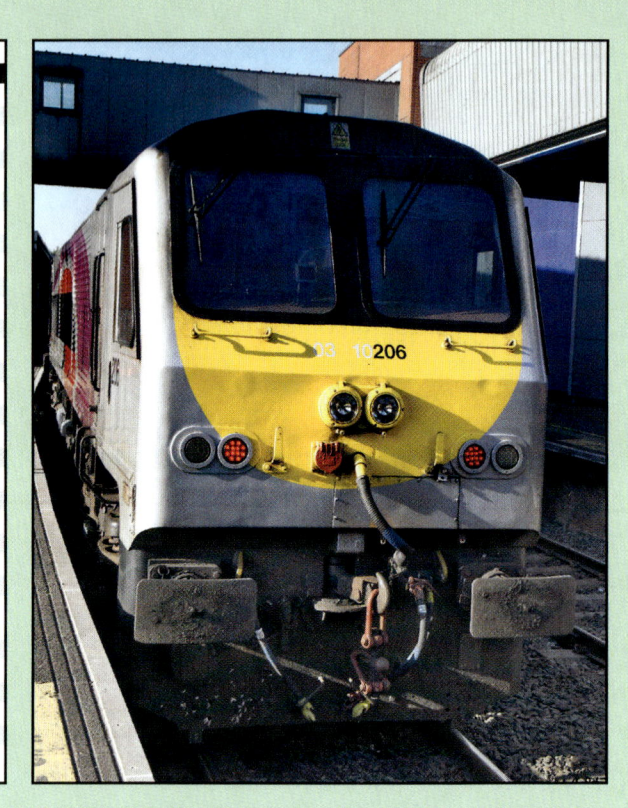

Above: *In 1994-1995 Irish Rail sought new main line diesel locos and returned to General Motors/EMD to provide the answer, this came in a fleet of 34 JT42HCW locos, a twin-cabbed design incorporating a 12-cylinder 710 series power unit. The front ends housed typical GM headlights, AAR jumper connections and both air and vacuum brake connections. No. 206 is illustrated.* **CJM**

Left Upper and Left Below: *After introduction, it was agreed to apply cast names to the entire fleet, using names cast in both English and Irish of rivers, this at one time the fleet became known as the 'River Class'. The cast plates were applied above the cab side windows in a trapezium shaped plate. A number of locos are now missing of one or both plates. The plates from No. 233 River Clare are shown. Both:* **CJM**

Class 201 Fleet List

Number	Name (Irish)	Name (English)	Works No.	Builder	Notes
201(S)	Abhainn na Sionnainne	River Shannon	928303-01	EMD-DD, Canada	
202(S)	Abhainn na Laoi	River Lee	928303-02	EMD-DD, Canada	
203(S)	Abhainn na Coiribe	River Corrib	928303-03	EMD-DD, Canada	
204(S)	Abhainn na Bearu	River Barrow	928303-04	EMD-DD, Canada	
205(S)	Abhainn na Feoire	River Nore	928303-05	EMD-DD, Canada	
206	(Abhainn na Life)	(River Liffey)	948500-01	EMD-DD, Canada	Enterprise use, push pull
207	Abhainn na Bóinne	River Boyne	948500-02	EMD-DD, Canada	Enterprise use, push pull
8208		River Lagan	948435-01	EMD-DD, Canada	Enterprise use, push pull. NIR owned
209			948435-02	EMD-DD, Canada	Enterprise use, push pull. NIR owned
210(S)	Abhainn na hEirne	River Erne	928303-06	EMD-DD, Canada	
211(S)	Abhainn na Suca	River Suck	928303-07	EMD-DD, Canada	
212(S)	Abhainn na Slaine	River Slaney	928303-08	EMD-DD, Canada	
213(S)	Abhainn na Muaidhe	River Moy	928303-09	EMD-DD, Canada	
214(S)	Abhainn na Broshai	River Brosna	928303-10	EMD-DD, Canada	
215	An Abhainn Mhor	River Avonmore	938403-01	EMD-DD, Canada	InterCity, push pull
216	Abhainn na Dothra	River Dodder	938403-02	EMD-DD, Canada	InterCity, push pull. Grand Hibernian loco
217	Abhainn na Fleisce	River Flesk	938403-03	EMD-DD, Canada	InterCity, push pull
218	Abhainn na Garbhoige	River Garavogue	938403-04	EMD-DD, Canada	InterCity, push pull
219	(Abhainn na Tulchann)	River Tolka	938403-05	EMD-DD, Canada	InterCity, push pull
220	An Abhainn Dhubh	River Blackwater	938403-06	EMD-DD, Canada	InterCity, push pull
221	Abhainn na Feilge	River Fealge	938403-07	EMD-DD, Canada	InterCity, push pull
222	(Abhainn na Dargaile)	River Dargle	938403-08	EMD-DD, Canada	InterCity, push pull
223	Abhainn na hAinnire	River Anner	938403-09	EMD-DD, Canada	InterCity, push pull
224	(Abhainn na Féile)	(River Feale)	938403-10	EMD-DD, Canada	InterCity, push pull
225(S)	Abhainn na Daoile	River Deel	938403-11	EMD-DD, Canada	InterCity, push pull
226	(Abhainn na Siuire)	(River Suir)	938403-12	EMD-DD, Canada	InterCity, push pull
227	(Abhainn na Leamhna)	River Laune	938403-13	EMD-DD, Canada	Enterprise use, push pull
228	(An Abhainn Bhui)	(River Owenboy)	938403-14	EMD-DD, Canada	Enterprise use, push pull
229	Abhainn na Mainge	River Maine	938403-15	EMD-DD, Canada	InterCity, push pull
230	(Abhainn na Bandan)	(River Bandon)	938403-16	EMD-DD, Canada	Enterprise use, push pull
231	(Abhainn na Maighe)	(River Maigue)	938403-17	EMD-DD, Canada	Enterprise use, push pull
232	(Abhainn na Chaomaraigh)	River Cummeragh	938403-18	EMD-DD, Canada	InterCity, push pull
233	Abhainn na Chlair	River Clare	938403-19	EMD-DD, Canada	Enterprise use, push pull
234	(Abhainn na hEatharlai)	River Aherlow	938403-20	EMD-DD, Canada	InterCity, push pull
Names in brackets are currently not applied					

Above: The only Irish General Motors locos to be built at the GM plant in London, Ontario, Canada were the Class 201s. On 6 April 2002, No. 228 approaches Cherryville Junction, Kildare with a service to Galway. At this point the line to Kilkenny and Waterford spurs off from the main line. **Brian Solomon**

Left: In the days when the Dublin-Galway trains were still loco-hauled, rather than formed of DMU stock, No. 222 departs from Galway on 8 September 2003 with the 18.20 to Dublin Heuston. **John Whiteley**

'201' Fact File

- Only Irish GMs built in Canada.

- Some locos now fitted with knuckle couplings at one end to operate push-pull trains.

- Loco No. 216 dedicated to the Belmond Pullman 'Grand Hibernian' train.

Left: Class 201 locos Nos. 206-209/215-226/228/229-234 have been modified with knuckle couplings and retractable buffers at one end to attach to passenger stock. This view shows the connection between a loco and Mk4 passenger rake, note the AAR connection is coupled to allow 'push-pull' operation. **CJM**

Below: When the Class 201s were constructed at the GM Diesel Division plant in London, Ontario, Canada, special facilities had to be provided as the locos were 5ft 3in gauge rather than the US standard of 4ft 8½in. Here a fitted out body is seen mounted on works accommodation trucks, while being moved around the plant on 29 July 1994. **CJM-C**

Traction Transition - GM/EMD power in the UK and Ireland　　25

Above: *Some sections of the rail network within the GM plant in London, Canada were equipped with multi-gauge tracks allowing the Irish locos to operate with their intended trucks. However, temporary US style knuckle couplings had to be fitted. Loco No. 205 fresh from the paint shop is seen in the works yard on 15 August 1994.* **CJM-C**

Left and Below: *Apart from delivery of the first loco No. 201, which was flown to Ireland, the other 33 were transported by rail and ship. On the left, No. 215 is seen mounted on a flat car, awaiting shipment from the Canadian Pacific (CP) yard in London on 5 December 1994. In the view below, the size difference between the Irish Class 201 and North American power is very evident. Class 201 No. 228 is seen coupled to BN 9513 and EMDX7003, both EMD SD70MACs. The SD70s, were on route for painting, while the 201 was on delivery.* **CJM-C**

Traction Transition - GM/EMD power in the UK and Ireland

Above: Today, apart from some Dublin Heuston to Cork services, all Irish Rail passenger duties are formed of DMU stock, long distance services using high-quality Mitsui/Rotem Class 22000 stock. In the days of loco-haulage, Class 201 No. 215 passes Muine Bheag (Bagenalstown) on 3 September 2003 with the 11.35 Dublin Heuston to Waterford service. **Gavin Morrison**

Below: It is not uncommon on Irish Rail for reversals to be required to reach passenger stations. One such location is Killarney on the Mallow to Tralee line. Trains travelling towards Tralee drive off the mainline into the terminal station and after station work is complete, propel back out to a junction and continue towards the trains destination, trains from Tralee, pass the station on a higher level line and then propel back into the platform. On 6 September 2003, Class 201 No. 219 leaving Killarney having just reversed from the station to the main line with the 15.00 Cork to Tralee service. **John Whiteley**

Traction Transition - GM/EMD power in the UK and Ireland

Above: *During the transition period between using the BREL designed and built Mk3 stock and the new CAF vehicles, InterCity-liveried Class 201s could be found powering rakes of orange-liveried Mk3s. On 14 April 2006, InterCity No. 216 is seen with a Mk3 rake near Sallins and Naas powering the 07.50 Limerick to Dublin Heuston.* **Robin Ralston**

Below: *After the BR-design Mk3 loco-hauled stock was withdrawn from the Dublin-Cork route, new CAF-built Mk4 vehicles were introduced in 2006, with eight sets (67-vehicles) built. These push-pull trains usually operate with the loco coupled by way of a knuckle coupling at the Cork end of formations and the driving van at the Dublin end. At the time of introduction a number of Class 201s were repainted in the new InterCity colours of silver and two-tone green. On 18 May 2017, No. 226 is seen near Garryncoonagh North near Charleville, forming the 18.00 Dublin Heuston to Cork.* **Robin Ralston**

Above: With a yellow background to its River Fealge cast nameplate, No. 221 takes the middle road through Kildare on 4 July 2018, bringing up the rear of the 11.25 Cork to Dublin Heuston. CJM

Right: The same loco as illustrated in the above picture, but obviously before a repaint with new branding and revision of number style, No. 221 is captured at Mallow on 20 April 2016 with the 12.25 Cork to Dublin Heuston. The vacuum brake system on these locos has been retained, but is currently not in use. CJM

Below: Sufficient stock exists to form eight InterCity Mk4 push-pull sets, but usually four or five are formed up at one time. With its InterCity bodyside branding clearly showing, applied to a panel attached to the ribbed bodyside. No. 217 is seen arriving at Dublin Heuston on 18 August 2015 on rear of 10.20 from Cork. Frequently one or two of the Class 201s can be found stabled in the station area, with a large number to be found at the nearby main depot and works at Inchicore. CJM

Traction Transition - GM/EMD power in the UK and Ireland

Left Top: *Painted in early 'Enterprise' (Belfast-Dublin express) livery, Class 201 No. 230 is recorded near Sallins and Naas, close to Kildare on 5 May 2006 powering a Mk2 passenger rake and a train supply generator coach behind the loco, forming the 06.45 Limerick to Dublin Heuston.*
Robin Ralston

Left Middle: *In a slightly revised livery to that shown in the above illustration, No. 233 has an all yellow front end, rather than having a black panel extending around the upper front. No. 233 is seen at Belfast Central station, since renamed as Belfast Lanyon Place station, on 18 August 2015, with the 08.00 service to Dublin Connolly. On the Belfast-Dublin 'Enterprise' service, the locos are usually coupled at the Belfast end of train formations, making exchange of locos in Dublin easy.* **CJM**

Below: *During 2015-2017, the 'Enterprise' Mk4 stock was given a major refurbishment, including attention to the Class 201s, which saw a revised livery applied. On 3 July 2018, No. 207 approaches Moira, leading the 13.20 Dublin Connolly to Belfast Central.* **CJM**

Above: *With its* River Boyne / Abhainn na Bóinne *cast nameplates above the cab side windows, revised liveried Class 201 No. 207 stands in the 'Enterprise' platform at Dublin Connolly on 6 July 2018 after arriving with the 08.00 from Belfast.* **CJM**

Right: *If for any reason one of the 'Enterprise' dedicated Class 201s is not available for service, one of the InterCity liveried locos will be substituted, as long as its fitted with Northern Ireland cab equipment. On 20 August 2017, IC No. 227 is seen on an 'Enterprise' service at Belfast Central.* **CJM**

In 2016, luxury train operator Belmond launched a high end land cruise train in Ireland, formed of 10 totally rebuilt former Irish Rail Mk3 coaches. The train, known as the Grand Hibernian, operates on selected dates each summer over the scenic routes, carrying a limited number of usually American and Japanese tourists. To power the train Irish Rail have dedicated Class 201 No. 216 to the duty, repainting it is Belmond dark blue and applying cast Grand Hibernian decals to the cab sides. On 5 July 2018 the loco and train are seen at Portarlington. **CJM**

Traction Transition - GM/EMD power in the UK and Ireland

Mendip 'Switchers'

In 1980, Mendip aggregate producer Foster Yeoman sought to improve yard operations at their expanding Torr Works, Merehead Quarry, and invited tenders to built new traction. Prior, the company had used old second or third hand ex BR 350hp 0-6-0 locos which did not meet the aspirations of the company.

The specification issued, demanded 24 hour cover with high availability, combined with low running costs. Although a handful of UK builders responded, Foster Yeoman decided to go to the US loco market, where they knew such locos were available.

General Motors/EMD offered an 'off-the-shelf' SW1001 'Switcher' and guaranteed that it would provide 100 per cent availability between its booked maintenance.

The Bo-Bo (four axle) offering would be powered by an 8-cylinder 645E engine set to deliver 1,000hp.

After discussions to incorporate some customisation, a single loco was ordered in mid-1980. It was constructed at GMs La Grange site in Chicago, Illinois during October 1980. After works testing, it was shipped via Southampton Docks, arriving at Merehead Quarry on 12 January 1981. Records show it cost just £330,000.

One or two technical design changes had to be incorporated, the GM standard continuous bodyside handrails were not fitted to meet width reduction, cab windows were revised in a style to allow a good view of the draw gear, dual air/vacuum brakes were fitted and a drop-head knuckle coupling was fitted. A novel feature was an operational US loco bell, mounted on the roof with a pneumatic striker, controlled from a push switch in the cab.

The loco was allocated the identity of No. 44 and was named *Western Yeoman II*.

In 2000 a second Switcher was purchased by ARC/Hanson in the form of a secondhand loco, built to works No. 37903 of 1972. Once delivered it was numbered as 120 and usually operates at the Whatley Quarry site. Originally named *Whatley Endeavour*, but was renamed *Kennith John Witcombe* in June 2015 in memory of a staff member. ∎

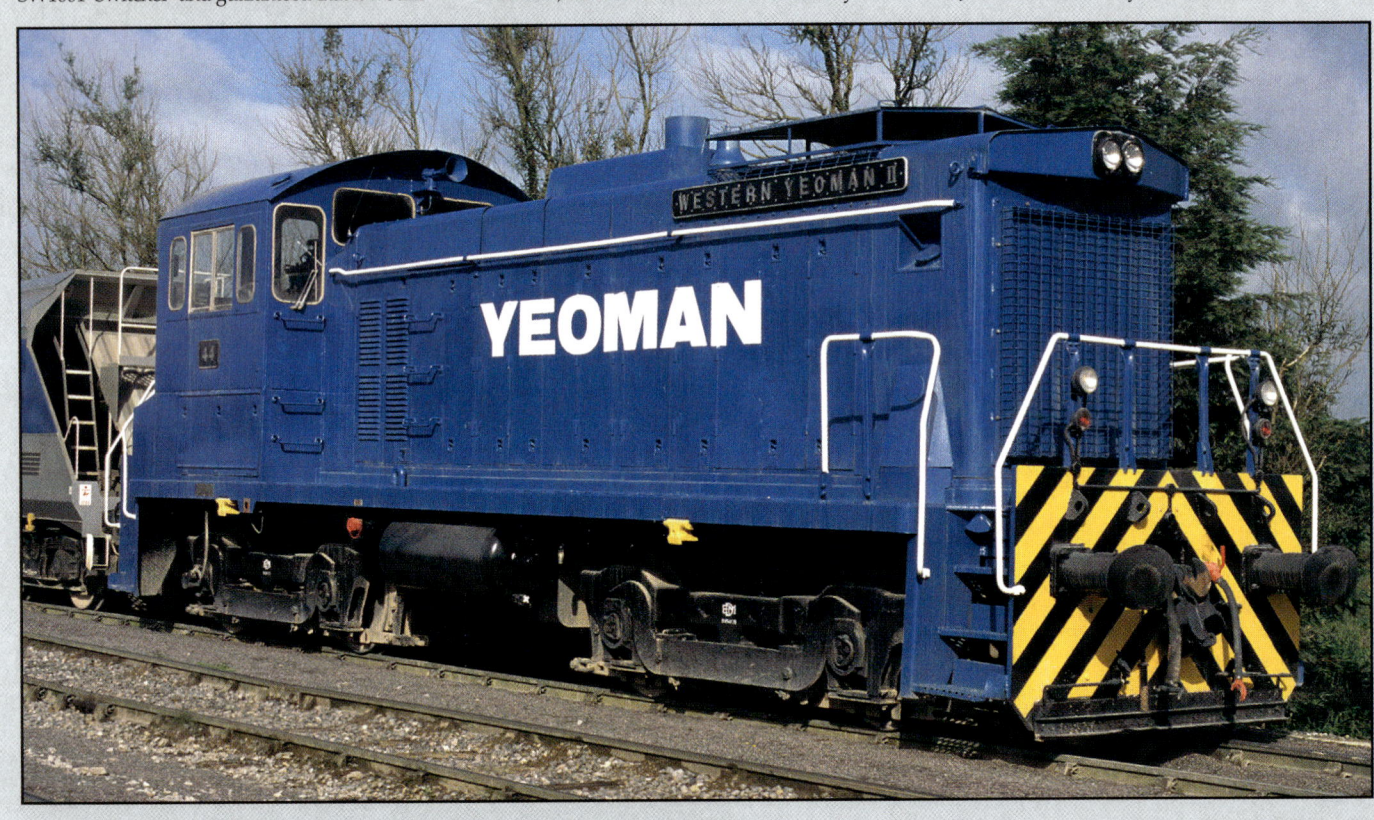

Above: *Painted in Foster Yeoman mid-blue livery, off-set by the Yeoman name in white on the bodyside, with a cast number plate '44' on the cab side and the* Western Yeoman II *Western Class 52 style nameplate on the bodyside. The loco is seen just after a repaint at Merehead summer 2008.*
CJM

Left: *The driving cab incorporated in the Foster Yeoman SW1001 was of the standard design, but included vacuum brake equipment, a fitting not on the US or Canada models. Standard design EMD power and master switch controllers are seen on the right, with the brake valve to the left.*
CJM

SW1001 Fact File

■ Standard North American 'Switch' loco design, derived from the SW1 of 1939.

■ A total of 174 SW1001s were built at the La Grange facility.

■ The design has a low height 15ft 3in and the locos are powered by the 8-cylinder 645 power unit set to 1,000hp.

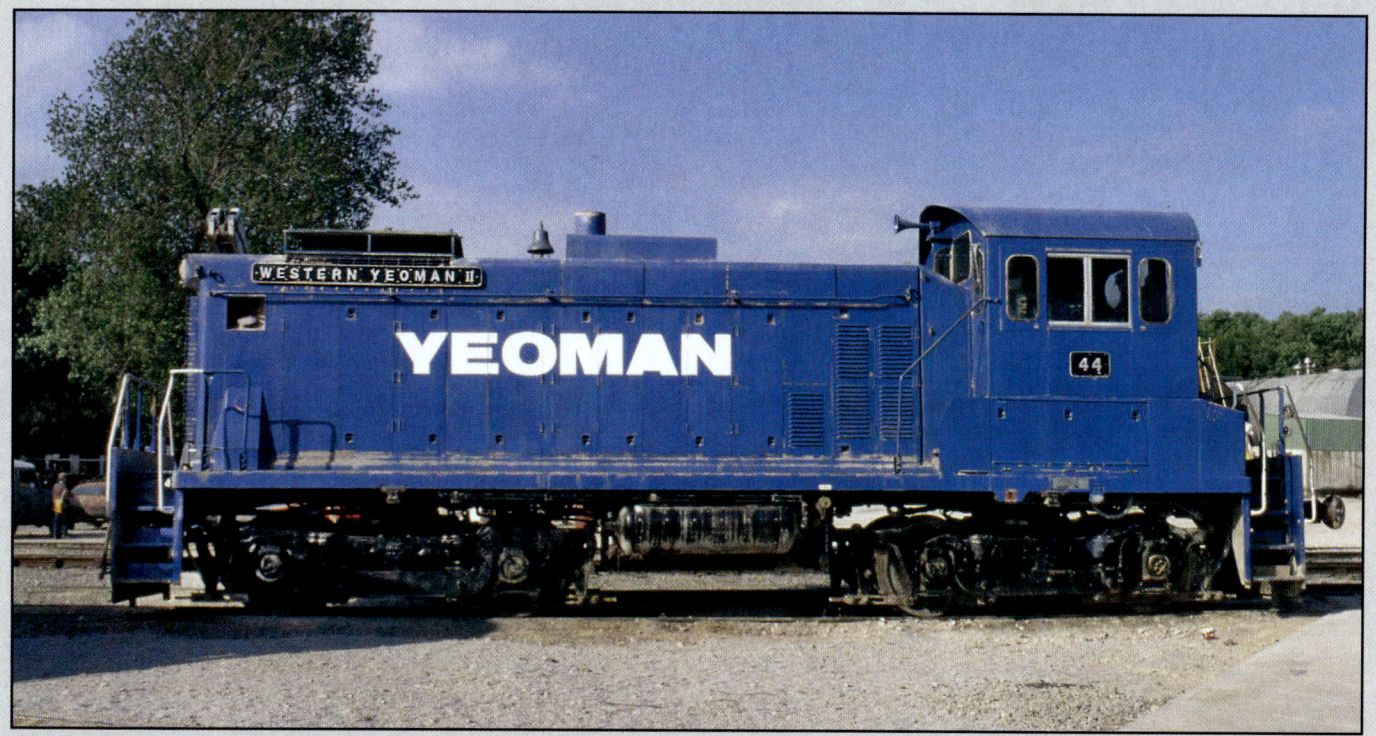

Above: *Profile view of No. 44 Western Yeoman II. This design of GM/EMD switcher was chosen for the Yeoman contract due to its reduced height of 14ft 3in compared to 15ft 1in for the SW 1500 design. The overall length is 44ft 8in. It is fitted with AAR Type A switcher trucks (bogies) which incorporate two GM D77 traction motors in each.* **CJM**

Right: *To facilitate coupling to a wide diversity of stock, the loco was fitted with drop-head knuckle couplings and standard UK design buffers. Main reservoir and brake pipes together with a vacuum brake hose were fitted to the buffer beam. To keep width to a minimum, no bodyside rails were fitted.* **CJM**

Below: *In 2000, a second SW1001 switcher was obtained to operate in the Mendips, with Whatley-based Hanson Aggregates (previously ARC-Southern). This loco, built to works No. 37903 in 1972 for Companie de Bauxite de Guinea (Boke) in Guinea, West Africa as No. 204. In 1982 it was involved in an accident and the remains were shipped back to the US. It was then rebuilt by National Rail Equipment and sold to Hanson as their No. 120. The loco is seen at Whatley.* **Stew Cronin**

Traction Transition - GM/EMD power in the UK and Ireland

The Class 59 Fleet

In the early 1980s Mendip aggregate company Foster Yeoman became concerned about the locos BR were providing for their trains, failures were common and the market position of company could be at stake. Foster Yeoman and the BR Railfreight arm agreed, that if possible all Yeoman trains would be rostered for then new Class 56 locos from May 1983.

This was a poor decision, as the Western Region Class 56 availability was rapidly decreasing, at times availability figures were only 30%. This reflected on Yeoman's operations. Records show that at times Yeoman trains were only running 60 per cent to time.

Foster Yeoman carried out a traction survey in mid-1983 and found 34 different locos from a variety of classes operated their trains in just one week, with poor quality and defective locos provided.

Discussions took place in autumn 1983 between Foster Yeoman and the BR freight business, seeking a rapid improvement in service. Yeoman knew from previous private wagon ownership, that with their privately-owned and dedicated wagon fleet availability was around 95 per cent. With this in mind, it was suggested to the then BR Railfreight Director Henry Sanderson that a privately owned loco fleet would be the answer to address these issues.

In many circles this was considered a joke, but in fact this was far from the case, Yeoman having carried out detailed research into private loco ownership and operation. Based on 1983 train consists, a fleet of six locos was considered, offering a fleet availability of 95%.

At the time, it was unlikely that BR or trade unions would agree to such a scheme. However, such was the strength of the Foster Yeoman contract, that agreement was eventually reached for Yeoman to own its own locos, but use BR drivers and seconded BR staff for maintenance.

At the time of Railfreight's agreement to Yeoman entering the private block train market, other block train operators were closely observing progress. Many had poor experiences of BR traction provision.

The strength of a private company in main line loco ownership, gave Yeoman the ability to make stringent demands on availability and performance. The most important was the ability of the fleet to move four million tonnes per annum, with a 'proven' 95% availability. When Yeoman started shopping, the British offers were almost none existent. Engineers involved with the Class 56 and 58 fleets, saying availability under controlled maintenance 'could be' 95%, but in practice this figure had never been met. British companies, including BREL, Brush and GEC were all given the chance to tender for the order, but little interest was shown when the stringent terms on availability and reliability were given, this was compounded by a small fleet size.

Yeoman knew that a 95% availability figure was in place with North American companies. US technology had already proved itself to Foster Yeoman, following the purchase of a GM-EMD 'Switcher'.

With no satisfaction from any UK company, Yeoman went to General Motors (GM), who were known to Yeoman, and offered the stipulated availability with their successful SD40-2 product line. GM then spent thousands of hours scaling down the SD40 design to meet the UK loading gauge.

Original talks between BR and Yeoman were on the basis of buying British locos, so when they turned to the US issues emerged, the trade unions objected to US traction, at a time when British works were closing. However, integral to the deal, was a new 15-year contract offered to BR for the annual movement of 4.5 million tonnes of aggregate. BR could not afford to lose such a lucrative deal and talks reached agreement in mid-1984 on the GM loco contract, with agreement for a 15 year train movement contract signed in November 1984.

The structural design and specification for the GM locos, was set by Yeoman. It was suggested the front end style should follow that of the 'Western' Class 52, but, had to meet stringent requirements by the BR Director of Mechanical & Electrical Engineering (DM&EE). This required a Route Availability of 7, a 21.5t maximum axle load, and a 3.2 ride index.

US cab design was not suitable for UK use and BR stipulated the latest Westinghouse DWB2 brake system and a Class 58 'style' driving desk. ➡

Left: *One of the original design specifications placed by Foster Yeoman was for 'ribbed' body sides, thus matching the design of their new aluminium Procor bogie wagon fleet. The exterior of the UK product was thus set, even though the matching wagon fleet soon fell out of favour. The ribbed body design was kept for the 1990s order for Irish Class 201s and later for the EWS Class 66 and Euro 66 fleets. This was one of the early offerings produced by the GM drawing office in Chicago, which was soon the subject of Foster Yeoman's red pen, with the 'Western' Class 52 style being followed in terms of curvature on subsequent designs.* **GM/EMD**

Below: *The Class 59 locomotive layout, GM were quite amazed as to how much equipment could be squeezed into the very restrictive body profile, determined by the UK gauge envelope. The only item which GM wanted to offer was dynamic brakes, but no space could be found for the equipment.* **CJM-C**

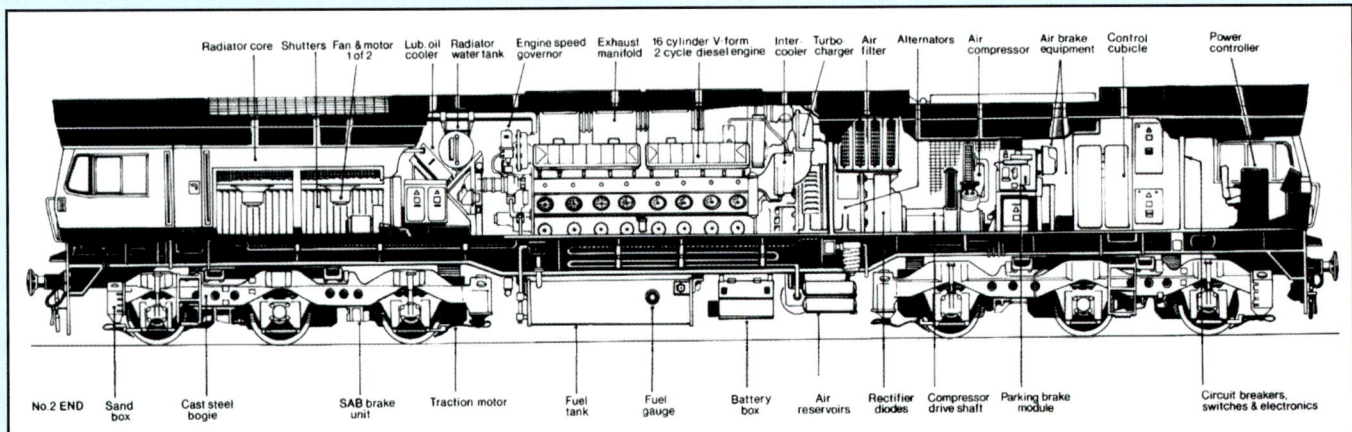

Control of exhaust noise was required, with a 84 dBa level in the cab and an external level of 107 dBa. Due to space limitations, the Yeoman fleet were unable to benefit from dynamic brake equipment, having to rely on friction brakes.

The final design included EMD's latest 'Super Series Creep' control system, this permitted haulage of heavier trains than previously possible, permitting consists of up to 4,300 tonnes without the need for double heading.

The superior performance and availability of GM's offering, saw a major rethink of Yeoman's traction needs, this saw just four locos ordered. The formal order contract No. 848002 was signed between Foster Yeoman, BR and General Motors on 16 November 1984. The new locos were classified by BR as Class 59, in US terms they were classified JT26CW-SS, the GM classification was derived from the builders model codes - 'J' indicating a double cab loco, 'T' indicating turbo charging, '26' was the engine type, 'C' was for three axles each end, 'W' was for standard gauge and 'SS' denoted Super Series.

The power unit selected for the '59' was a ⇨

Below: *The classic erecting shop view at General Motor's La Grange plant in Chicago. Illinois, with the historic wheeling of the first '59' No. 59001. The entire weight of the body is supported by a massive roof mounted gantry crane, holding the body by its four prime lifting points. The marrying up of the first loco of a new design with the bogies is always a major and very precise operation requiring the body to be lowered millimeter by millimeter onto the mounting pads of the bogie to ensure no problems exist.* **CJM-C**

Sub-class:	59/0	59/1	59/2
Number range:	59001-59005	59101-59104	59201-59206
GM model:	JT26CW-SS	JT26CW-SS	JT26CW-SS
Built by:	GM-EMD, La Grange, Illinois, USA	GM-DD, London, Ontario, Canada	GM-DD, London, Ontario, Canada
Years introduced:	1985-1989	1990	1994-1995
Wheel arrangement:	Co-Co	Co-Co	Co-Co
Maximum speed:	60mph (97km/h)	60mph (97km/h)	75mph (121km/h)
Length:	70ft 0½in (21.34m)	70ft 0½in (21.34m)	70ft 0½in (21.34m)
Height:	12ft 10in (3.91m)	12ft 10in (3.91m)	12ft 10in (3.91m)
Width:	8ft 8¼in (2.65m)	8ft 8¼in (2.65m)	8ft 8¼in (2.65m)
Weight:	121 tonnes	121 tonnes	121 tonnes
Wheelbase:	56ft 9in (17.29m)	56ft 9in (17.29m)	56ft 9in (17.29m)
Bogie wheelbase:	13ft 7in (4.14m)	13ft 7in (4.14m)	13ft 7in (4.14m)
Bogie pivot centres:	43ft 6in (13.25m)	43ft 6in (13.25m)	43ft 6in (13.25m)
Wheel diameter (new):	3ft 6in (1.06m)	3ft 6in (1.06m)	3ft 6in (1.06m)
Min curve negotiable:	4 chains (80.46m)	4 chains (80.46m)	4 chains (80.46m)
Engine type:	EMD 16-645E3C	EMD 16-645E3C	EMD 16-645E3C
Engine output:	3,000hp (2,237kW)	3,000hp (2,237kW)	3,000hp (2,237kW)
Power at rail:	2,533hp (1,889kW)	2,533hp (1,889kW)	2,533hp (1,889kW)
Tractive effort:	122,000lb (542kN)	122,000lb (542kN)	122,000lb (542kN)
Cylinder bore:	9$1/16$in (230mm)	9$1/16$in (230mm)	9$1/16$in (230mm)
Cylinder stroke:	10in (250mm)	10in (250mm)	10in (250mm)
Transmission:	Electric	Electric	Electric
Traction alternator:	EMD AR11	EMD AR11	EMD AR11
Companion alternator:	EMD D14A	EMD D14A	EMD D14A
Aux alternator:	EMD 3A8147	EMD 3A8147	EMD 3A8147
Traction motor type:	EMD D77B	EMD D77B	EMD D77B
No. of traction motors:	6	6	6
Gear ratio:	62:15	62:15	62:15
Brake type:	Air	Air	Air
Brake force:	69 tonnes	69 tonnes	69 tonnes
Route availability:	7	7	7
Heating type:	Not fitted	Not fitted	Not fitted
Multiple coupling type:	AAR (59, 66, 67, 70)	AAR (59, 66, 67, 70)	AAR (59, 66, 67, 70)
Fuel tank capacity:	1,000gal (4,546lit)	1,000gal (4,546lit)	1,000gal (4,546lit)
Lub oil capacity:	202gal (918lit)	202gal (918lit)	202gal (918lit)
Cooling water capacity:	212gal (964lit)	212gal (964lit)	212gal (964lit)
Sanding equipment:	Pneumatic	Pneumatic	Pneumatic
Sub-class variations:	Original fleet purchased by Foster Yeoman	Second batch of locos purchased by ARC Southern	Final derivative for National Power, sold to EWS (DB-C).

Traction Transition - GM/EMD power in the UK and Ireland

FREE 98-page digital sample issue

MODERN railways

Your favourite magazine is also available digitally.

DOWNLOAD THE APP NOW FOR FREE

FREE APP
with sample issue
IN APP ISSUES £3.99

SUBSCRIBE & SAVE
Monthly £2.99
6 issues £19.99
12 issues £34.99

SEARCH: Modern Railways

Read on your iPhone & iPad | Android | PC & Mac | kindle fire | Windows 10

ALSO AVAILABLE FOR DOWNLOAD

SEARCH RAILWAYS ILLUSTRATED
FREE APP with sample issue
IN APP ISSUES £3.99

SEARCH MODERN LOCOMOTIVES ILLUSTRATED
FREE APP with sample issue
IN APP ISSUES £3.99

FREE Specials App

IN APP ISSUES £3.99

Simply download to purchase digital versions of your favourite aviation specials in one handy place! Once you have the app, you will be able to download new, out of print or archive specials for less than the cover price!

SEARCH: Aviation Specials

How it Works.

Simply download the Modern Railways app and receive your sample issue completely free. Once you have the app, you will be able to download new or back issues (from January 2011 onwards) for less than newsstand price or, alternatively, subscribe to save even more!

Don't forget to register for your Pocketmags account. This will protect your purchase in the event of a damaged or lost device. It will also allow you to view your purchases on multiple platforms.

Available on iTunes | Available on the App Store | Available on Google play | Available on kindle fire | Available on PC, Mac & Windows 10

Available on PC, Mac, Blackberry and Windows 10 from **pocketmags.com**

Requirements for app: registered iTunes account on Apple iPhone, iPad or iPod Touch. Internet connection required for initial download. Published by Key Publishing Ltd. The entire contents of these titles are © copyright 2018. All rights reserved. App prices subject to change. 780/18

16-cylinder, 645E3C, a turbo-charged two-stroke, set to deliver 3,300hp, it was identical to that used in the SD40-2. The alternator came from the GM SD50 series, this was selected by GM to meet the work specification for the '59'. Bogies and traction motors for the '59' were modified versions of the SD40-2 type.

The most interesting part of the Class 59s was in its 'Creep' or 'Super Series' adhesion control system. Its operation is complicated, but in simple terms, if an accelerating loco from a stand can develop between 33-50% more tractive effort if its powered wheels are permitted to rotate or 'creep' under controlled conditions. This slip is finely tuned, as it must only be approximately 1- 2 mph above the true adhesion speed. The 'Super Series Creep' system was devised by US engineer Bruce Meyer, and was proven to improve adhesion. Electronics within the 'creep' system introduce a selective feature, with the leading axle given a higher degree of 'creep', friction, it is then increased on the rear axle. Speed detection for 'Super Series' is monitored by 'Doppler Radar', an eye, with a speed accuracy within +/- 1 mph.

When a train is started using 'Super Series' up to 1.5 mph Independent Detection And Correction (IDAC) is used - the driver's use of the power controller and sand application. Above 1.5 mph 'Super Series' takes over, and above 4 mph driver control sand application is shut off. Thus all adhesion characteristics above 4 mph are looked after by the 'Super Series' equipment.

At ordering, Yeoman specified a one year delivery time, with a 95% availability - these demands were met - surprisingly in the light of protracted planning. However, many items were supplied from the UK, including the Automatic Warning System, Driver's Safety Device, Westinghouse brakes, fuel gauges and drawgear.

As the Class 59s were not a standard GM product they were built by a dedicated team of 21 staff at the GM La Grange plant in Chicago Illinois. This team built all four locos in just under 26 weeks.

Main construction was at La Grange, but a number of components came from outside companies. For example, the carbodies were supplied by Super Steel of Milwaukee, Wisconsin. By November 1985 all four locos were complete and a major test period started.

The United States Department of Transportation Federal Railroad Administration (FRA) issued a certificate to allow No. 59001 to operate over the Burlington Northern Railroad on 10 December 1985. This allowed a small number of mainly light loco trials at night through the suburbs of Chicago!

Around Christmas 1985 the locos were inspected by Yeoman and BR, before being de-bogied and packed for shipment. Due to the small size of the locos, it was possible to haul them 'piggy-back' style from La Grange to Newport News in ⇨

Top: On 11 December 1985, the pioneer loco of the fleet No. 59001 stands on the transfer track between, La Grange and the Burlington Northern system after performing overnight trials. To conform with FRA regulations the loco No. 59001 is stencilled on the cab side. The wording at the cab side gives the name and address details of General Motors Corporation. Within a couple of days of this picture being recorded the loco was de-greased and put through the GM paint shop. **CJM-C**

Right: *The Yeoman 'follow-on' order, No. 59005 was delivered to Felixstowe Docks in June 1989 and is seen in the rail yard after being placed on is bogies ready for transfer to the RTC Derby and eventually Merehead for use.* **CJM**

Traction Transition - GM/EMD power in the UK and Ireland   37

Class 59 Fleet List

Number	Assembly Plant	Works No.	Build Date	Shipping Port	Transport Ship	Shipping Date	Port of UK Arrival	Arrival Date	Original Owner
Class 59/0									
59001	La Grange, IL, USA	848002-1	12/85	Newport News, VA	MV *Fairlift*	8 Jan 1986	Southampton	21 Jan 1986	Foster Yeoman
59002	La Grange, IL, USA	848002-2	12/85	Newport News, VA	MV *Fairlift*	8 Jan 1986	Southampton	21 Jan 1986	Foster Yeoman
59003	La Grange, IL, USA	848002-3	12/85	Newport News, VA	MV *Fairlift*	8 Jan 1986	Southampton	21 Jan 1986	Foster Yeoman
59004	La Grange, IL, USA	848002-4	12/85	Newport News, VA	MV *Fairlift*	8 Jan 1986	Southampton	21 Jan 1986	Foster Yeoman
59005	La Grange, IL, USA	878039-1	05/89	Baltimore, MD	MV *American Condor*	16 May 1989	Felixstowe	4 June 1989	Foster Yeoman
Class 59/1									
59101	London, Ont, Canada	878029-1	09/90	Halifax, NS	MV *Stellamare*	3 Oct 1990	Newport	19 Oct 1990	ARC
59102	London, Ont, Canada	878029-2	09/90	Halifax, NS	MV *Stellamare*	3 Oct 1990	Newport	19 Oct 1990	ARC
59103	London, Ont, Canada	878029-3	09/90	Halifax, NS	MV *Stellamare*	3 Oct 1990	Newport	19 Oct 1990	ARC
59104	London, Ont, Canada	878029-4	09/90	Halifax, NS	MV *Stellamare*	3 Oct 1990	Newport	19 Oct 1990	ARC
Class 59/2									
59201	London, Ont, Canada	918273-1	01/94	Halifax, NS	MV *Haskerland*	31 Jan 1994	Hull KGV	17 Feb 1994	National Power
59202	London, Ont, Canada	948519-1	06/95	Halifax, NS	MV *Condock V*	16 Jul 1995	Hull KGV	4 Aug 1995	National Power
59203	London, Ont, Canada	948519-2	06/95	Halifax, NS	MV *Condock V*	16 Jul 1995	Hull KGV	4 Aug 1995	National Power
59204	London, Ont, Canada	948519-3	06/95	Halifax, NS	MV *Condock V*	16 Jul 1995	Hull KGV	4 Aug 1995	National Power
59205	London, Ont, Canada	948519-4	06/95	Halifax, NS	MV *Condock V*	16 Jul 1995	Hull KGV	4 Aug 1995	National Power
59206	London, Ont, Canada	948519-5	06/95	Halifax, NS	MV *Condock V*	16 Jul 1995	Hull KGV	4 Aug 1995	National Power

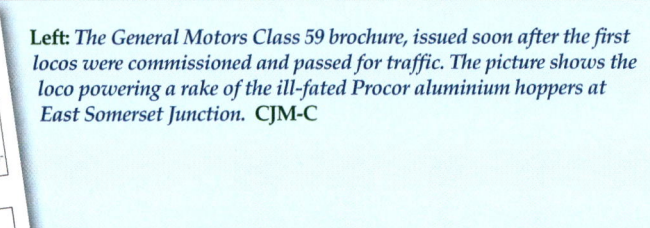

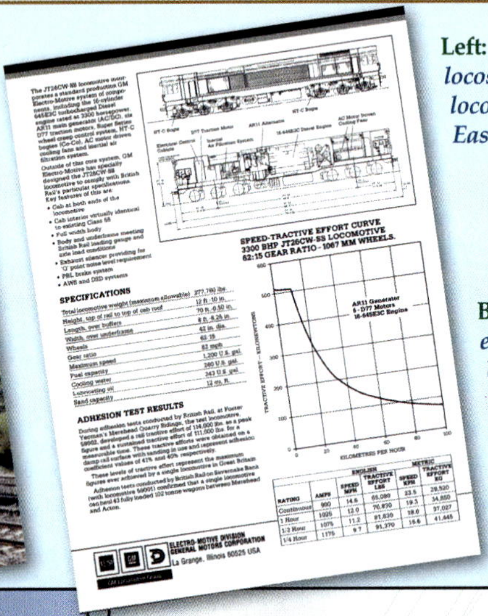

Left: *The General Motors Class 59 brochure, issued soon after the first locos were commissioned and passed for traffic. The picture shows the loco powering a rake of the ill-fated Procor aluminium hoppers at East Somerset Junction.* **CJM-C**

Below: *All three of the Class 59 sub-classes have slightly different equipment positions, some directed by the requirement to follow UK Rail Group Standards. However, the equipment remains the same. 1: Lamp bracket, 2: Tethering lugs for shipment, 3: Air horns behind grille, 4: Headlight, 5: Marker light, 6: Tail light, 7: AAR multiple control jumper socket (cable stored in engine bay), 8: Screw coupling hook and shackle, 9: Air brake pipe (red), 10: Main reservoir pipe (yellow), 11: Drop-head knuckle coupling, 12: Knuckle coupling release linkage. All:* **CJM**

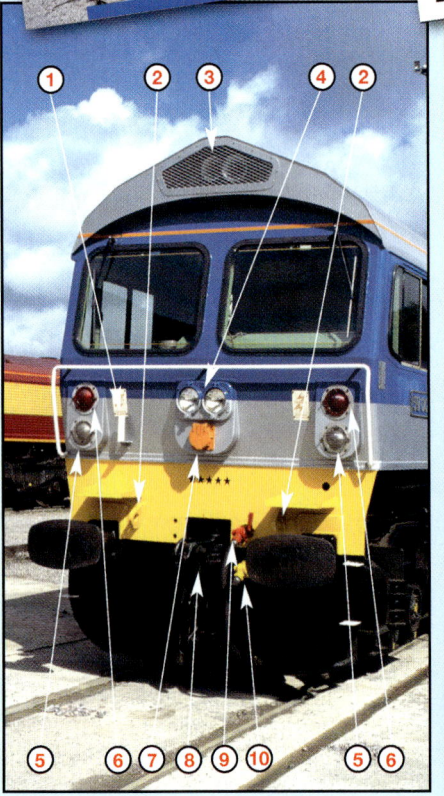

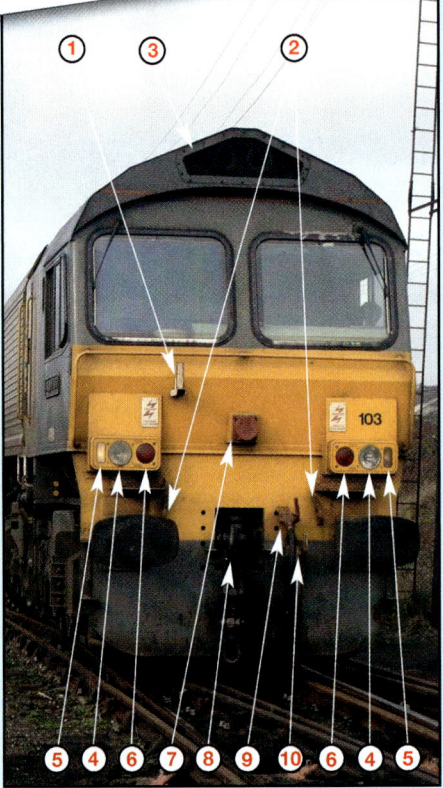

Traction Transition - GM/EMD power in the UK and Ireland

Class 59 Fact File

- First use of US-built main line locos in England, ordered by Foster Yeoman to increase reliability of traction on Mendip traffic.

- ARC Southern later purchased four locos.

- National Power ordered one loco, with a follow-on order for five to operate power station flows, locos later sold to EWS (DB-C).

- Currently all three Class 59 sub-classes operate from Merehead/Whatley on Mendip aggregate flows.

- No. 59003 operated for a period in Eastern Europe and is now back in the UK, working for GBRf.

Name	Date Named	2019 Operator
Yeoman Endeavour	28/6/86	Aggregate Industries
Alan J Day	21/6/96	Aggregate Industries
Yeoman Enterprise	28/6/86-20/6/96	
Yeoman Highlander	28/6/86	GB Railfreight, previously HHPI, Germany
Paul A Hammond	21/6/96	Aggregate Industries
Yeoman Challenger	28/6/86-20/6/96	
Kenneth J Painter	25/6/89	Aggregate Industries
Village of Whatley	9/5/92	Hanson
Village of Chantry	15/9/91	Hanson
Village of Mells	18/8/91	Hanson
Village of Great Elm	14/9/91	Hanson
Vale of York	3/3/94	DB-C
Vale of White Horse	28/9/96-11/13	DB-C
Alan Meddows Taylor MD Mendip Rail Limited	12/13	
Vale of Pickering	2/9/95	DB-C
Vale of Glamorgan	18/11/96	DB-C
Vale of Evesham	14/6/96-12/3/98	DB-C
Keith McNair	28/3/98	
Pride of Ferrybridge	28/6/97-12/08	DB-C
John F. Yeoman Rail Pioneer	01/09	

Virginia for a sea journey to England arriving in Southampton on 21 January 1986.

After being hauled to Westbury and Merehead for commissioning, all four were taken to the Engineering Development Unit (EDU) at the Railway Technical Centre, Derby for type test approval.

Following authorisation and staff training test and trial running commenced, with a service introduction on 17 February 1986. By mid 1996, the average daily tonnage hauled by the '59s' was 17,468.5 tonnes, equating to a yearly average of 4,541,810.00 tonnes (on a 260 day operational year). Performance in the first year was staggering, with each loco averaging 68,332 miles with a 99.3% availability. The highest figure ever recorded for a main line loco fleet in history.

With an increase in business, Yeoman authorised the purchase of a fifth loco in the summer of 1988. This was built at La Grange to order No. 878039 between March and May 1989 and shipped to the UK in June 1989.

Following the Foster Yeoman / British Rail partnership, a number of other operators saw benefits from owning their own locos. The first was Mendip-based aggregate producers ARC Southern. They ordered a fleet of four locos in 1987, to order 878029. By the time of production, General Motors had transferred its main assembly work from La Grange in Chicago to Canada, where General Motors had its Electro Motive Diesel Division headquarters in London, Ontario.

London assembly commenced in May 1990. Delivery from the London plant was by rail to the port of Halifax where on 3 October 1990 they were loaded on the Jumbo ship *MV Stellamare* and arrived at Newport Docks 19 October 1990. The four were soon tested, commissioned and introduced, entering revenue service on 5 November 1990.

The only other company to buy Class 59s was National Power (NP), who could see benefits from owning its own traction. Based in Ferrybridge, Yorkshire, NP ordered one loco, number 59201 in 1991 to haul limestone between Peak Forest and Drax power station. The loco was built at the Diesel Division plant in London, Ontario and shipped to Hull Docks in February 1994. After commissioning, it entered traffic in Spring 1994. The NP loco was slightly different from the previous Canadian build, the body structure was the same as on the Class 59/1, but drop-head knuckle couplers were fitted, a carbon-dioxide fire fighting system replaced the Halon system, NiCd batteries replaced lead-acid and a more advanced slow speed control system was fitted.

Soon after introduction, NP saw that additional locomotives and extra high-capacity wagons could save huge sums of money if deployed on coal transport to National Power generating plants, thus NP soon ordered five extra locomotives (Nos. 59202-206) in 1994 which were delivered in 1995. These were built at the London, Ontario plant, they were shipped from Halifax to Hull and allocated to a new purpose-build National Power depot at Ferrybridge.

After three years of operating with NP and following privatisation of the UK freight industry, National Power sold its entire rail operation to EWS in April 1998. The Class 59/2s lost their distinctive blue livery for standard EWS maroon and gold. The locos were redeployed from Ferrybridge to the London area to operate stone traffic in the Hither Green, Acton and Westbury areas, alongside the Yeoman/ARC 'Mendip Rail' pool. From 2005 a revised maintenance policy was launched with the Class 59/2s maintained under contract at Merehead depot by Mendip Rail/Foster Yeoman staff.

A number of changes have taken place since the '59s' were introduced. In addition to the formation of Mendip Rail as an operating business, both Yeoman and ARC have seen new owners. Yeoman eventually became part of the much larger Aggregate Industries operation and ARC came part of Hanson.

With EWS later being taken over by German based DB, the Class 59/2s were repainted in DB red and grey livery and until late 2019 continued to operate mainly on Mendip aggregate traffic. However, a major change to Mendip Class 59s was announced in late 2018, when Freightliner took over the provision of locos and staff for Mendip Rail trains from late 2019, this included the sale of all eight locos to Freightliner from the start of 2019. The six EWS locos will no longer be required in the Mendip area and DB have said the fleet will be transferred to other duties.

One loco of special interest is No. 59003, In 1997 this loco was selected to take part in a joint Foster Yeoman/DB venture, with the loco being repainted in a joint Yeoman/DB livery and shipped to Germany to power aggregate trains. The venture ceased in 1999 and the loco was sold to Heavy Haul Power International (HHPI) who ⇨

Right: *During the early talks between Foster Yeoman, BR and General Motors it was established that the standard SD 40 or any US driving cab design was not acceptable for UK operations. At the time the UK Class 58 was establishing a new standard cab design, and a revised version of this was adopted for the heads up displays and left side brake controllers. The standard design of GM power controller pedestal was installed on the driver's right side.* **CJM**

MAGAZINE SPECIALS

ESSENTIAL READING FROM KEY PUBLISHING

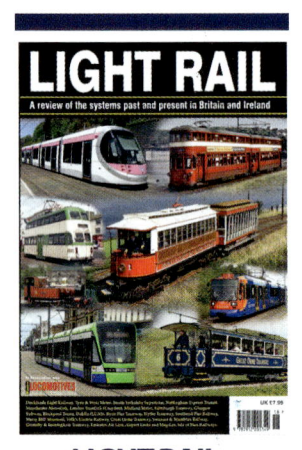

LIGHT RAIL
A review of the systems past and present in Britain and Ireland.
£7.99 inc FREE P&P*

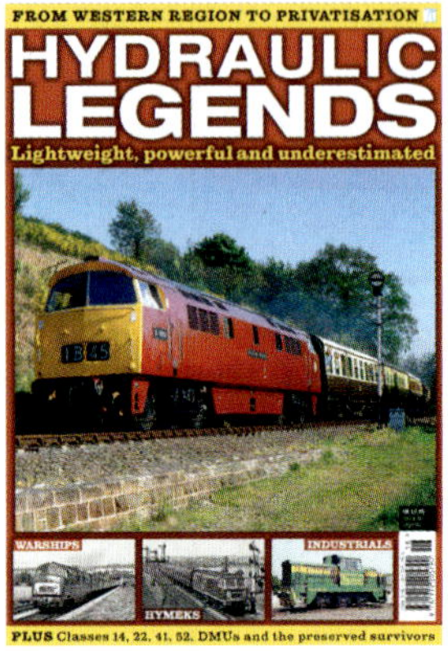

HYDRAULIC LEGENDS
Charting the inspiration, development and careers of some of British Railways' most enigmatic locomotives.
£6.99 inc FREE P&P*

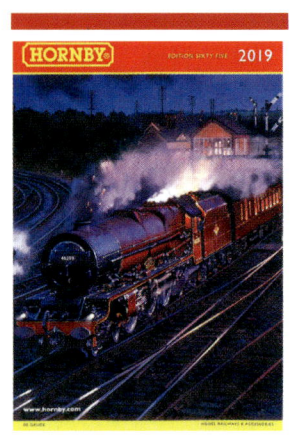

HORNBY 2019 CATALOGUE
A perfect showcase for everything the 2019 range has to offer.
£8.99 inc FREE P&P*

HORNBY MAGAZINE SKILLS GUIDE – LAYOUTS
This 132-page publication will become an essential workbench manual for modellers of all abilities.
£6.99 inc FREE P&P*

HORNBY MAGAZINE GREAT LAYOUTS 2
Featuring 26 favourites from the pages of Hornby Magazine, and scales from 'N' to Gauge 3.
£6.99 inc FREE P&P*

HORNBY MAGAZINE LOCO MANUAL
From the Hornby Magazine team, Locomotive Manual covers all you need to know to enhance your express steam locomotives.
£6.99 inc FREE P&P*

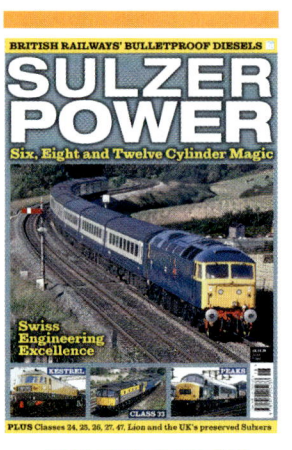

SULZER POWER
This Bookazine celebrates diesel locomotives, as well as the two Sulzer-powered prototypes, Lion and Kestrel.
£6.99 inc FREE P&P*

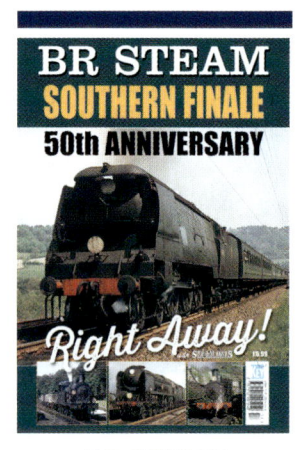

BR STEAM
The Southern was the final region on British Railways to operate steam-hauled express from a London terminus.
£6.99 inc FREE P&P*

MAGAZINE SPECIALS
ESSENTIAL reading from the teams behind your FAVOURITE magazines

HOW TO ORDER

VISIT www.keypublishing.com/shop

OR

PHONE
UK: 01780 480404
ROW: (+44)1780 480404

*Prices correct at time of going to press. Free 2nd class P&P on all UK & BFPO orders. Overseas charges apply. Postage charges vary depending on total order value.

FREE Aviation Specials App

Simply download to purchase digital versions of your favourite aviation specials in one handy place! Once you have the app, you will be able to download new, out of print or archive specials for less than the cover price!

IN APP ISSUES **£3.99**

291/19

operated a one stop shop in terms of block train operation in Germany, Poland, France and the Benelux countries. By 2015 with a decline in work, HHPI sold No. 59003 to UK railfreight operator GB Railfreight and it was returned to the UK, overhauled, upgraded and is now part of the GBRf fleet. ■

Right Top: *As with all new products from the Diesel Division Plant in London, Ontario, they spent a few hours on the test track at the rear of the works, proving all systems were operational. On 13 September 1990 ARC Nos. 59103 and 59102 are put through their paces. Note the temporary US style knuckle couplers. Moments after this picture was recorded the locos overshot the siding and went through the catch points leaving No. 59102 hanging precariously above an embankment.* **CJM-C**

Right Middle Upper: *On 26 September 1990, all four locos of the ARC Southern order are seen in the delivery yard awaiting to be hauled to the Port of Halifax for shipment to the UK.* **CJM-C**

Right Middle Lower: *Shipping to the UK saw the bodies separated from bogies, with despatch from Canadian soil via the Port of Halifax and arriving in the UK at Hull King George V Dock. Here, the body of No. 59202 is seen at CN London on 23 June 1995 mounted on flat car No. 639985. It is awaiting shipment for painting and transfer to Halifax.* **CJM-C**

Below: *Diesel Division plant switcher No. 57, a SW9 of 1951 vintage, is seen shunting one of the ARC Southern locos around the Diesel Division plant on 21 August 1990. The '59' is still in workshop primer and awaits its turn through the paint shop. The SW9 was originally operated by the Toronto, Hamilton and Buffalo railroad.* **CJM-C**

Traction Transition - GM/EMD power in the UK and Ireland

Above: *Passing Longfield Road crossover between Ealing Broadway and West Ealing on 10 February 1987, No. 59003 Yeoman Highlander heads west on the down slow line with the 11.21 Purfleet to Westbury empty aggregate train, formed of Yeoman high-capacity box wagons. This was the scene of the dreadful and fatal crash on 19 December 1973 when 'Western' No. D1007* **Western Talisman** *derailed while working the 17.18 Paddington to Oxford claiming 10 lives.* **CJM**

Below: *Approaching Hungerford and passing Hungerford up loop, No. 59004 Yeoman Challenger heads west to Westbury and eventually Merehead Quarry on 23 June 1989 with the returning Purfleet empty box vans. This loco was later renamed* **Paul A Hammond** *in June 1996 in recognition of one of Foster Yeoman's best aggregate customers.* **CJM**

42 Traction Transition - GM/EMD power in the UK and Ireland

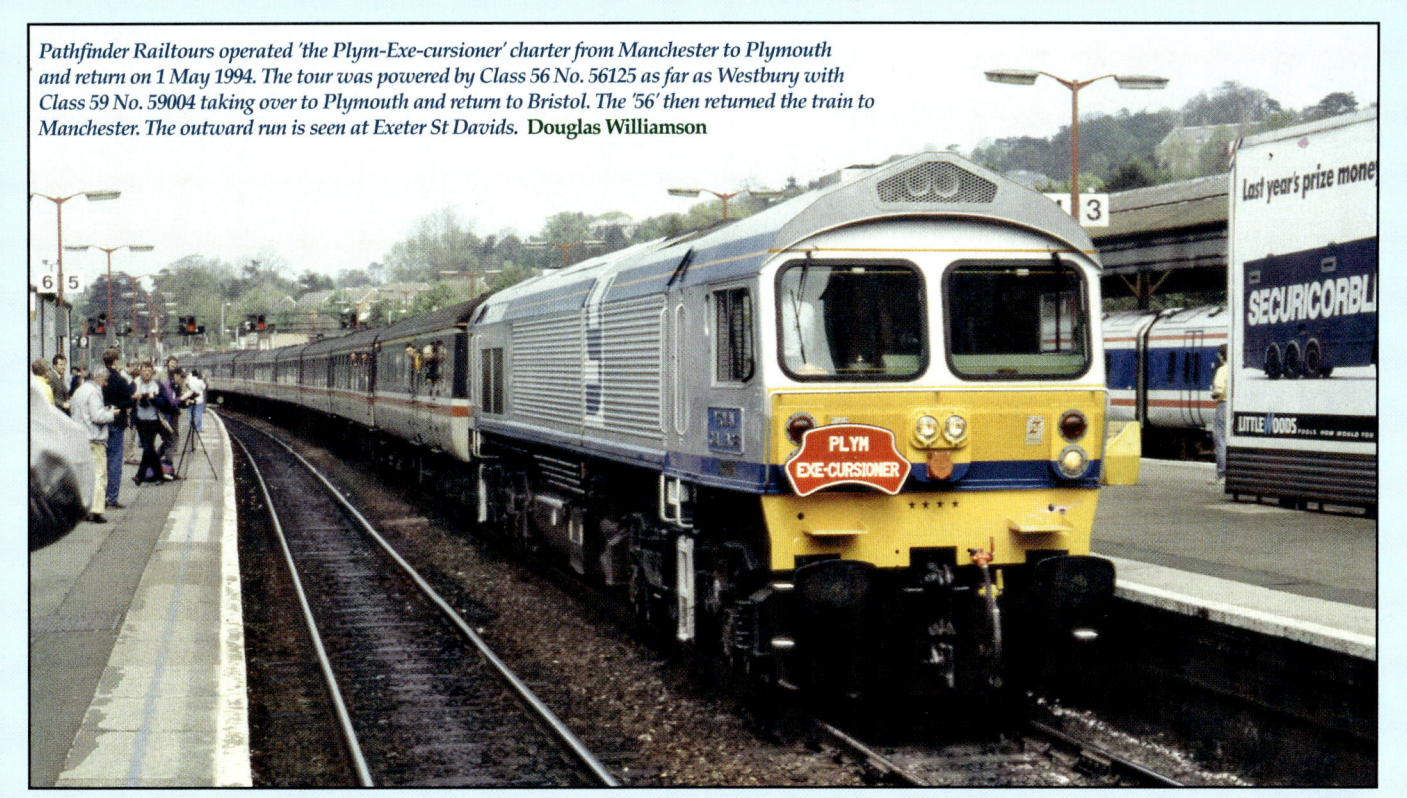

Pathfinder Railtours operated 'the Plym-Exe-cursioner' charter from Manchester to Plymouth and return on 1 May 1994. The tour was powered by Class 56 No. 56125 as far as Westbury with Class 59 No. 59004 taking over to Plymouth and return to Bristol. The '56' then returned the train to Manchester. The outward run is seen at Exeter St Davids. **Douglas Williamson**

Right: *The fifth Class 59 No. 59005, delivered in June 1989 was named Kenneth J. Painter, after Foster Yeoman's Rail Director in a ceremony, before it entered service. The loco is seen stabled outside Merehead shed on 28 September 1989.* **CJM**

Below: *To enable German footplate staff, mainly Traction Inspectors, to be trained on the operation of Class 59s in advance of the Yeoman/DB joint deal in 1997, No. 59004 and five Yeoman hoppers were moved to the privately owned West Somerset Railway on 26 February 1997 for two days of training runs. On 27 February. The train is seen approaching Doniford Halt while running from Blue Anchor to Bishops Lydeard.* **CJM**

Traction Transition - GM/EMD power in the UK and Ireland

Above: *With a small fleet of just five locos, it was frequently possible at weekends to arrange for the entire fleet to be 'on shed' at Merehead. From left to right we see Nos. 59001, 59002, 59005, 59003 and 59004 lined up in immaculate condition on 25 June 1989.* **CJM**

Left: *Displaying its as built ARC Southern mustard livery, No. 59104 Village of Great Elm is seen passing Berkley on 9 April 1996 with the 12.20 Whatley Quarry to Southall loaded stone, formed of a matching rake of new hopper wagons.* **CJM**

Below: *Painted in revised Foster Yeoman blue and silver livery, with a much reduced yellow warning end area, No. 59002 Alan J Day (the original Yeoman Enterprise) is seen near Twyford on 1 April 2009 bound for Acton yard with a mixed hopper and box train. This part of the GW network is now fully electrified and thus photography from bridges is very difficult due to the heavyweight overhead power equipment installed.* **Darren Ford**

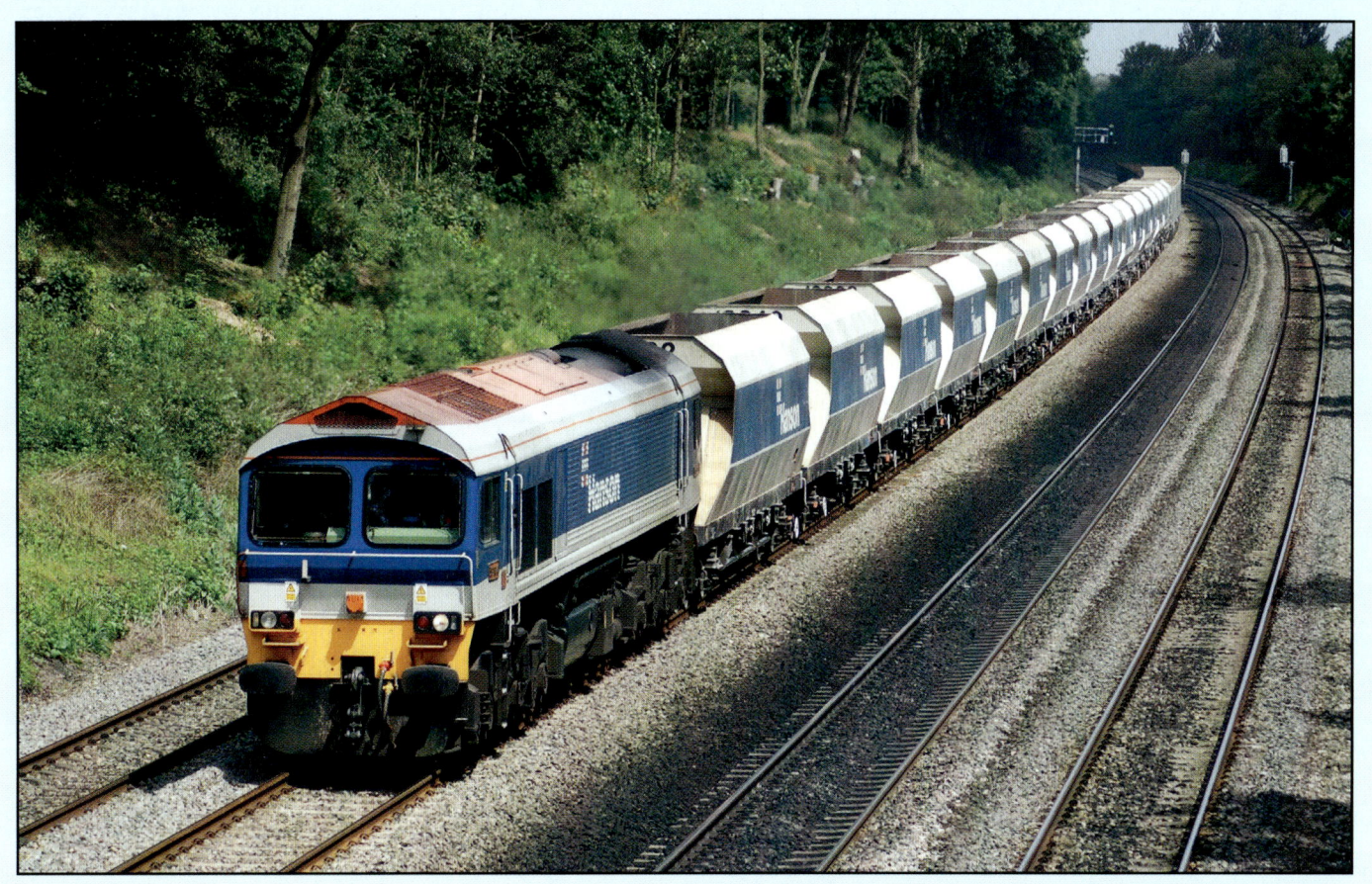

Above: In January 1999, after ARC had become part of the huge Hanson group, a re-livery policy was launched with a similar style paint design to the Yeoman fleet but using Hanson colours.. Heading towards Reading on the down slow line on 21 June 2006, No. 59104 displays the livery well. Considering the Class 59/0 and 59/1 fleets were operated in a dusty quarry atmosphere, they were and still are always kept clean. **Darren Ford**

Below: The first of the National Power Class 59/2s No. 59201 was delivered to the Port of Hull on 17 February 1994 and after inspection at the Railway Technical Centre, Derby and the operation of a dynamic test train, the loco was given an official launch at the National Railway Museum, York on 3 March 1994 when it was named **Vale of York**, *while positioned in the Great Hall of the museum. No. 59201, much the same as 59001 a few years earlier, was presented with a US style loco bell, mounted on the front end. These bells are non operational.* **CJM**

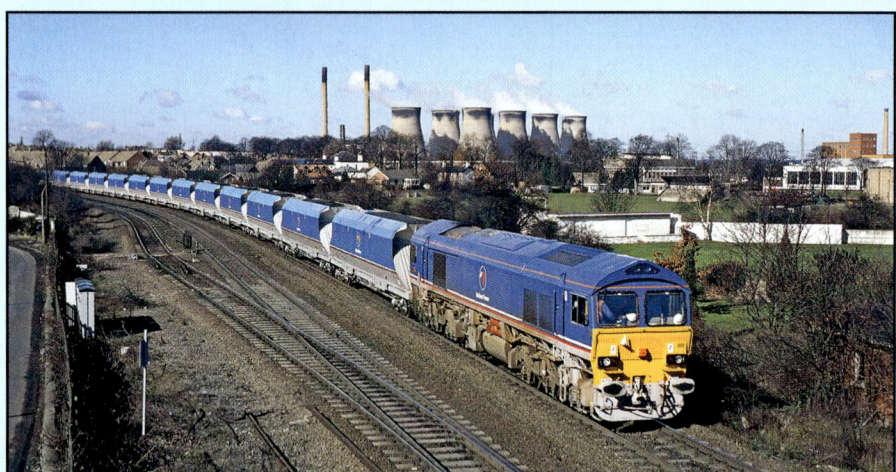

Above: National Power adopted a most stunning mid-blue livery for their fleet, which with a yellow end suited the body style well. With a rake of like liveried hoppers, No. 59201 passes Whitley Bridge Junction with a Drax to Tunstead working on 26 February 1996. **John Whiteley**

Left: No. 59202, un-named at the time, is captured soon after passing Knottingley on 7 March 1996. The loco is powering a Gascoigne Wood to Drax duty. **John Whiteley**

Below: To maintain the fleet of six Class 59/2s, National Power built a large depot at Ferrybridge, which opened just before arrival of the main fleet. On 18 August 1995 during the commissioning phase of the main fleet, Nos. 59202 and 59205 share depot space. **CJM**

Traction Transition - GM/EMD power in the UK and Ireland

For much of the journey between Reading and Crofton, the Berks and Hants line skirts the Kennet and Avon Canal, providing some excellent photographic locations. On 29 November 2012, Hanson No. 59102 Village of Chantry *passes Crofton with an Acton to Merehead service formed of Yeoman hoppers.* **John Whiteley**

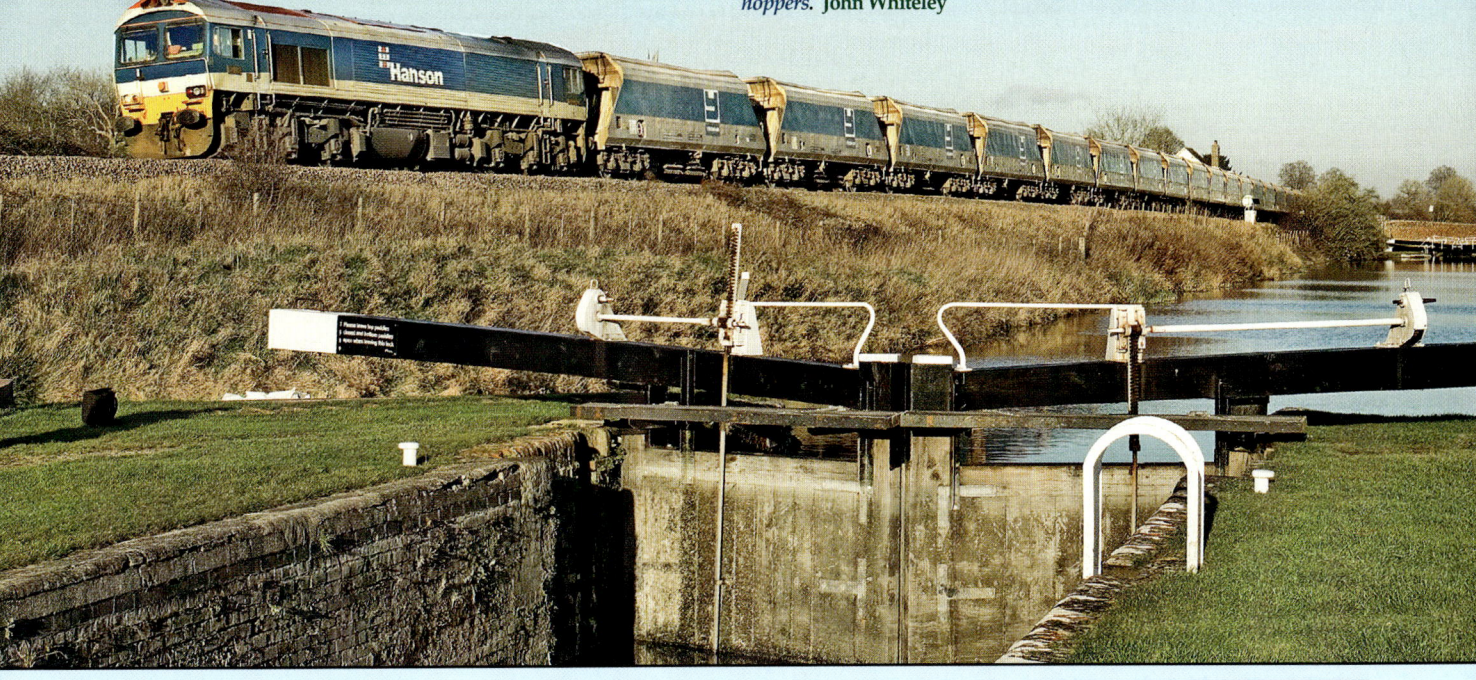

Right: *During the autumn and winter of 2010, Mendip Rail fulfilled a contract to supply 'rock armour' stone to the Minehead coastline with frequent trains operating between Merehead Quarry and Minehead using the West Somerset Railway to delivery the product close to the work site. On 26 November 2010, No. 59103* Village of Mells *approaches Blue Anchor on its return journey to the Mendips.* **Antony Christie**

Below: *All sub-classes of Class 59, together with Class 66 and 67 are fitted with AAR multiple control equipment and can operate in multiple. On 15 September 2011, Hanson No. 59104* Village of Great Elm *and EWS No. 59201 traverse the up slow line at West Drayton with a Merehead to Acton service.* **Mark V. Pike**

Traction Transition - GM/EMD power in the UK and Ireland 47

Above: *When the EWS Class 66s were delivered they sported a slightly different interpretation of the company maroon and gold livery to that applied to the like styled Class 59/2s. The '59/2' having a straight upper gold band, whereas the '66s' had a 'flash' gold band. The two livery styles are clearly shown in this view of Nos. 59205* L. Keith McNair *piloting No. 66007. The train, seen passing Coaley between Standish Junction and Cam & Dursley is the daily fuel train from Robeston to Westerleigh.* **Russell Ayre**

Below: *After EWS was taken over by German based Deutsche Bahn (DB) Schenker, the corporate red and grey livery was quickly applied, replacing the EWS maroon and gold. In immaculate condition with its silencer end closest to the camera, No. 59206* John F. Yeoman Rail Pioneer *is seen near Westerleigh on 2 August 2010 with the loaded oil train from Robeston.* **Russell Ayre**

Traction Transition - GM/EMD power in the UK and Ireland

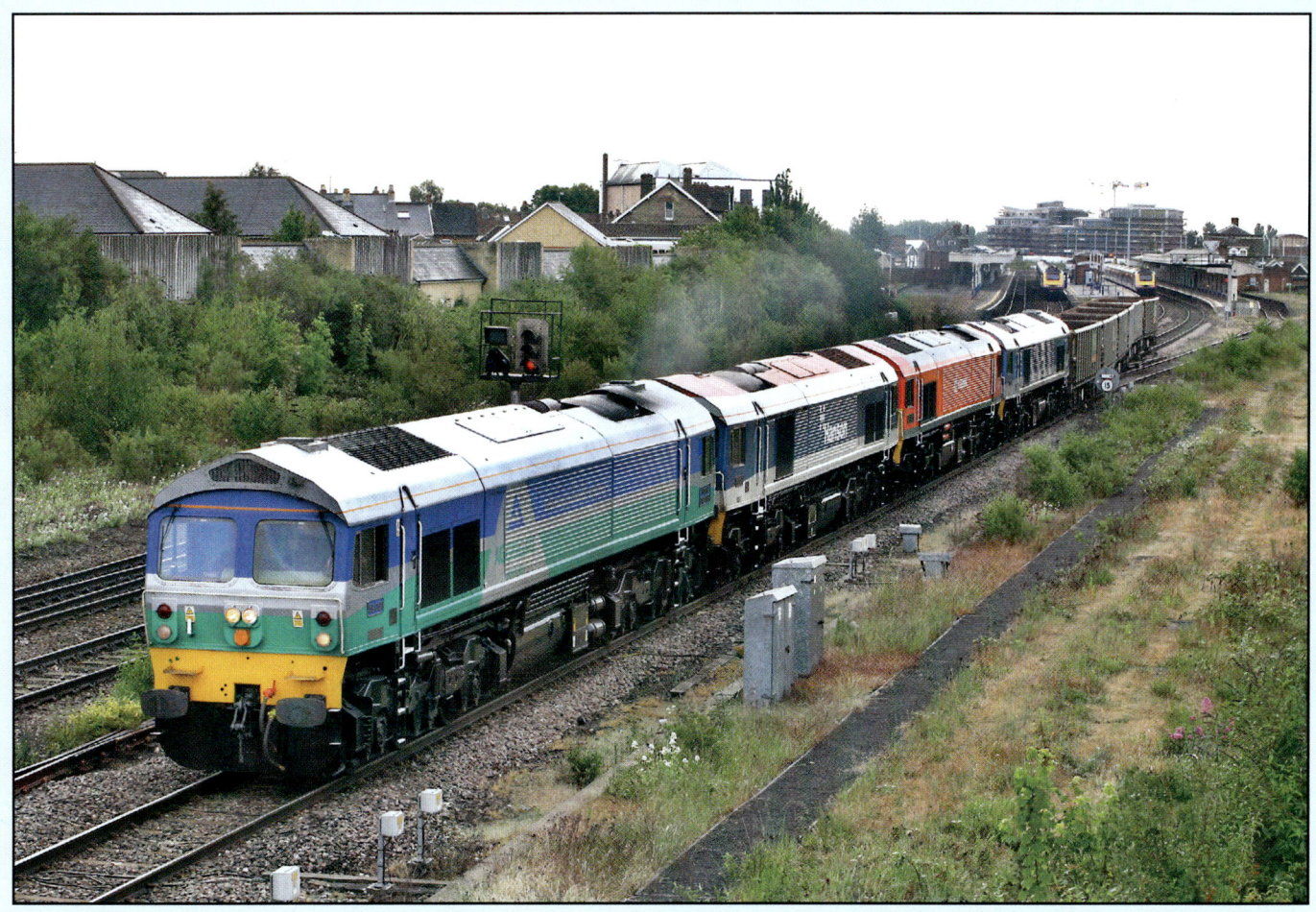

Above: *Well, you could not possibly get better than this for variety and rarity. On 10 June 2011, four Class 59s, Nos. 59001, 59103, 59206 and 59002 plus six JNA box wagons, are recorded passing Taunton, on route from Merehead to Bishops Lydeard. The locos (and wagons) were visiting the West Somerset Railway to take part in their 'Mixed Traffic Weekend' which coincided with the 25th anniversary of the original Class 59/0s.* **Brian Garrett**

Below: *Today, freight on the former L&SWR main line between Salisbury and Exeter is very rare, however due to an engineering blockage for three weeks in February-March 2019, many timetabled services were diverted, including the Merehead to Exeter aggregate train. DB Class 59/2 No. 59206, heads away from the former Seaton Junction and climbs Honiton bank passing Wilmington on 1 March 2019 with train 7C27, the 14.30 Westbury to Exeter Riverside.* **Antony Christie**

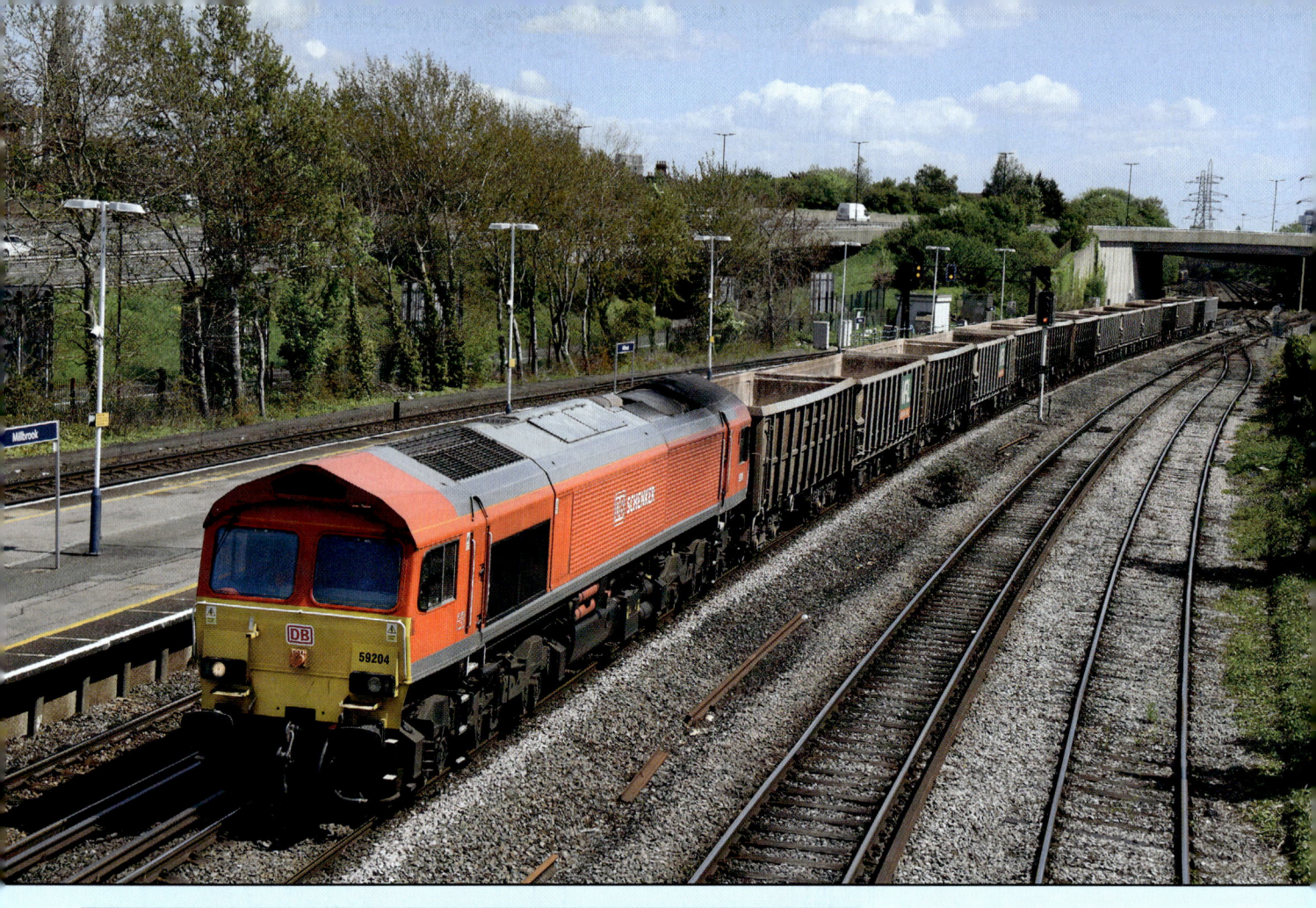

Above: The Mendip quarries now operated by Aggregate Industries and Hanson provide a large number of southern and western area terminals with product, seeing the '59s' work to a number of different locations. On 10 May 2018, No. 59204 passes Millbrook near Southampton with the 12.41 Chichester to Merehead. **CJM**

Left: On 25 May 2017, DB No. 59205 leads Aggregate Industries No. 59002 into Westbury station and yard, with train 7C64, the 15.24 Acton Yard to Merehead Quarry, which stopped at Westbury for a crew change. **CJM**

Below: It is very rare to find the Mendip Rail Class 59s deep into the West Country. They frequently work as far west as Exeter, but beyond that, reports are few. On 13 January 2014, No. 59005 emerges from Kennaway Tunnel, Dawlish with the 11.48 Burngullow to Exeter Riverside, formed of sand filled Mendip Rail box wagons. **CJM**

Traction Transition - GM/EMD power in the UK and Ireland

Above: Anyone wishing to record Class 59 workings, one of the best locations, apart from Westbury in on the stations between Acton and Reading, where most days between eight and 10 '59' powered trains operate. On 19 June 2017, No. 59004 passes Ealing Broadway on the up slow line with train, 7A09, the 07.12 Merehead Quarry to Acton Yard. **CJM**

Right Middle: No. 59003 Yeoman Highlander was selected by Foster Yeoman to be the loco involved in the joint Foster Yeoman - DB contract in 1997. The loco received major attention at Eastleigh Works including a repaint in to joint Yeoman/DB livery as well as technical work. After operating on DB for a short time, the venture ended in 1999. No. 59003 was then sold to Heavy Haul Power International (HHPI), owned by Richard Painter, the son of Foster Yeoman Rail Director Ken Painter. The loco then operated a 'one stop shop' basis powering block train in Germany, Poland, France and the Benelux countries. By 2015, with a decline in work, HHPI sold No. 59003 to UK railfreight operator GB Railfreight and it was returned to the UK, overhauled, upgraded and repainted in GBRf livery. No. 59003 is seen at Merehead Quarry prior to shipment. **CJM**

Right Below: After major attention at Eastleigh Works, No. 59003, retaining its original Yeoman Highlander nameplates was repainted in GBRf livery and deployed on some of their heaviest trains. After a while the loco settled down to operating GBRf aggregate trains from the Westbury area, where it was conveniently very close to the Class 59 experts at Mendip Rail. On 13 June 2018, No. 59003 awaits departure from Westbury with an aggregate service to Stud Farm. **Mark V. Pike**

Traction Transition - GM/EMD power in the UK and Ireland

GREAT SUBSCRIPTION OFFERS FROM KEY

SUBSCRIBE
TO *YOUR* FAVOURITE MAGAZINE
AND SAVE

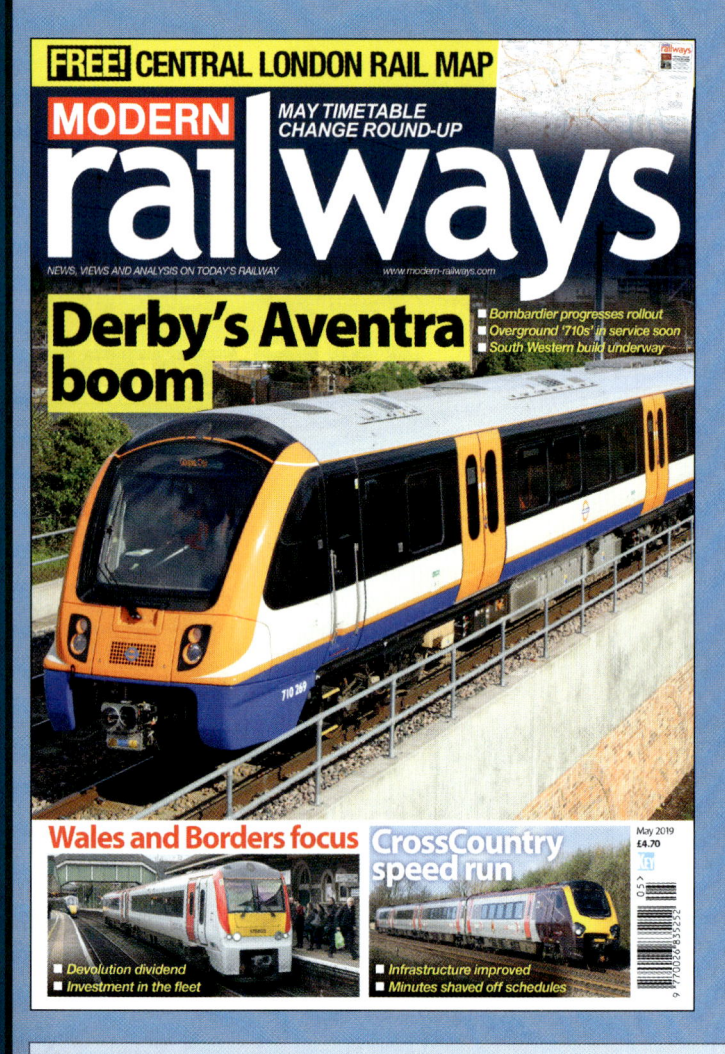

News, Views and Analysis on Today's Railway

Established for 50 years, **Modern Railways** has earned its reputation in the industry as a highly respected railway journal. Providing in-depth coverage of all aspects of the industry, from traction and rolling stock to signalling and infrastructure management, Modern Railways carries the latest news alongside detailed analysis, making it essential reading for industry professionals and railway enthusiasts alike.

www.modern-railways.com

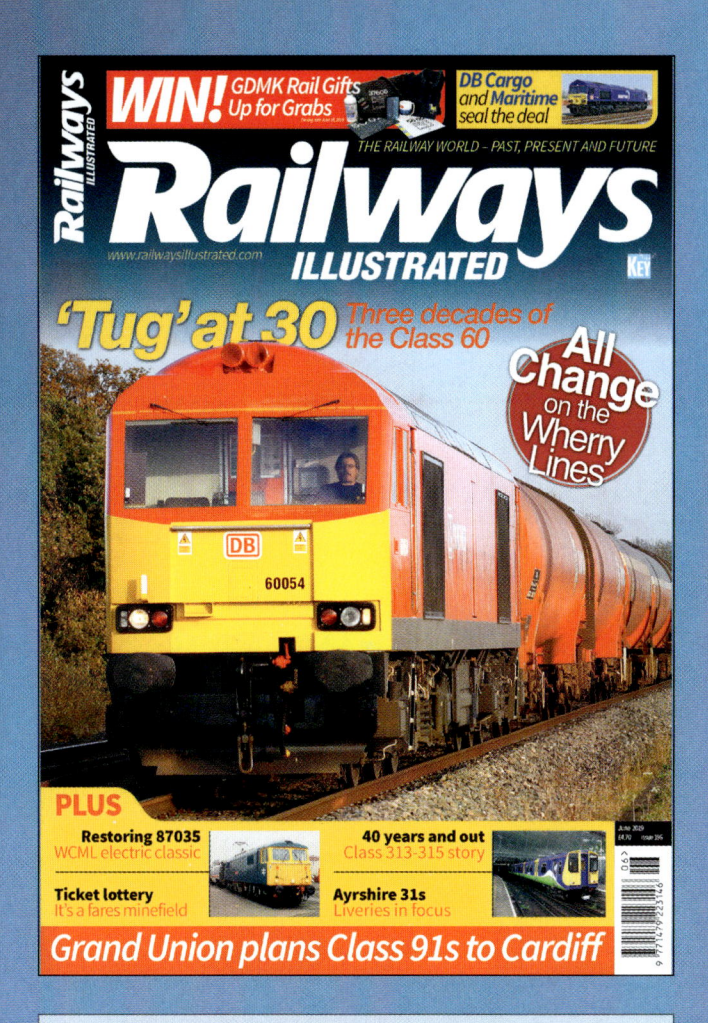

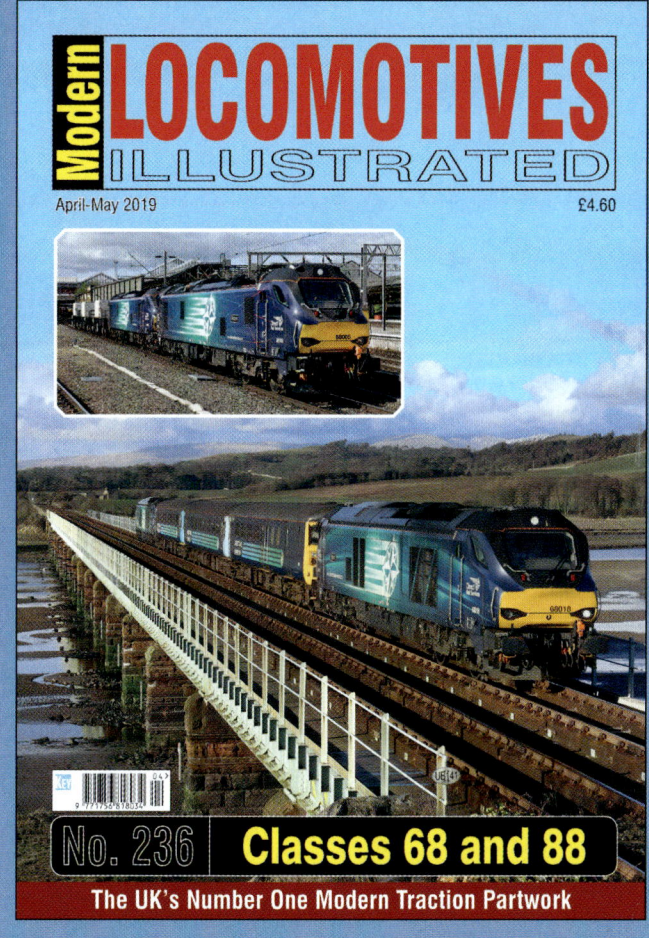

The best coverage of today's railway scene

Each issue of **Railways Illustrated** offers a comprehensive round-up of the latest news and topical events from the UK across the present-day railway, including heritage traction in operation on the main lines. Railways Illustrated reflects the energy and vitality of the present-day railway scene.

www.railwaysillustrated.com

The UK's Number One Modern Traction Partwork

Modern Locomotives Illustrated is a bi-monthly modern traction magazine, dedicated to recording the development, operation and disposal of the UK diesel and electric fleets. First published in June 2008, MLI will over a 10-year period cover all modern traction classes of locomotive and multiple unit trains.

www.modernlocomotives.co.uk

ALSO AVAILABLE DIGITALLY:

Available on iTunes · Available on the App Store · Available on Google play · Available on kindle fire · Available on PC, Mac & Windows 10

Available on PC, Mac and Windows 10 from pocketmags.com

290/19

FOR THE LATEST SUBSCRIPTION DEALS

VISIT: www.keypublishing.com/shop

PHONE: (UK) 01780 480404 (Overseas) +44 1780 480404

Traction Transition - GM/EMD power in the UK and Ireland

Class 57 Re-Engineering

Major re-engineering of an existing fleet of main line diesel locos in the UK was virtually unheard of until a joint Freightliner/Porterbrook project was announced in December 1997 to rebuild Class 47s into Class 57s. In the US and other parts of the world, such large-scale rebuilds were common.

With the privatised railway in the UK coming to grips with its traction assets, most of the 'new' operators sought new or improved traction. The cost of purchasing new locos was high and the long lead in time from design through delivery to deployment could not be underwritten. This was compounded by no UK builder offering an 'off-the-shelf' medium output diesel loco.

European or North American builders were the only option, however, due to the restrictive space envelope in the UK any loco selected would have to be scaled down. One exception however, was the General Motors Class 59 design, detailed in the previous chapter.

This design, in a revised form, was available in the General Motors (EMD) catalogue, as time progressed some UKs operators went down this road, in ordering Class 66s.

However, operators such as Freightliner, wanted a lower cost, ready to run 'new' loco and delivered in a relatively short timescale. A major problem in the UK rail industry is certification, this was becoming increasingly complex, time consuming and costly.

With this in mind, Freightliner, in partnership with Porterbrook Leasing entered negotiations on a possible re-engineering project for a small number of existing main line locos.

Various classes were considered for re-engineering, in the main these were owned by train operators rather than lease companies. However, members of the most numerous diesel class, the Class 47, were available through either direct ownership by Porterbrook or by Freightliner.

Brush Traction, Loughborough was quickly brought on board and a major Class 47 re-engineering project was launched.

The '47' body was in relatively good condition, some corrosion needed to be repaired, but the internals were the major cause of problems. A new or revised design of power unit was required, but with little major rebuilding of established UK power units having been undertaken and few offering an improvement on the existing Sulzer engine used in the '47', the project turned to the North American market where, rebuilding of prime movers had a long history.

A number of established engine suppliers existed in the US, with VMV, based in Paducah, Kentucky being one of the largest. During the early planning for the '47' rebuild project, various American power units were considered, space was a limiting factor. Products from the two leading US engine builders - General Electric and General Motors were considered, with the General Motors 12 cylinder 645-12E3 selected. This was of the same design as installed in the GM Class 59s.

To provide power it was agreed to use an alternator rather than a generator. The type selected for the rebuild project was a modified version of the Brush BA1101A, previously used in the UK Class 56. With this class being withdrawn, a number of alternator groups were available, these could be modified and refurbished by Brush and married up with the US supplied engines.

Traction output for the 'new' locos was to incorporate a 'state-of-the-art' anti wheel-slip system, together with wheel/rail interface sanding.

Since construction of the Class 47s, huge advances had been made in electronic tractive effort control and diagnostics and this a new electronics system was installed.

The Class 47s had over the years experienced problems with radiators, so a new design of hydrostatic fan was installed, together with improved brake frame giving easy access together with the provision of a large engine oil filter.

A major initiative was launched to upgrade the driving cab, removing all unwanted and obsolete equipment, installing a desk mounted radio and improving the equipment layout. The original style Brush power controller stand and brake valves were retained. Prior to the rebuild project being authorised, Freightliner had carried out cab improvement work on Class 47 No. 47270 which included draft proofing, this paved the way for cab refurbishment.

Once design work was complete Porterbrook and Freightliner agreed to rebuild six locos, these were given the new TOPS classification of Class 57/0.

The first six locos selected for re-engineering were Nos. 47356, 47322, 47317, 47347, 47350 and 47187. They arrived at Brush in early 1998 being gutted of all original equipment. A major redesign of the equipment bays was needed to accommodate the General Motors power unit.

The 'new' engines were ordered from VMV in late 1997, with the first, fully bench tested arriving at Loughborough in February 1998. This allowed the new engine to be trial fitted into No. 57001 on 16 March 1998. Reworking of the first '57' was rapid, most work was complete by early July, allowing Vehicle Acceptance Board (VAB) certification in early July, with No. 57001 rolled out at Loughborough on 21 July 1998.

After initial trials, the original order for six locos was extended to 12, with an order placed ⇨

Right: *Brush Traction, in partnership with Porterbrook were keen to promote their 'new' product and produced a promotional brochure.* **CJM-C**

Below: *Class 57/0 equipment layout. 1: Driving cab, 2: Fire discharge point, 3: Feed cut-off valve (No. 1 cab), 4: Fan speed bypass cock, 5: Engine overspeed trip, 6: Power unit with alternator (right), 7: Battery isolating switch, 8: Electric control panel, 9: Aux voltage relay, 10: Feed cut-off valve (No. 2 cab), 11: Fault panel, 12: Horn/wiper isolating cocks, 13: Fire discharge point, 14: Air isolating cocks, 15: Switch panel, 16: Brake selector switch, 17: Engine governor, 18: Local engine start/stop buttons, 19: Main reservoir isolating cock, 20: Water gauge, 21-23: Compressor and brake equipment, 24: Brake overcharge valve, 25: DSD isolating cock.* **CJM-C**

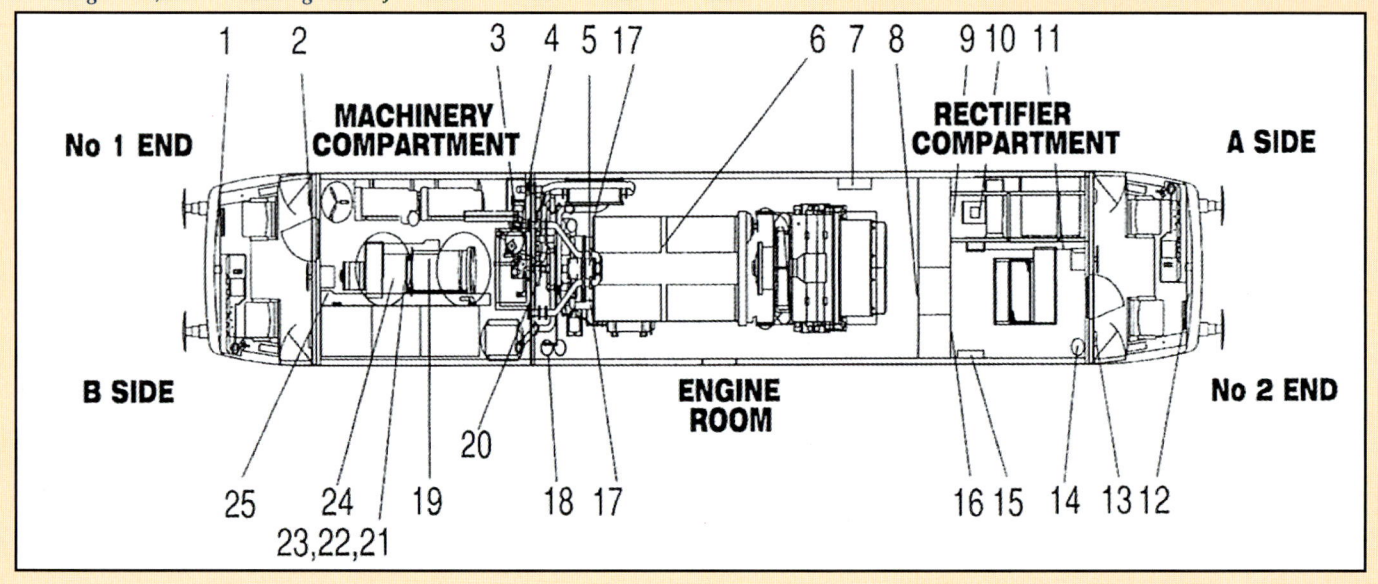

Sub-class:	57/0	57/3	57/6	57/6
Number range:	57002, 57003, 57007	57301-57316	57601	57602-57605
Rebuilt by:	Brush Traction	Brush Traction	Brush Traction	Brush Traction
Originally built by:	Brush	Brush	Brush	Brush
Years introduced – as Class 47:	1962-1964	1962-1964	1962-1964	1962-1964
Years introduced – as Class 57:	1998-1999	2002-2005	2001	2002-2003
Wheel arrangement:	Co-Co	Co-Co	Co-Co	Co-Co
Maximum speed:	75mph (121km/h)	95mph (153km/h)	95mph (153km/h)	95mph (153km/h)
Length:	63ft 6in (19.35m)	63ft 6in (19.35m)	63ft 6in (19.35m)	63ft 6in (19.35m)
Height:	12ft 10⅜in (3.92m)	12ft 10⅜in (3.92m)	12ft 10⅜in (3.92m)	12ft 10⅜in (3.92m)
Width:	9ft 2in (2.79m)	9ft 2in (2.79m)	9ft 2in (2.79m)	9ft 2in (2.79m)
Weight:	120.6 tonnes	117 tonnes	121 tonnes	117 tonnes
Wheelbase:	51ft 6in (15.70m)	51ft 6in (15.70m)	51ft 6in (15.70m)	51ft 6in (15.70m)
Bogie wheelbase:	14ft 6in (4.41m)	14ft 6in (4.41m)	14ft 6in (4.41m)	14ft 6in (4.41m)
Bogie pivot centres:	37ft 0in (11.28m)	37ft 0in (11.28m)	37ft 0in (11.28m)	37ft 0in (11.28m)
Wheel diameter (new):	3ft 9in (1.14m)	3ft 9in (1.14m)	3ft 9in (1.14m)	3ft 9in (1.14m)
Min curve negotiable:	4 chains (80.46m)	4 chains (80.46m)	4 chains (80.46m)	4 chains (80.46m)
Engine type:	General Motors 645-12E3	General Motors 645-12F3B	General Motors 645-12E3	General Motors 645-F3B-12
Engine output:	2,500hp (1,864kW)	2,750hp (2,051kW)	2,500hp (1,864kW)	2,750hp (2,051kW)
Power at rail:	2,025hp (1,510kW)	2,200hp (1,641kW)	2,025hp (1,510kW)	2,200hp (1,641kW)
Tractive effort:	55,000lb (244.6kN)	55,000lb (244.6kN)	55,000lb (244.6kN)	55,000lb (244.6kN)
Cylinder bore:	9¹/₁₆in (230mm)	9¹/₁₆in (230mm)	9¹/₁₆in (230mm)	9¹/₁₆in (230mm)
Cylinder stroke:	10in (250mm)	10in (250mm)	10in (250mm)	10in (250mm)
Transmission:	Electric	Electric	Electric	Electric
Main alternator type:	Brush BA1101A	Brush BA1101A	Brush BA1101E	Brush BA1101G
Aux alternator type:	Brush BAA602A	Brush BAA602A	Brush BAA602A	Brush BAA602A
ETS alternator type:	-	Brush BAA	Brush	Brush
Traction motor type:	Brush TM68-46	Brush TM68-46	Brush TM68-46	Brush TM68-46
No. of traction motors:	6	6	6	6
Gear ratio:	66:17	66:17	66:17	66:17
Brake type:	Air	Air	Air	Air
Brake force:	80 tonnes	60 tonnes	60 tonnes	60 tonnes
Route availability:	6	6	6	6
Heating type:	Not fitted	Electric - index - 100	Electric - index - 95	Electric - index - 100
Multiple control type:	DRS system	DRS system	Not fitted	Not fitted
Fuel tank capacity:	1,221gal (5,551lit)	1,295gal (5,887lit)	720gal (3,273lit)	1,295gal (5,887lit)
Lub oil capacity:	190gal (864lit)	190gal (864lit)	190gal (864lit)	190gal (864lit)
Cooling water capacity:	298gal (1,355lit)	298gal (1,355lit)	298gal (1,355lit)	298gal (1,355lit)
Sanding equipment:	Pneumatic	Pneumatic	Pneumatic	Pneumatic
Sub-class variations:	Porterbrook sponsored rebuild of Class 47 with rebuilt GM power units supplied by VMV	Porterbrook/Virgin funded '47' rebuilds for 'Thunderbird' work. Operated today by DRS and WCRC	Revised specification with prototype electric train supply	Rebuilt for use on Great Western sleeper services

Left: *General Motors 645-12E3 engines for the Class 57 contract were supplied fully refurbished by VMV Enterprises, based in Paducah, Kentucky, USA. The engines had all previously been used in American road power, with several of the engines reported to have come from a batch of re-worked GM SD40-2s operating for Southern Pacific.* **CJM**

Below: *The first of the Class 57 fleet, No. 57001 was rolled-out to the transport press and guests at Brush Traction, Loughborough on 21 July 1998. The loco was painted in the new Freightliner house colours of British Racing Green, with reflective bodyside branding. As this was the first of a new generation of locos, a Freightliner staff competition was held to find a name,* **Freightliner Pioneer** *was selected, with all locos receiving a Freightliner prefixed name on release from conversion.* **CJM**

in July 1999.

Freightliner were 'very pleased' with their 'new' traction, providing a business case existed and there was growth in their container and Heavy Haul businesses, they projected a fleet of 25 loco. However, the company then decided that brand new power was more suitable and General Motors Class 66s were ordered.

To coincide with the roll-out of No. 57001, Freightliner introduced a new livery, based on British Racing Green, offset by yellow lettering and a new logo.

The deployment of the Class 57s was quite successful for Freightliner, failures were greatly reduced, heavier trains could be operated and train crews were impressed with the refined driving cab. The fleet soon found work on the core Intermodal routes linking Ipswich, Southampton, Lawley Street, Cardiff and Leeds.

Such was the success of the Class 57 project, that Porterbrook made plans to further the project, by offering a version fitted with electric train supply. Porterbrook funded a speculative conversion, with the knowledge that several passenger operators had a need for passenger equipped Type 4 or Type 5s.

Porterbrook used Class 47 No. 47825, which was taken out of traffic on 28 March 2000 and transferred it to Brush, some structural work was required to repair corrosion, with the entire between cab area stripped and in the same way as the Class 57/0 a VMV rebuilt GM 645 power unit was fitted, together with a fully upgraded Class 56 alternator group. In the original steam heating boiler bay a new rectifier bank was installed, based on the design previously fitted to the Brush Class 60s.

The cab was given a major rebuild, the original design power controller and brake arrangement was retained, but a total revision to display and switch gear was made.

Externally the Electric Train Supply (ETS) rebuild incorporated a revised front end, the original route display panel was removed and two new large high-intensity headlights fitted one above each buffer, two dual tail/marker light units were also installed, together with a roof height marker light. New ETS jumper and socket boxes were positioned on the buffer beam, while vacuum brake and steam heat connections were removed.

During the rebuild of the first ETS Class 57, classified 57/6 and numbered 57601, talks took place with First Great Western (FGW) regarding using the loco on the London Paddington-Plymouth-Penzance route on both daytime and overnight services.

It was well known that FGW needed to replace their aging Class 47s, and the Class 57 was an effective option.

Porterbrook saw the ETS version of the '57' as a low-cost option to provide new traction to train operators to power regular timetabled services, or to act as a 'Thunderbird' rescue loco.

Following completion, No. 57601 was handed over to Porterbrook in Loughborough on 26 March 2001. The loco was painted in a striking silver and purple livery based on the Porterbrook house colours.

Virgin Trains, as part of its modernisation of the West Coast Main route, required a fleet of main line 'Thunderbird' locos to rescue Pendolino sets, or more importantly haul Pendolino sets when the overhead power equipment was isolated for maintenance.

Virgin entered talks with Porterbrook, who at the same time were discussing with FGW their future loco needs.

At one time these talks looked at one fleet of 16 locos based in London, to act as a common user pool for the two operators. This was dropped in favour of two fleets, built to specific needs. Therefore two batches of ETS Class 57 were ordered, 12 for Virgin, classified as 57/3 and four for FGW classified as 57/6.

The Class 57/3s were fitted with a slightly more powerful engine set to deliver 2,750hp (2,050kW) to cater for extra hotel power needed.

Porterbrook identified suitable locos from those being taken off lease with Virgin as Voyager stock was introduced, with additional locos supplied from those recently used by Freightliner.

Conversion work commenced in October 2001 with the arrival of No. 47845. During the course of the project, Virgin found extra need for the '57' fleet, with the order increased from 12 to 16 locos.

When originally rebuilt, the Virgin Class 57/3s retained conventional drawgear However, in the immediate post delivery period, it was agreed to fit auto couplers, with Brush designing a complex and unsightly auto drop-head Dellner coupler, which could be attached to a Pendolino coupling and via jumpers, provide hotel power for the train.

All 12 of the original Class 57/3 batch were therefore retro-fitted with drop head couplers, while the final four of the build were fitted from new.

All Class 57/3s were painted in Virgin Trains silver and red, in keeping with the Pendolino and Voyager stock. Soon after delivery, a novel and slightly humorous naming policy was announced - with the entire fleet named after characters and equipment from the 1960s cult TV series Thunderbirds.

The FGW Class 57/6 locos were ordered by operator after three years of using No. 57601, these four were converted at the Brush plant between November 2003 and September 2004 and based at Old Oak Common for commissioning and training. They were painted in the then standard FGW green.

In summer 2004 FGW announced a naming policy for the fleet, using a theme of west ➪

Left: *By 16 March 1998 a major milestone in the Class 57 project was reached, when a trial installation was carried out of the first General Motors 645-12E3 engine supplied by VMV was lowered into the bodyshell of former Class 47 No. 47356. The detailed and time consuming operation was performed in the presence of a small number of railway technical journalists, the MLI editor being one. This view shows the engine inside the bodyshell, as viewed from the flange end, onto which the Brush supplied alternator would subsequently be attached.* **CJM**

Class 57 Fact File

- Design introduced as joint venture between Porterbrook Leasing, Freightliner and Brush to upgrade Class 47 with refurbished EMD prime movers.

- Original design refined for fitting ETH (No. 57601).

- Two ETH production fleets 57/3 for Virgin Trains and 57/6 for Great Western emerged.

- Virgin locos later sold to Direct Rail Services and West Coast Railway.

- DRS hold a contract to supply 57/3s to Virgin Trains to act as 'Thunderbirds' for Pendolino stock as required.

Right: *Class 57 driving cab layout, the loco shown is the pioneer Class 57/6 No. 57601.* 1: Emergency brake valve, 2: Straight air brake valve, 3: Train brake valve (proportional on loco), 4: General fault light (blue), 5: Wheelslip warning light, 6: Engine stopped warning light, 7: Brake timing light, 8: Derate warning light, 9: Main reservoir gauge, 10: Bogie brake cylinder pressure gauge, 11: Brake pipe pressure gauge, 12: Drivers reminder appliance, 13: Speedometer, 14: Alternator output (traction), 15: Parking brake on button, 16: Electric train heat on button, 17: Electric train heat on indicator, 18: Electric train heat fault light. 19: Cab heat switch, 20: Headlight flasher (hazard warning), 21: Electric Train Supply earth indicator lights, 22: Electric Train Supply off button, 23: Parking brake off button, 24: Cab radio handset, 25: Radio loudspeaker, 26: Ashtray (now removed), 27: Master key socket, 28: Master switch, 29: Power controller, 30: AWS indicator, 31: Windscreen washer button, 32: Fire alarm test button, 33: Warning horn valve, 34: National Radio Network cab set, 35: AWS reset button, 36: Windscreen wiper control, 37: Engine start/stop buttons, 38: DSD pedal, 39: Headlight control switch, 40: Headlight/marker/tail light indicator, 41: TPWS panel, 42: OTMR indicator, 43: OTMR interface panel. **CJM**

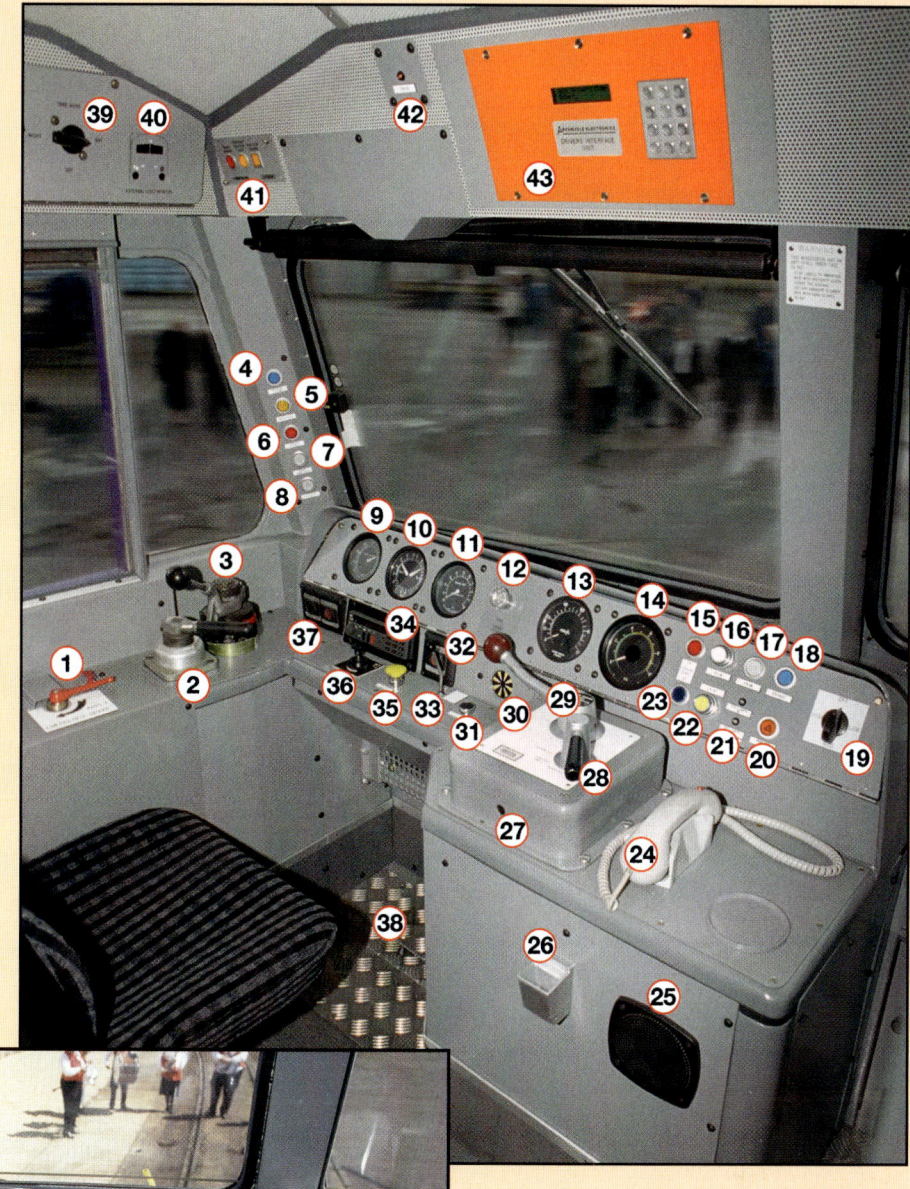

Left: *The driving cab layout of the first 47-57 conversions was not done to the same level as later rebuilds. Here the finished cab of No. 57001 is illustrated.* **CJM**

country castles.

In the immediate period prior to the four production Class 57/6s being delivered to FGW, the pioneer loco No. 57601 was returned to Porterbrook. Being a 'one off' trials loco no new placement could be found and after a short while it was sold to Carnforth based West Coast Railway Co (WCRC) in April 2003. WCRC painted the loco in their house colours of maroon.

In early 2007, after Freightliner received a significant number of Class 66s, Class 57/0s No. 57006-57012 were returned to Porterbrook Leasing. They were soon taken up by Carlisle-based Direct Rail Services (DRS). By Summer 2007 Freightliner returned the first six Class 57/0s to Porterbrook.

DRS were offered the rest of the fleet, but did not require them, over time DRS did take on nine of the 12. The DRS locos received DRS modifications. Two locos, Nos. 57005/006 were sold in January 2008 to Advenza Freight a part of the Cotswold Group based in Gloucester for general freight operations. The pair were repainted into Advenza mid-blue livery and branding. After Advenza and Cotswold Rail were wound up, the pair together with 57001 were sold to WCRC.

Following introduction on FGW, the four Class 57/6s settled down well in powering the overnight sleeping car express services between London Paddington and Penzance, sadly many problems were experienced with frequent failures and fault. A position which continues to the present day.

With completion of the main West Coast modernisation work, and the decision to cease using Class 57s to haul the Euston-Holyhead services forward from Crewe in 2010-2011, capacity existed in the Virgin operated fleet.

The spare capacity in the Virgin operation allowed Arriva Trains Wales (ATW) to hire two locos on a daily basis from December 2008 to operate on a new weekday express service linking Holyhead and Cardiff using Mk2/3 stock. ATW sub-leased a pair Nos. 57314 and 57315, these were repainted in Arriva Trains 'executive' blue livery.

Soon after, another pair Nos. 57313 and 57316 were painted in a 'neutral' blue/turquoise livery for use either on Arriva services or for Virgin Trains.

Later, the Virgin fleet Nos. 57301-57312 were transferred to Direct Rail Services for general use, with a proviso, that a batch were retained with drop-head couplings for emergency assistance of West Coast services if needed. The final four members of the fleet Nos. 57313-57316 were later sold to West Coast Railway Co, where their drop-head couplings were removed. ∎

Above: *Detail of larger size headlight and joint marker/tail light unit as fitted to Class 57/3 and 57/6 rebuilds.* **CJM**

Left and Below: *Each of the Class 57 sub-classes has a slightly different front end layout, but all equipment is in a standard position. The pioneer loco of the ETS-fitted build is shown left. 1: Loco to Land radio telephone aerial, 2: Warning horns behind grille, 3: Marker light (no high level light and separate low level marker/tail lights on Class 57/0), 4: Windscreen wipers, 5: Screen washer jets, 6: Headlight, 7: Electric Train Supply (ETS) jumper socket, 8: Main reservoir pipe (yellow), 9: Coupling shackle, 10: Brake pipe (red), 11: ETS jumper cable. Below from left to right we see the Freightliner Class 57/0 layout, with no high level marker light and retaining its original 'bolt-on' headlight assembly of the 1980s. In the middle is the early Class 57/3 front end without inset drop-head Dellner coupling as carried by Nos. 57301-57312. On the right is the fully modified Class 57/3 front end complete with remote operated drop-head Dellner coupling. All:* **CJM**

58   Traction Transition - GM/EMD power in the UK and Ireland

Above: *In as converted condition, the first of the Virgin Trains fleet No. 57301, rebuilt from No. 47845 is seen at Euston, note the Virgin 'shield' on the front end.* **CJM**

Right: *Class 57/3 No. 57304 Gordon Tracey leads 'Pendolino' Class 390/0 No. 390015 Virgin Crusader on the approaches to Ribblehead viaduct on 28 January 2006 with a diverted Glasgow Central to London Euston service. The core work for which the fleet were converted.* dieselimagegallery.com / Stan Withers

Below: *In addition to piloting 'Pendolino' stock, the Class 57/3s were also assigned to haul 'Voyager' Class 220 and 221 stock if needed, either due to failure or between depot movements. On 12 January 2005, No. 57304 hauls No. 220030 through South Brent, with a training special.* **CJM**

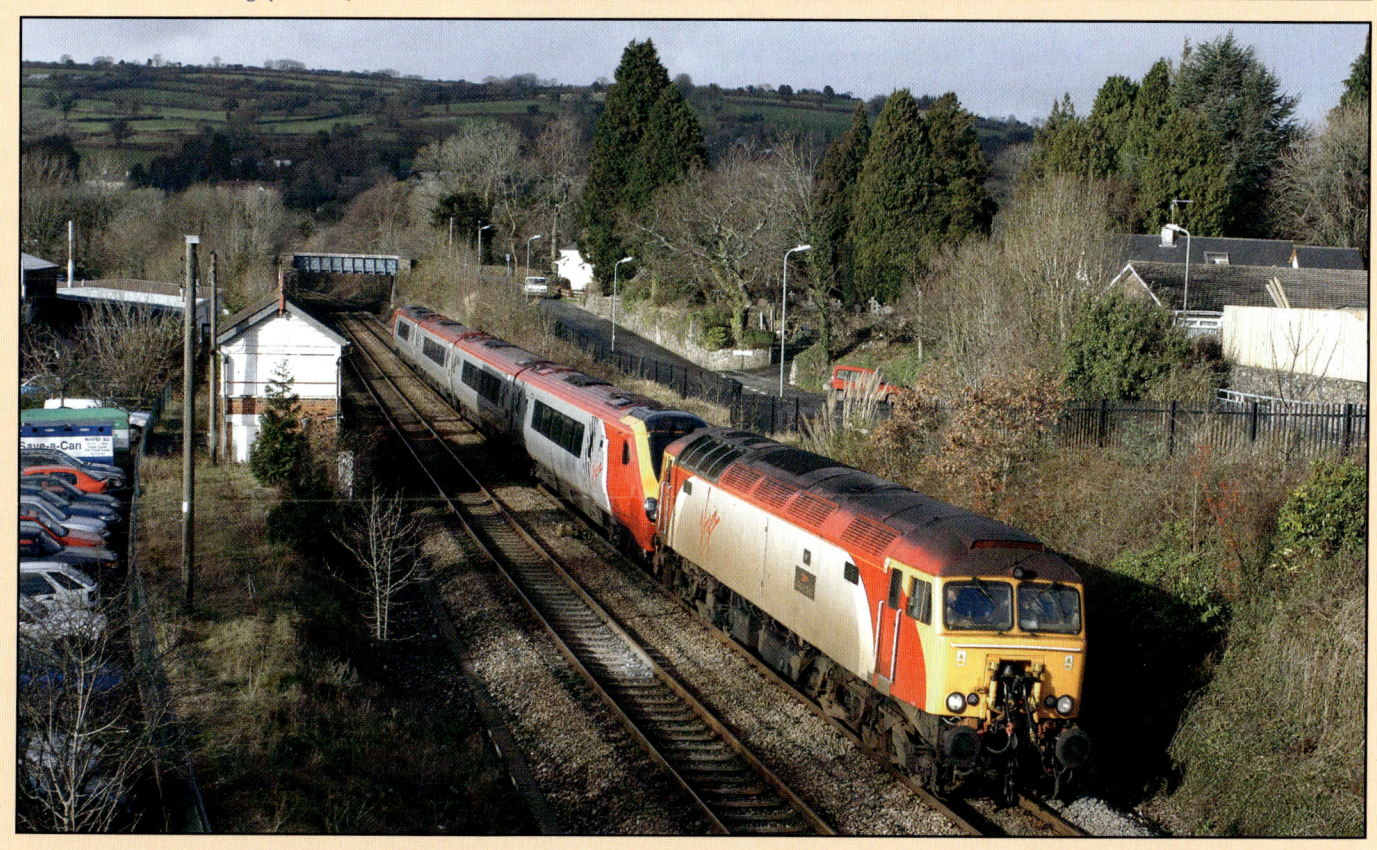

Traction Transition - GM/EMD power in the UK and Ireland

59

Class 57 Fleet List

Class 57/0

Number	Name	Introduced	Original Operator	Operator 2019	Converted From	Works No.	Original Introduction	Withdrawn as '47'
57001	Freightliner Pioneer 07/98-01/08	Jul-98	Freightliner	West Coast Railway	47356 (D1875)	637	Jul-65	Jul-98
57002	Freightliner Phoenix 10/98-12/07 Rail Express 12/16-	Oct-98	Freightliner	Direct Rail Services	47322 (D1803)	565	Jan-65	Jul-98
57003	Freightliner Evolution 11/98-12/07	Nov-98	Freightliner	Direct Rail Services	47317 (D1798)	560	Jan-65	Jul-98
57004	Freightliner Quality 12/98-01/08	Dec-98	Freightliner	Direct Rail Services	47347 (D1828)	590	Mar-65	Jul-98
57005	Freightliner Excellence 01/99-12/07	Jan-99	Freightliner	West Coast Railway	47350 (D1831)	593	May-65	Jun-98
57006	Freightliner Reliance 01/99-01/08	Jan-99	Freightliner	West Coast Railway	47187 (D1837)	599	May-65	Jul-98
57007	Freightliner Bond 09/99-04/07	Sep-99	Freightliner	Direct Rail Services	47332 (D1813)	575	Feb-65	Apr-99
57008	Freightliner Explorer 12/99-04/07 Telford International Railfreight Park June - 2009 06/09-04/13	Dec-99	Freightliner	Direct Rail Services	47060 (D1644)	-	Jan-65	Jun-99
57009	Freightliner Venturer 12/99-04/07	Dec-99	Freightliner	Direct Rail Services	47079 (D1664)	-	Mar-65	Jul-99
57010	Freightliner Crusader 01/00-04/07	Jan-00	Freightliner	Direct Rail Services	47231 (D1907)	669	Sep-65	Jul-99
57011	Freightliner Challenger 01/00-04/07	Jan-00	Freightliner	Direct Rail Services	47329 (D1810)	572	Jan-65	Jul-99
57012	Freightliner Envoy 02/00-04/07	Feb-00	Freightliner	Direct Rail Services	47204 [47308] (D1854)	-	Jul-65	Jul-99

Class 57/3

Number	Name	Introduced	Original Operator	Operator 2019	Converted From	Works No.	Original Intro'n	Withdrawn as '47'
57301	Scott Tracy 06/02-09/11 Goliath 10/14	Jun-02	Virgin Trains	Direct Rail Services	47069, 47638, 47845 (D1653)	-	Feb-65	Feb-02
57302	Virgil Tracy 07/02-03/12 Chad Varah 09/12	Jul-02	Virgin Trains	Direct Rail Services	47251, 47589, 47827 (D1928)	690	Feb-66	Feb-02
57303	Alan Tracy 02/03-09/11 Pride of Carlisle 09/14	Feb-03	Virgin Trains	Direct Rail Services	47261, 47554, 47705 (D1957)	619	Jan-67	Aug-02
57304	Gordon Tracy 10/02-03/12 Pride of Cheshire 06/12	Oct-02	Virgin Trains	Direct Rail Services	47055, 47652, 47807 (D1639)	-	Dec-64	Feb-02
57305	Alan Tracy 19/12/02-06/03/03 ¤ John Tracy 03/03-09/11, Northern Princess 10/14-	Feb-03	Virgin Trains	Direct Rail Services	47164, 47571, 47822 (D1758)	520	May-64	May-02
57306	Jeff Tracy 03/03 Her Majesty's Railway Inspectorate 175 11/15	Mar-03	Virgin Trains	Direct Rail Services	47242, 47659, 47814 (D1919)	681	Jan-66	May-02
57307	Lady Penelope 08/03	Aug-03	Virgin Trains	Direct Rail Services	47225 (D1901)	663	Oct-65	Sep-02
57308	Tin Tin 05/03 County of Staffordshire 08/13-06/17, Jamie Ferguson 07/17-	May-03	Virgin Trains	Direct Rail Services	47091, 47647, 47846 (D1677)	-	May-65	Jun-02
57309	Brains 06/03-03/12 Pride of Crewe 05/12	Jun-03	Virgin Trains	Direct Rail Services	47254, 47651, 47806 (D1931)	693	Mar-66	Jul-02
57310	Kyrano 07/03-09/11 Pride of Cumbria 07/14	Jul-03	Virgin Trains	Direct Rail Services	47036, 47563, 47831 (D1618)	-	Sep-64	Nov-02
57311	Parker 07/03-12/12 Thunderbird 05/13	Jul-03	Virgin Trains	Direct Rail Services	47032, 47662, 47817 (D1611)	-	Aug-64	Aug-02
57312	The Hood 09/03-09/11 Peter Henderson 10/11-09/14, Solway Princess 09/14-	Sep-03	Virgin Trains	Direct Rail Services	47330, 47390 (D1811)	573	Feb-65	Jun-03
57313	Tracy Island 11/04-12/08	Nov-04	Virgin Trains	West Coast Railway	47371 (D1890)	652	Jul-65	Jun-03
57314	Fire Fly 11/04-12/08	Nov-04	Virgin Trains	West Coast Railway	47372 (D1891)	653	Aug-65	Jun-03
57315	The Mole 12/04-12/08	Dec-04	Virgin Trains	West Coast Railway	47234 (D1911)	673	Nov-65	Apr-04
57316	Fab 1 12/04-12/08	Dec-04	Virgin Trains	West Coast Railway	47290 (D1992)	-	Mar-66	Mar-04

Class 57/6

Number	Name	Introduced	Original Operator	Operator 2019	Converted From	Works No.	Original Intro'n	Withdrawn as '47'
57601	-	Mar-01	First Great Western	West Coast Railway	47165, 47590, 47825 (D1759)	531	Aug-64	May-00
57602	Restormel Castle 09/04	Nov-03	First Great Western	First Great Western	47337 (D1818)	580	Feb-65	Jun-03
57603	Tintagel Castle 10/04	Dec-03	First Great Western	First Great Western	47349 (D1830)	592	Mar-65	Jun-03
57604	Pendennis Castle 10/04	Jan-04	First Great Western	First Great Western	47209, 47393 (D1859)	-	Aug-65	Jun-03
57605	Totnes Castle 09/04	Sep-04	First Great Western	First Great Western	47206 (D1856)	-	Aug-65	Apr-04

Left: *With much of the West Coast modernisation work complete and the need for Class 57/3s to haul 'Pendolino' stock on services away from an overhead power supply, work for the 16 Virgin-controlled '57s' was becoming thin on the ground. This led to some sub-lease work being found with Arriva Trains Wales and Great Western. On 4 May 2010 No. 57306 brings up the rear for a 'push-pull' formation with No. 57309 on the far end out of view, departing from Cardiff General, with the 14.00 to Taunton.* **CJM**

Above: *After Freightliner decided to opt for new main line traction in the form of General Motors Class 66/5s and 66/6s, the days for the original Class 57/0s were numbered. Advenza Freight, a part of Cotswold Rail, took on two locos, Nos. 57005 and 57006. On 4 May 2010, No. 57005 is seen stabled at Cardiff.* **CJM**

Right Middle: *From December 2008, to power a new weekday limited stop service linking Holyhead with Cardiff, using Mk2/3 stock, Arriva Trains Wales sub-leased a pair of 57/3s, Nos. 57314 and 57315. These were repainted in Arriva Trains 'executive' blue livery. Soon after, another pair Nos. 57313 and 57316 were re painted in a 'neutral' blue/turquoise livery and could be deployed on either Arriva Trains Wales or Virgin Trains services. On 4 May 2010, No. 57316 arrives at Newport with the 05.32 Holyhead to Cardiff service.* **CJM**

Right Below: *The four Class 57/6 locos for First Great Western, were delivered between November 2003 and September 2004 and were painted in the then standard FGW green and gold stripe livery. In addition to powering the overnight sleeper services between Paddington and Penzance and an occasional 'Motorail' duty, the locos were used as required to power stock movements between depots. On 4 July 2005, No. 57605 leads Class 43 No. 43124 a TGS coach and 43189 passed Horse Cove, Dawlish forming the 14.55 Bristol St Philips Marsh depot to Laira depot.* **CJM**

Traction Transition - GM/EMD power in the UK and Ireland

Above: *After FGW green and gold livery, the Class 57/6s on the GW roster were repainted into corporate blue livery, retaining their cast number and nameplates. Complete with two section yellow snowploughs, No. 57605* **Totnes Castle**, *departs from Totnes on 14 June 2014 with the 17.51 Exeter St Davids to Penzance, a train operated by a '57' and Mk3 stock for several years on peak Saturdays to ease a stock shortage.* **CJM**

Below: *Regrettably the reliability of the Great Western Class 57 fleet has not been good in recent years with frequent issues, often seeing the sleeper service cancelled or formed of non sleeping car stock. Making a rare appearance of a daytime sleeper train on 8 March 2018, No. 57603* **Tintagel Castle** *approaches Dawlish station and pulls away from Kennaway Tunnel with train 5A40, the 08.40 Newton Abbot to Reading depot, following failure of the up sleeper at Newton Abbot several hours prior.* **CJM**

Traction Transition - GM/EMD power in the UK and Ireland

Right Top: *Performing the work for which they were converted, powering the overnight sleeping car express service between London and the far west. On 20 September 2015, No. 57605 Totnes Castle 'top and tails' No. 57603 Tintagel Castle on the 'up' London Paddington bound sleeper at Plymouth.* **Antony Christie**

Right Middle: *In June 2010, No. 57604 Pendennis Castle was repainted in lined Brunswick green Great Western livery, as part of the railways celebrations to commemorate the 175th anniversary of the Great Western Railway. Displaying this livery, No. 57604 is seen arriving at Lostwithiel on 9 September 2017 with the Saturdays only 10.28 St Erth to Plymouth all stations service.* **Antony Christie**

Below: *With no less that three church spires in view (from left to right Our Lady & St Patrick's [Catholic], Teignmouth United Reformed and St Michaels [C of E]), this is the view looking at Teignmouth station from an over bridge at the west end. On 2 June 2018, No. 57605 Totnes Castle departs from the station call with the 17.51 Exeter St Davids to Penzance.* **CJM**

Traction Transition - GM/EMD power in the UK and Ireland

Above: *In 2010, Network Rail took on a small batch of Class 57/3s for snow train use and rescue purposes. The batch were soon taken over by DRS. Painted in Network Rail yellow, No. 57312 is seen working with Class 73 No. 73136 on the Swanage Railway during their diesel gala on 13 May 2012.* **Antony Christie**

Left: *Various styles of livery have been applied to the 21 Class 57s on the Direct Rail Services roster. No. 57308 shows the latest style with a shaded compass logo, together with the company name and logo replicated on the cab sides. No. 57308 Jamie Ferguson is seen at Crewe. The DRS-operated Class 57/3s retain their drop-head Dellner couplings.* **Antony Christie**

Below: *Currently, only a handful of the DRS-operated Class 57/0s are active, with many stored out of use. On 8 June 2017, Nos. 57007 and 57002 Rail Express pass Stafford, powering the 12.20 Crewe Basford Hall to Bescot engineers train. After take over by DRS, company jumper cables were installed to increase flexibility.* **CJM**

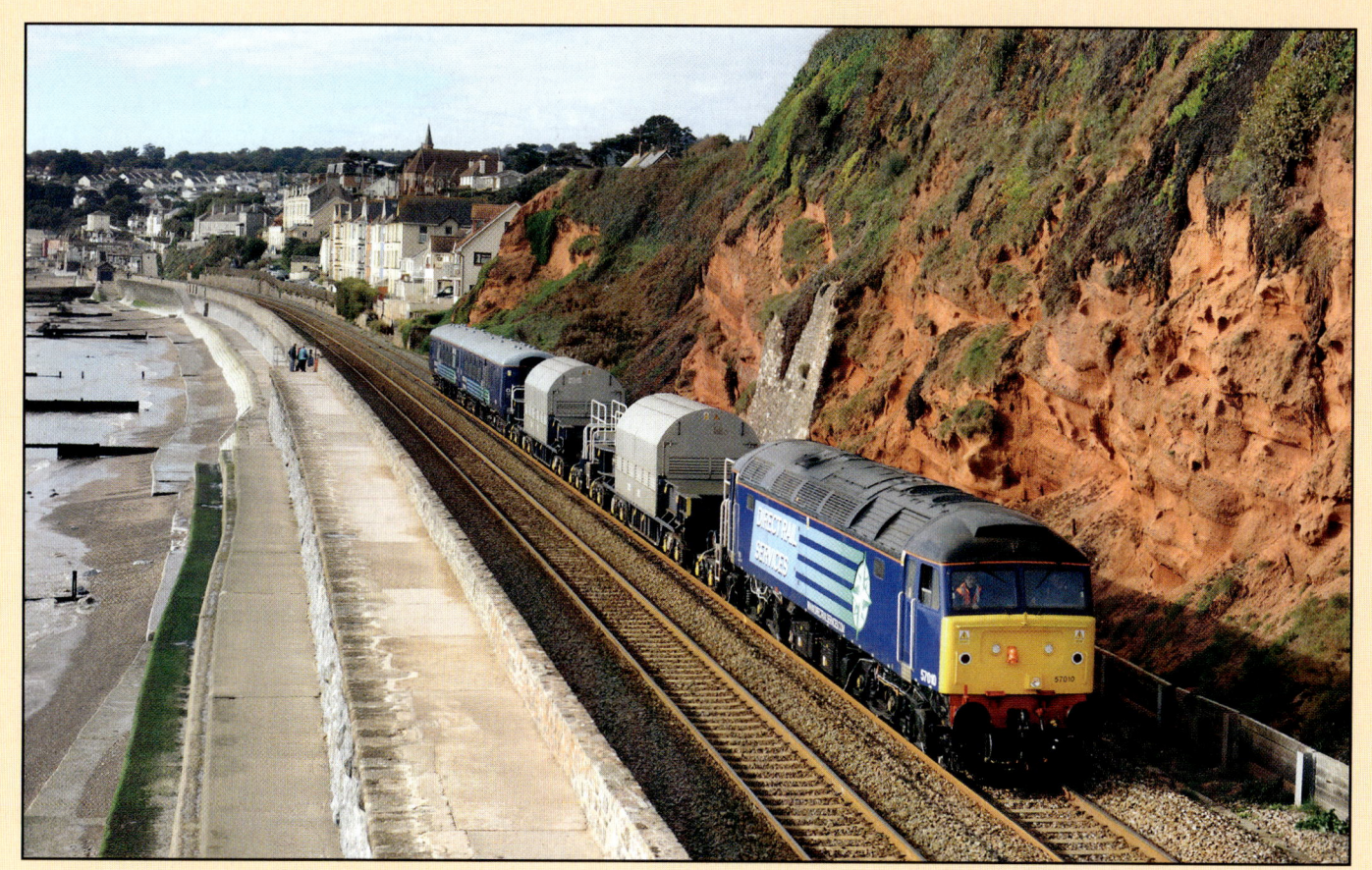

Above: The DRS Class 57s can be found operating a wide variety of train, from general freight services through departmental Network Rail services to the important flask trains, which are the companies core business. However, in 2019 more and more of these services have been placed in the hands of newer locomotives. Traversing the Dawlish sea wall at Rockstone bridge on 21 October 2010, No. 57010 forms train 6X50, the 09.35 Keyham Dock Yard (Plymouth Navel Base) to Carlisle, formed of flask wagons MODA95771 and MODA95770, with Mk2 escort vehicles Nos. 9419, 9428. **CJM**

Class 57 Fleet by Operator (04/19)

Direct Rail Services	57002-004 / 007-012, 57301-312
West Coast Railway	57001 / 005 / 006, 57313-316, 57601
Great Western	57602-605

Class 57 Sub-Class Details

Class 57/0 Original joint Porterbrook/Freightliner modification project taking Class 47 body shell and re-equipping with GM power unit and revised electrical systems. Later sold, with three locos going via Advenza to West Coast Railway and nine to Direct Rail Services.

Class 57/3 Originally 12 then increased to 16 locos, modified in similar way to Class 57/0 but incorporating train 'hotel' power supply for hauling Virgin Trains Class 390 stock away from electrified areas, fitted with drop-head Dellner couplings. After need diminished, four locos sold to West Coast Railway (drop-head couplers removed and 12 transferred to DRS who now provide cover for Virgin trains piloting operations.

Class 57/6 Similar modification to Class 57/3s, but modified for use on Great Western to power sleeper services. Originally one prototype loco converted with a follow-on batch of four. The original convert was later sold to West Coast Railway.

Right: The Carnforth-based West Coast Railway Co fleet of five electric train supply fitted locos are usually used to power charter trains, often in the 'top and tail' mode to reduce the need for shunting staff to run round trains. The four former Virgin Trains operated Class 57/3s have had their drop-head Dellner couplings removed, with a large space left on the front end. All carry West Coast maroon livery and No. 57601 carries Pullman colours. No. 57313 is seen passing Exminster on 30 April 2016 leading the return Cornish Explorer railtour which operated from Chester to Penzance and return. Sister loco No. 57315 is coupled on the rear of the train. **Antony Christie**

Traction Transition - GM/EMD power in the UK and Ireland

Traction Transition - GM/EMD power in the UK and Ireland
GM/EMD offer the Class 66

The Class 66, firmly has its history in the Foster Yeoman Class 59s from the mid-1980s, detailed earlier in this publication.

The '66' story emerged during the bidding process by Wisconsin Central (WC) for the UK rail freight operation under UK rail privatisation of the mid-1990s. Only two front line bidders were considered Wisconsin Central and OmniTrax. WC emerged as the winner, placing only £225.15 million on the table for the three shadow UK freight businesses, Mainline Freight, Transrail and Loadhaul, together with the parcels and charter business of Rail express systems.

The sale was marked by an event at London Marylebone on 24 February 1996, when the then BRB Chairman John Welsby handed over the freight businesses to Ed Burkhardt, President of Wisconsin Central.

At the launch event, Burkhardt said his new venture would be investing in 250 new freight locos, to replace 914 'heaps of junk' which he had just inherited. The new freight company was to be known as English Welsh & Scottish Railways (EWS).

Wisconsin Central a US short line, did not normally buy new locos, preferring to obtain secondhand locos and fund refurbishment. However, in this case EWS, there was nothing available to buy and a new order was the only option. WC were 'in bed' with General Motors (EMD), however to meet legalities many UK, European and other US builders, were given the chance to bid for the EWS order. This was against a very strict cost, performance and delivery specification. It was obvious that no UK or European builder could come close to the US companies, with General Motors having the Class 59 design fully certified in the UK, the company soon became preferred option.

In March/April 1996 many hours were spent by GM refining the design concept, at this time called the UK Class 61. In early April 1996, it emerged that EWS were seeking two designs of loco, 250 Co-Co freight engines and a less number of Bo-Bo high-speed mixed traffic locos, mainly for use on Royal Mail, parcels and passenger charter traffic.

WC dismissed a straight follow-on order for Class 59s, as the design and equipment was over 35 years old, and new 'state-of-the-art' technology was available.

To meet design certification of the Class 66, it was agreed to use the Class 59 underframe car-body and cab design, but with a totally new array of equipment. The prime mover adopted for the project was the GM/EMD 12N 710G3B. The main design was based of the current SD70 with a dual cab configuration.

Funding for the new fleet was arranged by Angel Trains Leasing and an official order was placed on 14 May 1996 for 250 locos, valued at around £375 million. Construction work was to undertaken at the Diesel Division production plant in London, Ontario, Canada. The first steel was cut in May 1997.

The massive Diesel Division plant was well used to large orders and the first stage of production was to create jigs to hold the various parts during assembly. It has to be remembered that the UK locos were much smaller than American builds and thus new tooling was required.

The first stage of assembly was the fabrication of frames, done in Department 513, when complete this was taken to the main assembly shop.

On works stands, the frame had an assembly rig attached which drilled and milled the various sections to take the bodywork, power unit, alternator and cooler group. Once this was finished, the rig was removed and the major pre-assembled components fitted. The cab sections and body sections were produced by contractor, Super Steel. The cab sections were formed as a separate assembly and part fitted prior to delivery to the production line. Once attached and the body sections installed, the main fitting out process and wiring began. The engines were supplied from GM from their La Grange plant in Chicago and brought together with items such as the cooler group, alternator and control equipment and assembled at the London site, on a just in time basis.

Once all equipment was installed, the body hoods were fitted and the loco mounted on a pair of EMD Radial bogies, assembled at the London factory. Radial or semi-steering bogies were ordered for the Class 66 as this was kinder to the track and gave improved performance and ride.

After the body was complete, it was moved to the paint facility, where spray painting was carried out and decals applied.

The next stage was a visit to the test area, this comprised of a period of static and dynamic tests involving operation over the works test track. Testing took several days to complete

Delivery of the complete locos was a major operation and involved the Goderich-Exeter Railway (GEXR) hauling a string of up to 12 locos at a time from London to Toronto via Stratford. From Canadian National's Toronto MacMillan Yard they were hauled to the port of export, usually Halifax.

The '66s' were fitted with the EM2000 advanced control system, which is based on a 32-bit microprocessor and used for traction control and fault diagnostics. Over 400 channels of data can be recorded on the EM2000 system which can either ➪

Below: *A view looking down at the main erecting shop at Diesel Division, London, Ontario, Canada, showing the main erecting shop of department 518 on 3 December 1998. Six EWS Class 66s are seen under assembly, including Nos. 66069, 66071 and 66073. In the foreground is one of the ill-fated SD90MAC-H locos for Union Pacific No. UP8513, later renumbered to 8923.* **CJM**

Right: *Either before or after a visit to the paint shop, new locos were put through their paces, at slow speed, on what was known at the Diesel Division Test Track, which was in fact a siding adjacent to the CP main line to the rear of the works. On 22 September 1998, No. 66019 in production primer is seen on the test track. Note the bolt-on knuckle coupling and temporary plastic windscreens. This loco was painted, packed and shipped, arriving at Newport, Wales on 31 October 1998.* **CJM-C**

be downloaded or remotely accessed.

Another new feature the class was 'Q-Tron' a data logging system or OTMR. On taking over a loco, a driver enters his personal ID, train details etc and the system will then monitor the drivers action and record actions with the power controller, AWS and braking.

The General Motors 12 cylinder two-stroke 710 series engine used for the Class 66, classified as 12N-710G3B-EC, is a breed of the GM two-stroke introduced in 1985 as a refinement to the 645 series, as fitted to the Class 59s. The 710 series engine has an excellent fuel efficiency, using an electronic fuel injection system.

To give an output of 3,300hp (2,460kW) an EMD turbo-charger was fitted. Coupled to the engine, is an EMD AR8 traction alternator and an auxiliary 6A6B alternator. Power from the traction alternator passes to six D43TR traction motors.

Braking on the Class 66 is of the Westinghouse PBL type.

The '66s' are fitted with Association of American Railroads (AAR) multiple jumper connection, using a single nose end mounted receptacle with a jumper cable stowed in the engine compartment when not in use.

It was a wish of EWS to install semi-auto couplers, with the locos designed to take a buckeye style connection. From loco No. 66201 swing head semi-auto couplers were installed, with pre-delivered locos being retro-fitted.

The first loco of the order to be complete, No. 66001 was tested at the EMD plant in early March 1998 and handed over to Ed Burkhardt on 23 March 1998. It was then shipped via the port of Albany on the Hudson River north of New York and arrived at ABP Immingham on 18 April. The loco was then transferred to Toton for an engineering inspection and commissioning.

The second of the build, No. 66002, was subject of major testing in the US and after completion Diesel Division was shipped on a flat car to the Association of American Railroads (AAR) test centre in Pueblo, Colorado, arriving on 1 June 1998. Here, extensive trials and performance tests were carried out, it remained at the test site for some eight weeks. In September 1998, No. 66002 was transferred to VMV in Paducah in Kentucky for upgrade before shipment to the UK, this was a protracted affair not arriving until 24 April 1999.

Production slowed after the first two locos were built to allow for type test approval by the then Railtrack. Testing of No. 66001 in the UK went well with a safety certificate issued on 14 July and a full approval one month later. Production of the order then gained momentum with three (Nos. 66003-005) shipped in September. Regular deliveries then followed with the final loco No. 66250 delivered on 23 June 2000.

By early 1999 Freightliner showed interest in the design, the official company line was that they were 'looking at all options', but in reality, only the '66' was available.

Freightliner soon opened talks with General Motors, but at that time only a protracted delivery date could be offered as all resources were placed on the EWS and US domestic orders. Eventually, a deal was struck in March 1999 for Freightliner through Porterbrook Leasing to order five locos, to be built alongside the EWS order following extra production capacity being created at the London site.

The first two Freightliner locos, allocated the Class 66/5 sub-class and numbered 66501-66502 were delivered alongside an EWS batch to Newport Docks on 17 July 1999, the remaining three followed one month later on 17 August 1999. All locos went directly into service following driver training.

Follow-on orders were soon announced, Freightliner ordering 15 locos, allocated numbers 66506-66520, these were delivered between June-November 2000 and funded on a lease back deal through Forward Trust Rail (later HSBC Rail).

The Class 66 design was now becoming popular and in early 1999 German operator Häfen Güterverkehr Köln, placed an order for two locos to power container trains between Germany and Rotterdam. At the time, as work was progressing well on the EWS order, and it was agreed to fulfil ➪

In all its glory, the first of the Class 66 build, No. 66001, stands outside the shed at Merehead on 27 June 1998, when it was the sole member of the design in the UK. **CJM**

Traction Transition - GM/EMD power in the UK and Ireland

Sub-class	66/0	66/3 and 66/4	66/5	66/6
Number range:	66001-66250	66301-66305, 66401-66434	66501-66599	66601-66625
Built by:	General Motors, EMDD, London, Canada	General Motors, EMDD, London, Canada	General Motors, EMDD, London, Canada	General Motors, EMDD, London, Canada
GM model:	JT-42-CWR	JT-42-CWR	JT-42-CWR	JT-42-CWR
Years introduced:	1998-2000	2003-2008	1999-2007	2000-2007
Wheel arrangement:	Co-Co	Co-Co	Co-Co	Co-Co
Design speed:	87.5mph (141km/h)	87.5mph (141km/h)	87.5mph (141km/h)	87.5mph (141km/h)
Maximum speed:	75mph (121km/h)	75mph (121km/h)	75mph (121km/h)	65mph (105km/h)
Length:	70ft 0½in (21.34m)	70ft 0½in (21.34m)	70ft 0½in (21.34m)	70ft 0½in (21.34m)
Height:	12ft 10in (3.91m)	12ft 10in (3.91m)	12ft 10in (3.91m)	12ft 10in (3.91m)
Width:	8ft 8¼in (2.65m)	8ft 8¼in (2.65m)	8ft 8¼in (2.65m)	8ft 8¼in (2.65m)
Weight:	126 tonnes	126 tonnes	126 tonnes	126 tonnes
Wheelbase:	56ft 9in (17.29m)	56ft 9in (17.29m)	56ft 9in (17.29m)	56ft 9in (17.29m)
Bogie wheelbase:	13ft 7in (4.14m)	13ft 7in (4.14m)	13ft 7in (4.14m)	13ft 7in (4.14m)
Bogie pivot centres:	43ft 6in (13.26m)	43ft 6in (13.26m)	43ft 6in (13.26m)	43ft 6in (13.26m)
Wheel diameter (new):	3ft 6in (1.06m)	3ft 6in (1.06m)	3ft 6in (1.06m)	3ft 6in (1.06m)
Min curve negotiable:	4 chains (80.46m)	4 chains (80.46m)	4 chains (80.46m)	4 chains (80.46m)
Engine type:	GM 12N-710G3B-EC	GM 12N-710G3B-U2	GM 12N-710G3B-EC§	GM 12N-710G3B-EC
Engine output:	3,300hp (2,460kW)	3,245hp (2,420kW)	3,300hp (2,460kW)	3,300hp (2,460kW)
Power at rail:	3,000hp (2,238kW)	3,000hp (2,238kW)	3,000hp (2,238kW)	3,000hp (2,238kW)
Tractive effort (max):	92,000lb (409kN)	92,000lb (409kN)	92,000lb (409kN)	105,080lb (467kN)
Tractive effort (cont):	58,390lb (260kN)	58,390lb (260kN)	58,390lb (260kN)	66,630lb (296kN)
Cylinder bore:	9¹/₁₆ (230mm)	9¹/₁₆ (230mm)	9¹/₁₆ (230mm)	9¹/₁₆ (230mm)
Cylinder stroke:	11in (279mm)	11in (279mm)	11in (279mm)	11in (279mm)
Traction alternator:	GM-EMD AR8	GM-EMD AR8	GM-EMD AR8	GM-EMD AR8
Companion alternator:	GM-EMD CA6	GM-EMD CA6	GM-EMD CA6	GM-EMD CA6
Traction motor type:	GM-EMD D43TR	GM-EMD D43TRC	GM-EMD D43TR	GM-EMD D43TR
No. of traction motors:	6	6	6	6
Gear ratio:	81:20	81:20	81:20	83:18
Brake type:	Air, Westinghouse PBL3	Air, Westinghouse PBL3	Air, Westinghouse PBL3	Air, Westinghouse PBL3
Brake force:	68 tonnes	68 tonnes	68 tonnes	68 tonnes
Bogie type:	HTCR Radial	HTCR Radial	HTCR Radial	HTCR Radial
Route availability:	7	7	7	7
Heating type:	Not fitted	Not fitted	Not fitted	Not fitted
Multiple coupling type:	AAR	AAR	AAR	AAR
Fuel tank capacity:	1,440gal (6,546lit)	1,133gal (5,150lit)	66501- 66584 1,440gal (6,546lit) 66585-66599 1,133gal (5,150lit)	66601-66622 1,440gal (6,546lit) 66623-66625 1,133gal (5,150lit)
Lub oil capacity:	202 gal (918lit)	202 gal (918lit)	202 gal (918lit)	202 gal (918lit)
Sanding equipment:	Pneumatic	Pneumatic	Pneumatic	Pneumatic
Special fittings:	EM2000 Q-Tron, GPS Combination coupler+, SSC	EM2000 Q-Tron, GPS low emission	EM2000 Q-Tron, GPS	EM2000 Q-Tron, GPS
Sub-class variations:	Standard DB-C	DRS & Freightliner	Standard Freightliner	Freightliner modified gearing
Note:	+ 66001/002 unable to be fitted with Combination couplers		§ 66585-66599 have a GM 12N-710G3B-U2 engine and GM-EMD D43TRC traction motors	

the HGK order quickly by taking two locos off the UK (EWS) production line, Nos. 66154 and 66155 and building these as HGK Nos. DE61 and DE62. Fresh bodies were built as replacement. More can be found on the Euro 66s in the last chapter of this book.

Freightliner, who operated heavier trains, wanted higher output locos with lower gearing and improved tractive effort. This was worked into a production modification and in the summer of 2000 six high output locos, classified as 66/6 emerged, numbered in the 666xx series.

At the start of 2000 another new operator came on the scene, that of GB Railfreight, then a part of GB Railways, who quickly closed a contract to secure funding from HSBC Rail for seven locos, classified Class 66/7, these were delivered to the UK in March 2001.

The next batch of UK locos were for Freightliner with 28 locos delivered between June and November 2001, funded by both Porterbrook and HSBC.

While Diesel Division were busy building in excess of 1,000 SD70s for Union Pacific, the Class 66 orders continued. GBRf business was booming and a further order for five locos (66713-717) was placed in November 2002. At around the same time, Carlisle-based Direct Rail Services (DRS) turned there interest to Class 66s.

And, at the tail end of 2002, when a deadline for emission standards came into force, a further 40 '66s' were ordered. DRS ordered 10 Class 66/4s in December 2002 funded by Porterbrook.

With emissions issues now so important GM/EMD offered low-emission locos, this called for a major engineering review, as the revised power unit, classified as 12N-710G3B-U2 and its cooler group, required considerable more space and called for a separate cooling system to reduce the temperature of the turbo-charged air, this required a bigger cooler assembly, taking up the space of the original cab to cab walkway. This was allowed, providing an extra door for engine room access was provided - and thus the five-door Class 66 was born. To cope with weight increase, the size of the fuel tank was reduced from 1,440gal (6,546lit) to 1,133gal (5,150lit), cutting the operating range by around 200 miles.

On 15 October 2003 DRS took delivery of the first five locos, the balance arriving on 20 November. These were finished in a new DRS 'Compass' livery.

At the end of 2003 Freightliner continued to add to its loco portfolio with more '66/5s' and '66/6s'.

In mid-2004 GBRf placed another order for five Class 66s, (66718-66722), these were low-emission type and would be funded by HSBC. A further order for 10 UK low-emission locos for DRS was placed in mid summer, these were allocated numbers 66411-66420.

In 2005, GBRf announced a major new contract to provide power and wagons for London Underground surface line engineering trains, this saw five extra locos ordered.

The Class 66 story took a major turn in 2005, when EWS Euro Cargo Rail (ECR) to operate in France and mainland Europe, quickly No. 66215 was taken out of service and modified for French use, including the fitting of KVB or French ATP, French radios, French OTMR, TPWS and AWS. In addition, modifications were made to the obstacle deflector plates, brake, fuel and bogie equipment. Work was carried out at Toton, with the loco going to France on 3 January 2006. Prior to this No. 66083 had made a brief visit to France on 11 October 2005 for static tests..

Full operating certification was granted to ECR on 31 August 2006 with the company placing a substantial order for 60 Euro '66s' classified as 77 in France.

In addition to Euro 66s a substantial number of UK Class 66s have been modified for use with EWS, later DB in France and Poland, these are detailed in the fleet table.

In March 2006 Freightliner placed a further order for 16 low emission locos.

A further delivery of '66s' was made to Newport on 29 May 2006 when DRS low-emission locos Nos. 66411-413 arrived.

An unexpected announcement came on 28 October 2006 when Carlisle-based DRS announced a further order for 10 Class 66s to be allocated numbers 66421-66430.

In 2007-2008 many further orders were announced by both GBRf and Freightliner.

In July 2007 another new operator emerged, ⇨

66/7	66/8	66/9
66701-66789	66846-66850	66951-66957
General Motors, EMDD. London, Canada & Caterpiller, Muncie, IN	General Motors, EMDD. London, Canada	General Motors, EMDD, London, Canada
JT-42-CWR	JT-42-CWR	JT-42-CWR
2001-2014	Orig: 2004, 66/8: 2011	2004, 2008
Co-Co	Co-Co	Co-Co
87.5mph (141km/h)	87.5mph (141km/h)	87.5mph (141km/h)
75mph (121km/h)	75mph (121km/h)	75mph (121km/h)
70ft 0½in (21.34m)	70ft 0½in (21.34m)	70ft 0½in (21.34m)
12ft 10in (3.91m)	12ft 10in (3.91m)	12ft 10in (3.91m)
8ft 8¼in (2.65m)	8ft 8¼in (2.65m)	8ft 8¼in (2.65m)
126 tonnes	126 tonnes	126 tonnes
56ft 9in (17.29m)	56ft 9in (17.29m)	56ft 9in (17.29m)
13ft 7in (4.14m)	13ft 7in (4.14m)	13ft 7in (4.14m)
43ft 6in (13.26m)	43ft 6in (13.26m)	43ft 6in (13.26m)
3ft 6in (1.06m)	3ft 6in (1.06m)	3ft 6in (1.06m)
4 chains (80.46m)	4 chains (80.46m)	4 chains (80.46m)
GM 12N-710G3B-EC§	GM 12N-710G3B-EC	GM 12N-710G3B-U2
3,300hp (2,460kW)	3,300hp (2,460kW)	3,300hp (2,460kW)
3,000hp (2,238kW)	3,000hp (2,238kW)	3,000hp (2,238kW)
92,000lb (409kN)	92,000lb (409kN)	92,000lb (409kN)
58,390lb (260kN)	58,390lb (260kN)	58,390lb (260kN)
9¹⁄₁₆ (230mm)	9¹⁄₁₆ (230mm)	9¹⁄₁₆ (230mm)
11in (279mm)	11in (279mm)	11in (279mm)
GM-EMD AR8	GM-EMD AR8	GM-EMD AR8
GM-EMD CA6	GM-EMD CA6	GM-EMD CA6
GM-EMD D43TR	GM-EMD D43TR	GM-EMD D43TR
6	6	6
81:20	81:20	81:20
Air, Westinghouse PBL3	Air, Westinghouse PBL3	Air, Westinghouse PBL3
68 tonnes	68 tonnes	68 tonnes
HTCR Radial	HTCR Radial	HTCR Radial
7	7	7
Not fitted	Not fitted	Not fitted
AAR	AAR	AAR
66701-66717/ 66733-66746 / 66780-66789 - 1,440gal (6,546lit) 66718-66722 – 1,220gal (5,546lit) 66723-66732/66747-66749 / 66773-66779 1,133gal (5,150lit)	1,440gal (6,546lit)	1,133gal (5,150lit)
202 gal (918lit)	202 gal (918lit)	202 gal (918lit)
Pneumatic	Pneumatic	Pneumatic
EM2000 Q-Tron, GPS	EM2000 Q-Tron, GPS	EM2000 Q-Tron, GPS
66718-772 - low emission GBRf	Ex-Freightliner now with Colas	Freightliner Low-emission locos 66951-66952 low-emission demo locos
§ 66718-66746 have a GM 12N-710G3B-U2 engine and GM-EMD D43TRC traction motors 66747-751 from Europe		

Right Upper and Middle: *Class 66 nose end equipment positions. 1: Warning horns behind grille, 2: High level marker light, 3: Lamp bracket, 4: Marker light, 5: Headlight, 6: Tail light, 7: AAR multiple control jumper socket, 8: Release linkage for 'swing head' coupling, 9: Swing head coupling, 10: Air brake pipe, 11: Main reservoir pipe, 12: Transit securing lugs, 13: Coupling hook and shackle. Both:* **CJM**

Below: *As part of emissions testing prior to delivery, No. 66001, painted in full EWS livery, is seen on the Diesel Division test track with an extension to its exhaust system, which would be coupled to monitoring equipment inside the test house. This unusual image was recorded on 26 March 1998.* **CJM-C**

Below: *Several different designs of builders or makers plates have been carried on the 66s. This is the 'stick-on' plate as fitted to GBRf No. 66722. The plates shows the point of manufacture and assembly as Canada, the official EMD model type as JT42WR-T1 its works number 20048652-005 and a date of construction 02-2006. This loco was delivered on 8 April 2006.* **CJM**

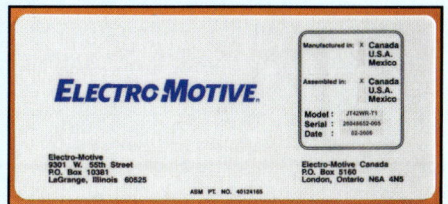

Traction Transition - GM/EMD power in the UK and Ireland

Above: The first of the Freightliner locos Class 66/5 No. 66501 makes one of its first shows in public on 10 June 1999. It is seen being switched at the front of the Diesel Division plate in London, Ontario by No. 0069 a SW900 'switcher' built in February 1955 as works No. 19703 and was originally an industrial loco at the General Motors Buick car plant. **CJM-C**

Jarvis, who through its FastLine Freight businesses ordered five locos with funding by Ellco to power coal trains for Eon. These locos arrived between June and November 2008 and were based at Roberts Road, Doncaster.

Sadly the company went into receivership in March 2010 and the locos were sold to CB Rail and leased to DRS.

Freightliner still wanted more locos and in late summer 2007 ordered a further five standard, five door locos, numbered 66595-66599, this order was increased to 10 with numbering extending from 66953-957.

One further new order emerged in 2007 for four Class 66/4s for DRS, these were built to order No. 20078946 and shipped to the UK for delivery in November 2008.

After just a short period of stability changes started to emerge. The Freightliner operation in Poland was doing well and more locos were needed. Several new Euro 66s had been delivered direct to Poland, but extra locos were required. It was decided to modify several UK locos and export them to Poland. The first to go were Nos. 66582/583/584/586 in June 2009, renumbered into the Freightliner Poland series as FPL66009/010/011/008. This was followed by several others (detailed in table).

The original 10 DRS Class 66/4s started to come off lease as newer locos were delivered in 2009, five were assigned Advenza Rail Freight, a part of the Cotswold Group, who were trying to be an open-access operator. Nos. 66406-409 were transferred in summer 2009, repainted in Advenza Freight blue and renumbered 66841-66845. Advenza Rail Freight and Cotswold went into liquidation on 7 October 2009 and the '66s' reverted to Porterbrook ownership.

After periods of spot hire to various companies including Colas, Nos. 66841-66845 together with ex-DRS Nos. 66401-66405 were taken over by GBRf and renumbered as Nos. 66733-66737 and 66742-66746.

Colas Rail Freight then obtained five off-lease Freightliner locos No. 66573-66577 which were overhauled and repainted into Colas colours as Nos. 66846-66850. At around the same time, four off-lease Freightliner locos Nos. 66578-66581 were taken on by GBRf and renumbered as 66738-66741

Such was the desire to obtain more '66s', GBRf obtained five original 'Euro 66s'. The first three to arrive in the UK, were works Nos. 20078968-04/06/07. In spring 2013, two further locos were obtained, works No. 20038513-01 which had previously been used by Rush Rail and works No. 20038513-04, owned by Beacon Rail, and previously used by Heavy Haul Power International.

It was considered that after the Diesel Division plant in London, Canada closed, no further locos of the design would be built, this was supported by emissions levels. However, such was the interest in the design, that in 2012 General Motors accepted an order for a further 28, all for GBRf to be constructed by the new owners of General Motors, Progress Rail, a subsidiary of Caterpillar at a new factory in Muncie, Indiana. These locos numbered 66752-66779 were delivered to the UK between July 2014 and February 2016.

In more recent times, EWS, now owned by German rail giant Deutsche Bahn have, through losses in traffic found they have more locos than are required and in 2018 sold 10 to GBRf. Further changes in owner/operator are likely in the future and as we closed for press a further four Euro locos are scheduled to be rebuilt and transfer to UK with GBRf as Nos. 66790-66793.

Love them or hate them, the Class 66 has been one of the most successful modern diesel-electric designs, frequently giving a reliability figure of around 93 per cent. ■

Below: The shipping of the Class 66s from the Diesel Division plant in London, Ontario was an interesting operation. Usually batches of between 4-12 locos were shipped together, being collected in the rail yard off Oxford Street, London and the tripped by the Goderich & Exeter Railway, a short line to Stratford and onto CN Mac Yard on the outskirts of Toronto. From here they were hauled by CN to the departing port, most usually, but not always, Halifax. In this 20 January 2007 view recorded at Stratford, from right to left we see Freightliner/Bardon Aggregates No. 66623, Euro 66s Nos. EU08 and EU09, Freightliner Poland Nos. EU02/03/04 (FL-Poland 66001/002/003), with 66625 on the rear out of picture. **CJM-C**

70   *Traction Transition - GM/EMD power in the UK and Ireland*

Cab Window Re-design

Original Design

Revised Design

During the course of construction, issues emerged with the cab window design, mainly involving the ingress of water. A revised design was produced and installed on locos 66301-66305, 66411-66434, 66582-66599, 66623-66624, 66718-66779, 66951-66957 from delivery, many others have now been retro-fitted.

Right Upper: *The 'little and large show'. This image clearly shows the size difference between a UK and North American size loco. On the left is Freightliner No. 66607, while on the right is Union Pacific SD70 No. 4716.* **CJM-C**

Right Lower: *Low emissions development loco No. 66951 was after completion at Diesel Division shipped, in base primer, by rail to La Grange, Chicago for testing, returning to London, Canada for completion. On 14 February 2004, the loco is seen in the Canadian National yard in London, after its return from the US, attached to CN GP40 No. 9424, about to make its way back to the Diesel Division plant. This loco was later delivered to Freightliner.* **CJM-C**

Above: *After completion at Diesel Division, the second '66' No. 66002 was loaded on a flat car and transported to the Association of American Railroads test centre in Pueblo, Colorado, arriving on 1 June 1998. Extensive trials and performance tests were carried out, it departed in September 1998 via VMV for upgrade work and arrived in the UK in April 1999. The loco is seen in the Canadian Pacific yard in London, Canada on 13 May 1998.* **CJM-C**

Above: *Recorded on 2 February 2005, Freightliner No. 66581 stands inside the main factory at Diesel Division, London awaiting movement to the port and shipping. This loco arrived in the UK on 15 May 2005. It worked with Freightliner until 2011 when it was transferred to GB Railfreight and is currently No. 66741.* **CJM**

Traction Transition - GM/EMD power in the UK and Ireland

Class 66 UK Fleet List

Numbers and renumbers	Name	Builder	Works No.	Date Delivered	Original Owner	2019 Oper'r	Notes UIC Number
66001		GM-EMD Ca	968702-1	18/04/98	ATL	DB-C	
66002	Lafarge Buddon Wood 09/02-03/03 Lafarge Quorn 03/03-01/15	GM-EMD Ca	968702-2	24/04/99	ATL	DB-C	
66003		GM-EMD Ca	968702-3	27/08/98	ATL	DB-C	
66004		GM-EMD Ca	968702-4	27/08/98	ATL	DB-C	
66005	Maritime Intermodal One 03/19	GM-EMD Ca	968702-5	27/08/98	ATL	DB-C	
66006		GM-EMD Ca	968702-6	04/10/98	ATL	DB-C	
66007		GM-EMD Ca	968702-7	04/10/98	ATL	DB-C	
66008 66780 09/18		GM-EMD Ca	968702-8	04/10/98	ATL	DB-C	
66009		GM-EMD Ca	968702-9	04/10/98	AT	DB-C	
66010 ●		GM-EMD Ca	968702-10	04/10/98	ATL	ECR-F	92 70 0666 010-4
66011		GM-EMD Ca	968702-11	04/10/98	ATL	DB-C	
66012		GM-EMD Ca	968702-12	31/10/98	ATL	DB-C	
66013 ●		GM-EMD Ca	968702-13	31/10/98	ATL	DB-C	
66014		GM-EMD Ca	968702-14	31/10/98	ATL	DB-C	
66015		GM-EMD Ca	968702-15	31/10/98	ATL	DB-C	
66016 66781 01/18		GM-EMD Ca	968702-16	31/10/98	ATL	DB-C	
66017		GM-EMD Ca	968702-17	31/10/98	ATL	DB-C	
66018		GM-EMD Ca	968702-18	31/10/98	ATL	DB-C	
66019		GM-EMD Ca	968702-19	31/10/98	ATL	DB-C	
66020		GM-EMD Ca	968702-20	31/10/98	ATL	DB-C	
66021		GM-EMD Ca	968702-21	31/10/98	ATL	DB-C	
66022 ●	Lafarge Charnwood 03/03-	GM-EMD Ca	968702-22	31/10/98	ATL	ECR-F	92 70 0666 022-9
66023		GM-EMD Ca	968702-23	01/12/98	ATL	DB-C	
66024		GM-EMD Ca	968702-24	01/12/98	ATL	DB-C	
66025		GM-EMD Ca	968702-25	01/12/98	ATL	DB-C	
66026 ●		GM-EMD Ca	968702-26	01/12/98	ATL	ECR-F	92 70 0666 026-0
66027		GM-EMD Ca	968702-27	01/12/98	ATL	DB-C	
66028 ●		GM-EMD Ca	968702-28	01/12/98	ATL	ECR-F	92 70 0666 028-6
66029 ●		GM-EMD Ca	968702-29	01/12/98	ATL	ECR-F	92 70 0666 029-4
66030		GM-EMD Ca	968702-30	01/12/98	ATL	DB-C	
66031 ●		GM-EMD Ca	968702-31	01/12/98	ATL	DB-C	
66032 ●		GM-EMD Ca	968702-32	01/12/98	ATL	ECR-F	92 70 0666 032-8
66033 ●		GM-EMD Ca	968702-33	01/12/98	ATL	ECR-F	92 70 0666 033-6
66034		GM-EMD Ca	968702-34	15/12/98	ATL	DB-C	
66035	Resourceful 02/18-	GM-EMD Ca	968702-35	15/12/98	ATL	DB-C	
66036 ●		GM-EMD Ca	968702-36	15/12/98	ATL	ECR-F	92 70 0666 036-9
66037		GM-EMD Ca	968702-37	15/12/98	ATL	DB-C	
66038 ●		GM-EMD Ca	968702-38	15/12/98	ATL	ECR-F	92 70 0666 038-5
66039		GM-EMD Ca	968702-39	15/12/98	ATL	DB-C	
66040		GM-EMD Ca	968702-40	15/12/98	ATL	DB-C	
66041		GM-EMD Ca	968702-41	15/12/98	ATL	DB-C	
66042 ●	Lafarge Buddon Wood 07/03-12/06	GM-EMD Ca	968702-42	15/12/98	ATL	ECR-F	92 70 0666 042-7
66043		GM-EMD Ca	968702-43	15/12/98	ATL	DB-C	
66044		GM-EMD Ca	968702-44	15/12/98	ATL	DB-C	
66045 ●		GM-EMD Ca	968702-45	04/01/99	ATL	ECR-F	92 70 0666 045-0
66046 66782 01/18		GM-EMD Ca	968702-46	04/01/99	ATL	DB-C	
66047	Maritime Intermodal Two 03/19	GM-EMD Ca	968702-47	04/01/99	ATL	DB-C	
66048	James the Engine 01/10-	GM-EMD Ca	968702-48	04/01/99	ATL	-	1
66049 ●		GM-EMD Ca	968702-49	04/01/99	ATL	ECR-F	92 70 0666 049-2
66050	EWS Energy 09/08-	GM-EMD Ca	968702-50	04/01/99	ATL	DB-C	
66051		GM-EMD Ca	968702-51	04/01/99	ATL	DB-C	
66052 ●		GM-EMD Ca	968702-52	04/01/99	ATL	ECR-F	92 70 0666 052-6
66053		GM-EMD Ca	968702-53	04/01/99	ATL	DB-C	
66054		GM-EMD Ca	968702-54	04/01/99	ATL	DB-C	
66055	Alan Thauvette 09/16-	GM-EMD Ca	968702-55	04/01/99	ATL	DB-C	
66056		GM-EMD Ca	968702-56	04/01/99	ATL	DB-C	
66057		GM-EMD Ca	968702-57	04/01/99	ATL	DB-C	
66058 66783 03/18	Derek Clark 08/15-10-/17 The Flying Dustman 03/18-	GM-EMD Ca	968702-58	04/01/99	ATL	DB-C	
66059		GM-EMD Ca	968702-59	04/01/99	ATL	DB-C	
66060		GM-EMD Ca	968702-60	04/01/99	ATL	DB-C	
66061		GM-EMD Ca	968702-61	04/02/99	ATL	DB-C	
66062 ●		GM-EMD Ca	968702-62	04/02/99	ATL	ECR-F	92 70 0666 062-5
66063		GM-EMD Ca	968702-63	04/02/99	ATL	DB-C	
66064 ●		GM-EMD Ca	968702-64	04/02/99	ATL	ECR-F	92 70 0666 064-1
66065		GM-EMD Ca	968702-65	04/02/99	ATL	DB-C	
66066	Geoff Spencer 09/16-	GM-EMD Ca	968702-66	04/02/99	ATL	DB-C	
66067		GM-EMD Ca	968702-67	04/02/99	ATL	DB-C	
66068		GM-EMD Ca	968702-68	04/02/99	ATL	DB-C	
66069		GM-EMD Ca	968702-69	04/02/99	ATL	DB-C	
66070		GM-EMD Ca	968702-70	04/02/99	ATL	DB-C	
66071 ●		GM-EMD Ca	968702-71	04/02/99	ATL	ECR-F	92 70 0666 071-6
66072 ●		GM-EMD Ca	968702-72	04/02/99	ATL	ECR-F	92 70 0666 072-4
66073 ●		GM-EMD Ca	968702-73	27/02/99	ATL	ECR-F	92 70 0666 073-2
66074		GM-EMD Ca	968702-74	27/02/99	ATL	DB-C	
66075		GM-EMD Ca	968702-75	27/02/99	ATL	DB-C	
66076		GM-EMD Ca	968702-76	27/02/99	ATL	DB-C	
66077	Benjamin Gimbet GC 06/04-12/16	GM-EMD Ca	968702-77	27/02/99	ATL	DB-C	
66078		GM-EMD Ca	968702-78	27/02/99	ATL	DB-C	
66079	James Nightall GC 06/04-	GM-EMD Ca	968702-79	27/02/99	ATL	DB-C	
66080		GM-EMD Ca	968702-80	27/02/99	ATL	DB-C	
66081 66784 01/18	Keighley & Worth Valley 08/18- Railway 50th Anniversary 1968-2018	GM-EMD Ca	968702-81	27/02/99	ATL	DB-C	

66082			GM-EMD Ca	968702-82	27/02/99	ATL	DB-C
66083			GM-EMD Ca	968702-83	12/04/99	ATL	DB-C
66084			GM-EMD Ca	968702-84	12/04/99	ATL	DB-C
66085			GM-EMD Ca	968702-85	12/04/99	ATL	DB-C
66086			GM-EMD Ca	968702-86	12/04/99	ATL	DB-C
66087			GM-EMD Ca	968702-87	12/04/99	ATL	DB-C
66088			GM-EMD Ca	968702-88	12/04/99	ATL	DB-C
66089			GM-EMD Ca	968702-89	12/04/99	ATL	DB-C
66090			GM-EMD Ca	968702-90	12/04/99	ATL	DB-C
66091			GM-EMD Ca	968702-91	24/04/99	ATL	DB-C
66092			GM-EMD Ca	968702-92	12/04/99	ATL	DB-C
66093			GM-EMD Ca	968702-93	12/04/99	ATL	DB-C
66094			GM-EMD Ca	968702-94	24/04/99	ATL	DB-C
66095			GM-EMD Ca	968702-95	24/04/99	ATL	DB-C
66096			GM-EMD Ca	968702-96	24/04/99	ATL	DB-C
66097			GM-EMD Ca	968702-97	24/04/99	ATL	DB-C
66098			GM-EMD Ca	968702-98	24/04/99	ATL	DB-C
66099			GM-EMD Ca	968702-99	24/04/99	ATL	DB-C
66100		*Armistice 100 1918-2018* 11/18	GM-EMD Ca	968702-100	24/04/99	ATL	DB-C
66101			GM-EMD Ca	968702-101	24/04/99	ATL	DB-C
66102			GM-EMD Ca	968702-102	24/04/99	ATL	DB-C
66103			GM-EMD Ca	968702-103	24/04/99	ATL	DB-C
66104			GM-EMD Ca	968702-104	24/04/99	ATL	DB-C
66105			GM-EMD Ca	968702-105	24/04/99	ATL	DB-C
66106			GM-EMD Ca	968702-106	29/05/99	ATL	DB-C
66107			GM-EMD Ca	968702-107	29/05/99	ATL	DB-C
66108			GM-EMD Ca	968702-108	29/05/99	ATL	DB-C
66109			GM-EMD Ca	968702-109	29/05/99	ATL	DB-C
66110			GM-EMD Ca	968702-110	29/05/99	ATL	DB-C
66111			GM-EMD Ca	968702-111	29/05/99	ATL	DB-C
66112			GM-EMD Ca	968702-112	29/05/99	ATL	DB-C
66113			GM-EMD Ca	968702-113	29/05/99	ATL	DB-C
66114			GM-EMD Ca	968702-114	29/05/99	ATL	DB-C
66115			GM-EMD Ca	968702-115	29/05/99	ATL	DB-C
66116			GM-EMD Ca	968702-116	29/05/99	ATL	DB-C
66117			GM-EMD Ca	968702-117	20/06/99	ATL	DB-C
66118			GM-EMD Ca	968702-118	20/06/99	ATL	DB-C
66119			GM-EMD Ca	968702-119	20/06/99	ATL	DB-C
66120			GM-EMD Ca	968702-120	20/06/99	ATL	DB-C
66121			GM-EMD Ca	968702-121	20/06/99	ATL	DB-C
66122			GM-EMD Ca	968702-122	20/06/99	ATL	DB-C
66123 ●			GM-EMD Ca	968702-123	20/06/99	ATL	ECR-F	92 70 0666 123-5
66124			GM-EMD Ca	968702-124	20/06/99	ATL	DB-C
66125			GM-EMD Ca	968702-125	20/06/99	ATL	DB-C
66126			GM-EMD Ca	968702-126	20/06/99	ATL	DB-C
66127			GM-EMD Ca	968702-127	20/06/99	ATL	DB-C
66128			GM-EMD Ca	968702-128	07/07/99	ATL	DB-C
66129			GM-EMD Ca	968702-129	07/07/99	ATL	DB-C
66130			GM-EMD Ca	968702-130	07/07/99	ATL	DB-C
66131			GM-EMD Ca	968702-131	07/07/99	ATL	DB-C
66132	66785 01/18		GM-EMD Ca	968702-132	07/07/99	ATL	DB-C
66133			GM-EMD Ca	968702-133	07/07/99	ATL	DB-C
66134			GM-EMD Ca	968702-134	07/07/99	ATL	DB-C
66135			GM-EMD Ca	968702-135	07/07/99	ATL	DB-C
66136			GM-EMD Ca	968702-136	07/07/99	ATL	DB-C
66137			GM-EMD Ca	968702-137	20/10/99	ATL	DB-C
66138			GM-EMD Ca	968702-138	17/08/99	ATL	DB-C
66139			GM-EMD Ca	968702-139	17/08/99	ATL	DB-C
66140			GM-EMD Ca	968702-140	17/08/99	ATL	DB-C
66141	66786 01/18		GM-EMD Ca	968702-141	17/08/99	ATL	DB-C
66142		*Maritime Intermodal Three* 03/19	GM-EMD Ca	968702-142	17/08/99	ATL	DB-C
66143			GM-EMD Ca	968702-143	17/08/99	ATL	DB-C
66144			GM-EMD Ca	968702-144	17/09/99	ATL	DB-C
66145			GM-EMD Ca	968702-145	17/08/99	ATL	DB-C
66146 P			GM-EMD Ca	968702-146	17/09/99	ATL	DB-P	92 70 0666 046-6
66147			GM-EMD Ca	968702-147	17/08/99	ATL	DB-C
66148			GM-EMD Ca	968702-148	17/09/99	ATL	DB-C
66149			GM-EMD Ca	968702-149	17/09/99	ATL	DB-C
66150			GM-EMD Ca	968702-150	17/09/99	ATL	DB-C
66151			GM-EMD Ca	968702-151	17/09/99	ATL	DB-C
66152		*Derek Holmes Railway Operator* 03/10-	GM-EMD Ca	968702-152	17/09/99	ATL	DB-C
66153 P			GM-EMD Ca	968702-153	17/09/99	ATL	DB-P	92 70 0666 153-2
66154			GM-EMD Ca	968702-154	14/01/00	ATL	DB-C
66155			GM-EMD Ca	968702-155	14/01/00	ATL	DB-C
66156			GM-EMD Ca	968702-156	20/10/99	ATL	DB-C
66157 P			GM-EMD Ca	968702-157	17/09/99	ATL	DB-P	92 70 0666 157-3
66158			GM-EMD Ca	968702-158	20/10/99	ATL	DB-C
66159 P			GM-EMD Ca	968702-159	20/10/99	ATL	DB-P	92 70 0666 159-9
66160			GM-EMD Ca	968702-160	20/10/99	ATL	DB-C
66161			GM-EMD Ca	968702-161	20/10/99	ATL	DB-C
66162			GM-EMD Ca	968702-162	20/10/99	ATL	DB-C
66163 P			GM-EMD Ca	968702-163	20/10/99	ATL	DB-P	92 70 0666 163-1
66164			GM-EMD Ca	968702-164	20/10/99	ATL	DB-C
66165			GM-EMD Ca	968702-165	20/10/99	ATL	DB-C
66166 P			GM-EMD Ca	968702-166	20/10/99	ATL	DB-P	92 70 0666 166-4
66167			GM-EMD Ca	968702-167	17/11/99	ATL	DB-C
66168			GM-EMD Ca	968702-168	17/11/99	ATL	DB-C
66169			GM-EMD Ca	968702-169	17/11/99	ATL	DB-C
66170			GM-EMD Ca	968702-170	17/11/99	ATL	DB-C
66171			GM-EMD Ca	968702-171	17/11/99	ATL	DB-C

66172			Paul Melleney 10/05-	GM-EMD Ca	968702-172 17/11/99	ATL	DB-C	
66173 P				GM-EMD Ca	968702-173 17/11/99	ATL	DB-P	92 70 0666 173-0
66174				GM-EMD Ca	968702-174 17/11/99	ATL	DB-C	
66175				GM-EMD Ca	968702-175 17/11/99	ATL	DB-C	
66176				GM-EMD Ca	968702-176 17/11/99	ATL	DB-C	
66177				GM-EMD Ca	968702-177 17/11/99	ATL	DB-C	
66178 P				GM-EMD Ca	968702-178 17/11/99	ATL	DB-P	92 70 0666 178-9
66179 ●				GM-EMD Ca	968702-179 24/12/99	ATL	ECR-F	92 70 0666 179-7
66180 P				GM-EMD Ca	968702-180 24/12/99	ATL	DB-P	92 70 0666 180-5
66181				GM-EMD Ca	968702-181 24/12/99	ATL	DB-C	
66182				GM-EMD Ca	968702-182 24/12/99	ATL	DB-C	
66183				GM-EMD Ca	968702-183 24/12/99	ATL	DB-C	
66184	66787	01/18		GM-EMD Ca	968702-184 24/12/99	ATL	DB-C	
66185			DP World London Gateway 09/13-	GM-EMD Ca	968702-185 24/12/99	ATL	DB-C	
66186				GM-EMD Ca	968702-186 24/12/99	ATL	DB-C	
66187				GM-EMD Ca	968702-187 24/12/99	ATL	DB-C	
66188				GM-EMD Ca	968702-188 24/12/99	ATL	DB-C	
66189 P				GM-EMD Ca	968702-189 24/12/99	ATL	DB-P	92 70 0666 189-6
66190 ●				GM-EMD Ca	968702-190 14/01/00	ATL	ECR-F	92 70 0666 190-4
66191 ●				GM-EMD Ca	968702-191 14/01/00	ATL	ECR-F	92 70 0666 191-2
66192				GM-EMD Ca	968702-192 14/01/00	ATL	DB-C	
66193 ●				GM-EMD Ca	968702-193 14/01/00	ATL	ECR-F	92 70 0666 193-8
66194				GM-EMD Ca	968702-194 14/01/00	ATL	DB-C	
66195 ●				GM-EMD Ca	968702-195 14/01/00	ATL	ECR-F	92 70 0666 195-3
66196 P				GM-EMD Ca	968702-196 29/02/00	ATL	DB-P	92 70 0666 196-1
66197				GM-EMD Ca	968702-197 29/02/00	ATL	DB-C	
66198				GM-EMD Ca	968702-198 29/02/00	ATL	DB-C	
66199				GM-EMD Ca	968702-199 29/02/00	ATL	DB-C	
66200			Railway Heritage 10/04-06/15 Committee	GM-EMD Ca	968702-200 29/02/00	ATL	DB-C	
66201 ●				GM-EMD Ca	968702-201 29/02/00	ATL	ECR-F	92 70 0666 201-9
66202 ●				GM-EMD Ca	968702-202 29/02/00	ATL	ECR-F	92 70 0666 202-7
66203 ●				GM-EMD Ca	968702-203 29/02/00	ATL	ECR-F	92 70 0666 203-5
66204 ●				GM-EMD Ca	968702-204 29/02/00	ATL	ECR-F	92 70 0666 204-7
66205 ●				GM-EMD Ca	968702-205 23/03/00	ATL	ECR-F	92 70 0666 205-0
66206				GM-EMD Ca	968702-206 23/03/00	ATL	DB-C	
66207				GM-EMD Ca	968702-207 23/03/00	ATL	DB-C	
66208 ●				GM-EMD Ca	968702-208 23/03/00	ATL	ECR-F	92 70 0666 208-4
66209 ●				GM-EMD Ca	968702-209 23/03/00	ATL	ECR-F	92 70 0666 209-2
66210 ●				GM-EMD Ca	968702-210 23/03/00	ATL	ECR-F	92 70 0666 210-0
66211 ●				GM-EMD Ca	968702-211 23/03/00	ATL	ECR-F	92 70 0666 211-8
66212 ●				GM-EMD Ca	968702-212 23/03/00	ATL	ECR-F	92 70 0666 212-6
66213 ●				GM-EMD Ca	968702-213 19/04/00	ATL	ECR-F	92 70 0666 213-4
66214 ●				GM-EMD Ca	968702-214 23/03/00	ATL	ECR-F	92 70 0666 214-2
66215 ●				GM-EMD Ca	968702-215 19/04/00	ATL	ECR-F	92 70 0666 215-9
66216 ●				GM-EMD Ca	968702-216 23/03/00	ATL	ECR-F	92 70 0666 216-7
66217 ●				GM-EMD Ca	968702-217 19/04/00	ATL	ECR-F	92 70 0666 217-5
66218 ●				GM-EMD Ca	968702-218 19/04/00	ATL	ECR-F	92 70 0666 218-3
66219 ●				GM-EMD Ca	968702-219 19/04/00	ATL	ECR-F	92 70 0666 219-1
66220 P				GM-EMD Ca	968702-220 19/04/00	ATL	DB-P	92 70 0666 220-9
66221				GM-EMD Ca	968702-221 19/04/00	ATL	DB-C	
66222 ●				GM-EMD Ca	968702-222 19/04/00	ATL	ECR-F	92 70 0666 222-5
66223 ●				GM-EMD Ca	968702-223 19/04/00	ATL	ECR-F	92 70 0666 223-3
66224 ●				GM-EMD Ca	968702-224 19/04/00	ATL	ECR-F	92 70 0666 224-1
66225 ●				GM-EMD Ca	968702-225 19/04/00	ATL	ECR-F	92 70 0666 225-8
66226 ●				GM-EMD Ca	968702-226 19/04/00	ATL	ECR-F	92 70 0666 226-6
66227 P				GM-EMD Ca	968702-227 19/04/00	ATL	DB-P	92 70 0666 227-4
66228 ●				GM-EMD Ca	968702-228 19/04/00	ATL	ECR-F	92 70 0666 228-2
66229 ●				GM-EMD Ca	968702-229 30/05/00	ATL	ECR-F	92 70 0666 229-0
66230				GM-EMD Ca	968702-230 30/05/00	ATL	DB-C	
66231 ●				GM-EMD Ca	968702-231 30/05/00	ATL	ECR-F	92 70 0666 231-6
66232 ●				GM-EMD Ca	968702-232 30/05/00	ATL	ECR-F	92 70 0666 232-7
66233 ●				GM-EMD Ca	968702-233 30/05/00	ATL	ECR-F	92 70 0666 233-2
66234 ●				GM-EMD Ca	968702-234 30/05/00	ATL	ECR-F	92 70 0666 234-0
66235 ●				GM-EMD Ca	968702-235 30/05/00	ATL	ECR-F	92 70 0666 235-7
66236 ●				GM-EMD Ca	968702-236 30/05/00	ATL	ECR-F	92 70 0666 236-5
66237 P				GM-EMD Ca	968702-237 30/05/00	ATL	DB-P	92 70 0666 237-3
66238	66788	01/18		GM-EMD Ca	968702-238 30/05/00	ATL	GBR	
66239 ●				GM-EMD Ca	968702-239 30/05/00	ATL	ECR-F	92 70 0666 239-9
66240 ●				GM-EMD Ca	968702-240 21/06/00	ATL	ECR-F	92 70 0666 240-7
66241 ●				GM-EMD Ca	968702-241 21/06/00	ATL	ECR-F	92 70 0666 241-5
66242 ●				GM-EMD Ca	968702-242 21/06/00	ATL	ECR-F	92 70 0666 242-3
66243 ●				GM-EMD Ca	968702-243 21/06/00	ATL	ECR-F	92 70 0666 243-1
66244 ●				GM-EMD Ca	968702-244 21/06/00	ATL	ECR-F	92 70 0666 244-9
66245 ●				GM-EMD Ca	968702-245 21/06/00	ATL	ECR-F	92 70 0666 245-4
66246 ●				GM-EMD Ca	968702-246 21/06/00	ATL	ECR-F	92 70 0666 246-4
66247 ●				GM-EMD Ca	968702-247 21/06/00	ATL	ECR-F	92 70 0666 247-2
66248 P				GM-EMD Ca	968702-248 21/06/00	ATL	DB-P	92 70 0666 248-8
66249 ●				GM-EMD Ca	968702-249 21/06/00	ATL	DB-C	92 70 0666 249-8
66250	66789	02/18	Robert K. Romak‡ 06/00-01/18 British Rail 1948-1997 02/18-	GM-EMD Ca	968702-250 21/06/00	ATL	GBR	
66301			Kingmoor TMD 07/17-	GM-EMD Ca	20078929-01 21/06/08	BRL	DRS	4
66302				GM-EMD Ca	20078929-02 05/11/08	BRL	DRS	4
66303				GM-EMD Ca	20078929-03 25/08/08	BRL	DRS	4
66304				GM-EMD Ca	20078929-04 21/06/08	BRL	DRS	4
66305				GM-EMD Ca	20078929-05 21/06/08	BRL	DRS	4
66401	66733	03/11	Cambridge PSB 09/14-	GM-EMD Ca	20038515-01 14/10/03	PTR	GBR	5
66402	66734	06/11	The Eco Express 01/12-07/12	GM-EMD Ca	20038515-02 14/10/03	PTR	-	5, 2
66403	66735	06/11		GM-EMD Ca	20038515-03 14/10/03	PTR	GBR	5
66404	66736	05/11	Wolverhampton Wanderers 12/11-	GM-EMD Ca	20038515-04 14/10/03	PTR	GBR	5
66405	66737	04/11	Lesia 05/11-	GM-EMD Ca	20038515-05 14/10/03	PTR	GBR	5

66406	66841	04/09	66742	Jul-11	Port of Immingham 05/12- Centenary 1912 - 2012	GM-EMD Ca	20038515-06 18/11/03	PTR	GBR	6
66407	66842	05/09	66743	Jul-11		GM-EMD Ca	20038515-07 18/11/03	PTR	GBR	6
66408	66843	06/09	66744	Jul-11	Crossrail 06/12-	GM-EMD Ca	20038515-08 18/11/03	PTR	GBR	6
66409	66844	07/09	66745	Jul-11	Modern Railways - 09/12- The First 50 Years	GM-EMD Ca	20038515-09 18/11/03	PTR	GBR	6
66410	66845	03/10	66746	Jul-11		GM-EMD Ca	20038515-10 18/11/03	PTR	GBR	6
66411	66013P 12/11				Eddie the Engine 09/06-07/11	GM-EMD Ca	20058700-01 25/05/06	LBG	FLP	92 70 0066-013FPL 5
	Exported to Poland 12/11 as 66013-FPL									
66412	66015P 12/12					GM-EMD Ca	20058700-02 25/05/06	LBG	FLP	92 70 0066-015FPL 5
	Exported to Poland 12/12 as 66013-FPL									
66413					Lest we Forget 11/18	GM-EMD Ca	20058700-03 25/05/06	LBG	FLT	5
66414					James the Engine 01/09-10/11	GM-EMD Ca	20058700-04 16/10/06	LBG	FLT	
66415						GM-EMD Ca	20058700-05 16/10/06	LBG	FLT	
66416						GM-EMD Ca	20058700-06 16/10/06	LBG	FLT	
66417	66014P Feb-12					GM-EMD Ca	20058700-07 16/10/06	LBG	FLP	92 70 0066-014FPL
	Exported to Poland 02/12 as 66014-FPL									
66418					Patriot 11/16-	GM-EMD Ca	20058700-08 16/10/06	LBG	FLT	
66419						GM-EMD Ca	20058700-09 16/10/06	LBG	FLT	
66420						GM-EMD Ca	20058700-10 16/10/06	LBG	FLT	
66421					Gresty Bridge TMD 07/18-	GM-EMD Ca	20068877-01 09/09/07	LBG	DRS	
66422						GM-EMD Ca	20068877-02 09/09/07	LBG	DRS	
66423						GM-EMD Ca	20068877-03 09/09/07	LBG	DRS	
66424						GM-EMD Ca	20068877-04 09/09/07	LBG	DRS	
66425						GM-EMD Ca	20068877-05 09/09/07	LBG	DRS	
66426						GM-EMD Ca	20068877-06 09/09/07	LBG	DRS	
66427						GM-EMD Ca	20068877-07 09/09/07	LBG	DRS	
66428						GM-EMD Ca	20068877-08 21/09/07	LBG	DRS	
66429						GM-EMD Ca	20068877-09 21/09/07	LBG	DRS	
66430						GM-EMD Ca	20068877-10 21/09/07	LBG	DRS	
66431						GM-EMD Ca	20078946-01 05/11/08	LBG	DRS	
66432						GM-EMD Ca	20078946-02 05/11/08	LBG	DRS	
66433						GM-EMD Ca	20078946-03 05/11/08	LBG	DRS	
66434						GM-EMD Ca	20078946-04 05/11/08	LBG	DRS	
66501					Japan 2001 07/01-	GM-EMD Ca	998106-01 17/07/99	PTR	FLT	
66502					Basford Hall 08/01- Centenary 2001	GM-EMD Ca	998106-02 17/07/99	PTR	FLT	
66503					The Railway Magazine 02/04-	GM-EMD Ca	998106-03 17/08/99	PTR	FLT	
66504						GM-EMD Ca	998106-04 17/08/99	PTR	FLT	
66505						GM-EMD Ca	998106-05 17/08/99	PTR	FLT	
66506					Crewe Regeneration 07/00-	GM-EMD Ca	998145-01 21/06/00	EVL	FLT	
66507						GM-EMD Ca	998145-02 21/06/00	EVL	FLT	
66508						GM-EMD Ca	998145-03 21/06/00	EVL	FLT	
66509						GM-EMD Ca	998145-04 21/06/00	EVL	FLT	
66510						GM-EMD Ca	998145-05 21/06/00	EVL	FLT	
66511						GM-EMD Ca	998145-06 14/08/00	EVL	FLT	
66512						GM-EMD Ca	998145-07 14/08/00	EVL	FLT	
66513						GM-EMD Ca	998145-08 14/08/00	EVL	FLT	
66514						GM-EMD Ca	998145-09 14/08/00	EVL	FLT	
66515						GM-EMD Ca	998145-10 14/08/00	EVL	FLT	
66516						GM-EMD Ca	998145-11 14/08/00	EVL	FLT	
66517						GM-EMD Ca	998145-12 14/08/00	EVL	FLT	
66518						GM-EMD Ca	998145-13 14/08/00	EVL	FLT	
66519						GM-EMD Ca	998145-14 11/11/00	EVL	FLT	
66520						GM-EMD Ca	998145-15 11/11/00	EVL	FLT	
66521						GM-EMD Ca	20008215-01 12/12/00	EVL	-	3
66522					east london express 11/04-10/18	GM-EMD Ca	20008215-02 12/12/00	EVL	FLT	
66523						GM-EMD Ca	20008215-03 12/12/00	EVL	FLT	
66524						GM-EMD Ca	20008215-04 12/12/00	EVL	FLT	
66525						GM-EMD Ca	20008215-05 12/12/00	EVL	FLT	
66526					Driver Steve 09/01- Dunn (George)	GM-EMD Ca	20008269-01 18/08/01	PTR	FLT	
66527					Don Raider 09/01-12/16	GM-EMD Ca	20008269-02 18/08/01	PTR	FLP	92 70 0066-016FPL
	Exported to Poland 03/16 as 66016-FPL									
66528						GM-EMD Ca	20008269-03 18/08/01	PTR	FLT	
66529						GM-EMD Ca	20008269-04 18/08/01	PTR	FLT	
66530						GM-EMD Ca	20008269-05 18/08/01	PTR	FLP	92 70 0066-017FPL
	Exported to Poland 03/16 as 66017-FP									
66531						GM-EMD Ca	20008269-06 18/08/01	PTR	FLT	
66532					P&O Nedlloyd Atlas 09/02-	GM-EMD Ca	20008269-07 10/10/01	PTR	FLT	
66533					Hanjin Express / 07/03- Senator Express	GM-EMD Ca	20008269-08 10/10/01	PTR	FLT	
66534					OOCL Express 06/03-	GM-EMD Ca	20008269-09 10/10/01	PTR	FLT	
66535						GM-EMD Ca	20008269-10 10/10/01	PTR	FLP	92 70 0066-018FPL
	Exported to Poland 03/16 as 66018-FPL									
66536						GM-EMD Ca	20008269-11 10/10/01	PTR	FLT	
66537						GM-EMD Ca	20008269-12 10/10/01	PTR	FLT	
66538						GM-EMD Ca	20008269-13 16/11/01	EVL	FLT	
66539						GM-EMD Ca	20008269-14 16/11/01	EVL	FLT	
66540					Ruby 01/06-	GM-EMD Ca	20008269-15 16/11/01	EVL	FLT	
66541						GM-EMD Ca	20008269-16 16/11/01	EVL	FLT	
66542						GM-EMD Ca	20008269-17 12/12/01	EVL	FLT	
66543						GM-EMD Ca	20008269-18 12/12/01	EVL	FLT	
66544						GM-EMD Ca	20008269-19 12/12/01	PTR	FLT	
66545						GM-EMD Ca	20008269-20 12/12/01	PTR	FLT	
66546						GM-EMD Ca	20008269-21 12/12/01	PTR	FLT	
66547						GM-EMD Ca	20008269-22 12/12/01	PTR	FLT	
66548						GM-EMD Ca	20008269-23 12/12/01	PTR	FLT	
66549						GM-EMD Ca	20008269-24 12/12/01	PTR	FLT	
66550						GM-EMD Ca	20008269-25 12/12/01	PTR	FLT	
66551						GM-EMD Ca	20008269-26 12/12/01	PTR	FLT	

Number	Renumbered	Name	Builder	Works No.	Date	Pool	Livery	Notes
66552		Maltby Raider 07/04-	GM-EMD Ca	20008269-27	12/12/01	PTR	FLT	
66553			GM-EMD Ca	20008269-28	12/12/01	PTR	FLT	
66554			GM-EMD Ca	20018342-01	28/03/02	EVL	FLT	7
66555			GM-EMD Ca	20018342-08	23/11/02	EVL	FLT	
66556			GM-EMD Ca	20018342-09	23/11/02	EVL	FLT	
66557			GM-EMD Ca	20018342-10	23/11/02	EVL	FLT	
66558			GM-EMD Ca	20018342-11	23/11/02	EVL	FLT	
66559			GM-EMD Ca	20018342-12	23/11/02	EVL	FLT	
66560			GM-EMD Ca	20018342-13	23/11/02	EVL	FLT	
66561			GM-EMD Ca	20018342-14	31/12/02	EVL	FLT	
66562			GM-EMD Ca	20018342-15	31/12/02	EVL	FLT	
66563			GM-EMD Ca	20018342-16	31/12/02	EVL	FLT	
66564			GM-EMD Ca	20018342-17	31/12/02	EVL	FLT	
66565			GM-EMD Ca	20018342-18	31/12/02	EVL	FLT	
66566			GM-EMD Ca	20018342-19	31/12/02	EVL	FLT	
66567			GM-EMD Ca	20028462-01	18/11/03	EVL	FLT	
66568			GM-EMD Ca	20028462-02	18/11/03	EVL	FLT	
66569			GM-EMD Ca	20028462-03	18/11/03	EVL	FLT	
66570			GM-EMD Ca	20028462-04	18/11/03	EVL	FLT	
66571			GM-EMD Ca	20028462-05	18/11/03	EVL	FLT	
66572			GM-EMD Ca	20028462-06	18/11/03	EVL	FLT	
66573	66846 Jul-11		GM-EMD Ca	20028462-13	13/12/03	COL	COL	8
66574	66847 Jul-11		GM-EMD Ca	20028462-14	13/12/03	COL	COL	8
66575	66848 Jul-11		GM-EMD Ca	20028462-15	19/04/04	COL	COL	8
66576	66849 Jul-11	Hamburg Sud 06/04-05/11 Advantage Wylam Dilly 07/11-	GM-EMD Ca	20028462-16	19/04/04	COL	COL	8
66577	66850 Jul-11	David Maidment OBE 07/13- www.railwaychildren.org.uk	GM-EMD Ca	20028462-17	19/04/04	COL	COL	8
66578	66738 May-11	Huddersfield Town 07/14-	GM-EMD Ca	20028462-18	15/05/05	GBR	GBR	8
66579	66739 May-11	Bluebell Railway 03/13-	GM-EMD Ca	20028462-19	15/05/05	GBR	GBR	8
66580	66740 May-11	Sarah 08/14-	GM-EMD Ca	20028462-20	15/05/05	GBR	GBR	8
66581	66741 May-11	Sophie 03/06-05/10 Swanage Railway 05/15-	GM-EMD Ca	20028462-21	15/05/05	GBR	GBR	8
66582	66009P Jan-09 Exported to Poland as 66009-FPL 01/09		GM-EMD Ca	20058772-04	26/03/07	EVL	FLP	92 70 0066-009FPL
66583	66010P Jun-09 Exported to Poland as 66010-FPL 06/09		GM-EMD Ca	20058772-05	26/03/07	EVL	FLP	92 70 0066-010FPL
66584	66011P Jun-09 Exported to Poland as 66011-FPL 06/09		GM-EMD Ca	20058772-06	26/03/07	EVL	FLP	92 70 0066-011FPL
66585		The Drax Flyer 10/07-11/17	GM-EMD Ca	20058772-07	26/03/07	LBG	FLT	
66586	66008P Jun-09 Exported to Poland as 66008-FPL 06/09		GM-EMD Ca	20058772-08	26/03/07	LBG	FLP	92 70 0066-008FPL
66587			GM-EMD Ca	20058772-09	20/04/07	LBG	FLT	
66588			GM-EMD Ca	20058772-10	20/04/07	LBG	FLT	
66589			GM-EMD Ca	20058772-11	20/04/07	LBG	FLT	
66590			GM-EMD Ca	20058772-12	20/04/07	LBG	FLT	
66591			GM-EMD Ca	20058772-13	20/04/07	LBG	FLT	
66592		Johnson Stephens Agencies 11/07-	GM-EMD Ca	20058772-14	20/04/07	LBG	FLT	
66593		3MG Mersey Multimodal Gateway 09/08-	GM-EMD Ca	20058772-15	20/04/07	LBG	FLT	
66594		NYK Spirit of Kyoto 06/07-	GM-EMD Ca	20058772-16	20/04/07	LBG	FLT	
66595	Exported to Poland as 66595-FPL 04/18		GM-EMD Ca	20068922-01	08/04/08	LBG	FLT	92 70 0066-595FPL
66596			GM-EMD Ca	20078922-02	08/04/08	LBG	FLT	
66597		Viridor 10/11-	GM-EMD Ca	20068922-03	08/04/08	EVL	FLT	
66598			GM-EMD Ca	20068922-04	21/06/08	LBG	FLT	
66599			GM-EMD Ca	20068922-05	21/06/08	LBG	FLT	
66601		The Hope Valley 11/00-	GM-EMD Ca	998175-01	11/11/00	LBG	FLT	
66602			GM-EMD Ca	998175-02	11/11/00	LBG	FLT	
66603			GM-EMD Ca	998175-03	11/11/00	LBG	FLT	
66604			GM-EMD Ca	998175-04	11/11/00	LBG	FLT	
66605			GM-EMD Ca	998175-05	11/11/00	LBG	FLT	
66606			GM-EMD Ca	998175-06	11/11/00	LBG	FLT	
66607			GM-EMD Ca	20018342-02	28/03/02	LBG	FLT	
66608	66603P Feb-11 Exported to Poland as 66603-FPL 02/11		GM-EMD Ca	20018342-03	28/03/02	LBG	FLP	92 70 0066-603FPL
66609	66605P Apr-11 Exported to Poland as 66605-FPL 04/11		GM-EMD Ca	20018342-04	28/03/02	LBG	FLP	92 70 0066-605FPL
66610			GM-EMD Ca	20018342-05	28/03/02	LBG	FLT	
66611	66604P Apr-11 Exported to Poland as 66604-FPL 04/11		GM-EMD Ca	20018342-06	28/03/02	LBG	FLP	92 70 0066-604FPL
66612	66606P Jul-11 Exported to Poland as 66606-FPL 07/11	Forth Raider 10/03-05/11	GM-EMD Ca	20018342-07	28/03/02	LBG	FLP	92 70 0066-606FPL
66613			GM-EMD Ca	20028462-07	13/12/03	LBG	FLT	
66614		1916 Poppy 2016 10/16-	GM-EMD Ca	20028462-08	13/12/03	EVL	FLT	
66615			GM-EMD Ca	20028462-09	13/12/03	EVL	FLT	
66616			GM-EMD Ca	20028462-10	13/12/03	EVl	FLT	
66617			GM-EMD Ca	20028462-11	13/12/03	EVL	FLT	
66618		Railways Illustrated 03/04- Annual Photographic Awards - Alan Barnes*	GM-EMD Ca	20028462-12	13/12/03	EVL	FLT	9
66619		Derek W Johnson MBE 02/06-	GM-EMD Ca	20028462-22	15/03/05	EVL	FLT	
66620			GM-EMD Ca	20028462-23	15/03/05	EVL	FLT	
66621			GM-EMD Ca	20028462-24	15/03/05	EVL	FLT	
66622			GM-EMD Ca	20028462-25	15/03/05	EVL	FLT	
66623		Bill Bolsover 11/07-03/19	GM-EMD Ca	20058772-01	05/02/07	LBG	FLT	
66624	66602P Jun-10 Exported to Poland as 66602-FPL 06/10		GM-EMD Ca	20058772-02	05/02/07	LBG	FLP	92 70 0066-602FPL
66625	66601P Oct-09 Exported to Poland as 66601-FPL 10/09		GM-EMD Ca	20058772-03	05/02/07	LBG	FLP	92 70 0066-601FPL

66701		Railtrack National 03/01-02/04 Logistics Whitemoor 05/04-06/11	GM-EMD Ca	20008201-01 09/03/01	EVL	GBR	
66702		Blue Lightning 08/02-	GM-EMD Ca	20008201-02 09/03/01	EVL	GBR	
66703		Doncaster PSB 12/02-1981-2002	GM-EMD Ca	20008201-03 09/03/01	EVL	GBR	
66704		Colchester Power 03/03- Signal Box	GM-EMD Ca	20008201-04 09/03/01	EVL	GBR	
66705		Golden Jubilee 06/02-	GM-EMD Ca	20008201-05 09/03/01	EVL	GBR	
66706		Nene Valley 04/03-	GM-EMD Ca	20008201-06 09/03/01	EVL	GBR	
66707		Sir Sam Fey / 08/03- Great Central Railway	GM-EMD Ca	20008201-07 09/03/01	EVL	GBR	
66708		Jayne 07/11-	GM-EMD Ca	20018356-01 21/06/02	EVL	GBR	
66709		Joseph Arnold Davies 07/02-04/12 Sorrento 04/12-	GM-EMD Ca	20018356-02 21/06/02	EVL	GBR	
66710		Phil Packar BRIT 10/10-	GM-EMD Ca	20018356-03 21/06/02	EVL	GBR	
66711		Sence 07/15-	GM-EMD Ca	20018356-04 21/06/02	EVL	GBR	
66712		Peterborough Power 10/06-Signalbox	GM-EMD Ca	20018356-05 21/06/02	EVL	GBR	
66713		Forest City 04/03-	GM-EMD Ca	20028454-01 25/05/03	EVL	GBR	
66714		Cromer Lifeboat 06/03-	GM-EMD Ca	20028454-02 25/05/03	EVL	GBR	
66715		Valour 11/03-	GM-EMD Ca	20028454-03 25/05/03	EVL	GBR	
66716		Willesden Traincare 09/04-12/10 Centre Locomotive & Carriage 05/11- Institution Centenary 1911 - 2011	GM-EMD Ca	20028454-04 25/05/03	EVL	GBR	
66717		Good Old Boy 09/06-	GM-EMD Ca	20028454-05 25/05/03	EVL	GBR	
66718		Gwyneth Dunwoody 01/07-11/13 Sir Peter Handy CBE 11/13-	GM-EMD Ca	20048652-01 08/04/06	EVL	GBR	
66719		Metro-Land 01/07-	GM-EMD Ca	20048652-02 08/04/06	EVL	GBR	
66720		Metronet Pathfinder 01/07-06/11	GM-EMD Ca	20048652-03 08/04/06	EVL	GBR	
66721		Harry Beck 01/07-	GM-EMD Ca	20048652-04 08/04/06	EVL	GBR	
66722		Sir Edward Watkin 01/07-	GM-EMD Ca	20048652-05 08/04/06	EVL	GBR	
66723		Chinook 09/08-	GM-EMD Ca	20058765-01 20/12/06	EVL	GBR	
66724		Drax Power Station 09/07-	GM-EMD Ca	20058765-02 20/12/06	EVL	GBR	
66725		Sunderland 08/07-	GM-EMD Ca	20058765-03 20/12/06	EVL	GBR	
66726		Sheffield Wednesday 09/09-	GM-EMD Ca	20058765-04 20/12/06	EVL	GBR	
66727		Andrew Scott CBE 09/08-09/16 Maritime One 09/16	GM-EMD Ca	20058765-05 20/12/06	EVL	GBR	
66728		Institution of Railway 04/08-Operators	GM-EMD Ca	20068902-01 08/04/08	PTR	GBR	
66729		Derby County 05/10-	GM-EMD Ca	20068902-02 08/04/08	PTR	GBR	
66730		Whitemoor 08/11-	GM-EMD Ca	20068902-03 08/04/08	PTR	GBR	
66731		interhubGB 03/11-	GM-EMD Ca	20068902-04 08/04/08	PTR	GBR	
66732		GBRF The First Decade 07/09-1999-2009 John Smith MD	GM-EMD Ca	20068902-05 08/04/08	PTR	GBR	
66733	See 66401						
66734	See 66402						
66735	See 66403						
66736	See 66404						
66737	See 66405						
66738	See 66578						
66739	See 66579						
66740	See 66580						
66741	See 66581						
66742	See 66406, 66841						
66743	See 66407, 66842						
66744	See 66408, 66843						
66745	See 66409, 66844						
66746	See 66410, 66845						
66747			GM-EMD Ca	20078968-07 21/12/12	GBR	GBR	10
66748		West Burton 50 09/16-	GM-EMD Ca	20078968-04 21/12/12	GBR	GBR	10
66749			GM-EMD Ca	20078968-06 21/12/12	GBR	GBR	10
66750		Bristol Panel Signal 10/15- Box	GM-EMD Ca	20038513-01 12/06/13	GBR	GBR	10
66751		Inspitation Delivered 04/15-Hitachi Rail Group	GM-EMD Ca	20038513-04 11/08/13	GBR	GBR	10
66752		The Hossier State 06/16-	PR-MI	20128816-01 10/07/14	GBR	GBR	
66753		EMD Roberts Road 12/14-	PR-MI	20128816-02 10/07/14	GBR	GBR	
66754		Northampton Saints 04/15-	PR-MI	20128816-03 10/07/14	GBR	GBR	
66755		Tony Berkley OBE 07/18-RFG Chairman 1997-2018	PR-MI	20128816-04 10/07/14	GBR	GBR	
66756		The Royal Corps 06/17- of Signals	PR-MI	20128816-05 10/07/14	GBR	GBR	
66757		West Somerset Railway 09/15-	PR-MI	20128816-06 06/09/14	GBR	GBR	
66758		The Pavior 09/18-	PR-MI	20128816-07 06/09/14	GBR	GBR	
66759		Chippy 10/15-	PR-MI	20128816-08 06/09/14	GBR	GBR	
66760		David Gordon Harris 07/16-	PR-MI	20128816-09 06/09/14	GBR	GBR	
66761		Wensleydale Railway 07/15 Association 25 years 1990-2015	PR-MI	20128816-10 06/09/14	GBR	GBR	
66762			PR-MI	20128816-11 06/09/14	GBR	GBR	
66763		Severn Valley Railway 05/16	PR-MI	20128816-12 06/09/14	GBR	GBR	
66764			PR-MI	20128816-13 06/09/14	GBR	GBR	
66765			PR-MI	20128816-14 06/09/14	GBR	GBR	
66766			PR-MI	20128816-15 06/12/14	GBR	GBR	
66767			PR-MI	20128816-16 06/12/14	GBR	GBR	
66768			PR-MI	20128816-17 06/12/14	GBR	GBR	
66769			PR-MI	20128816-18 06/12/14	GBR	GBR	
66770			PR-MI	20128816-19 06/12/14	GBR	GBR	

Number	Name	Builder	Works No.	Date	Owner	Operator	Other
66771		PR-MI	20128816-20	06/12/14	GBR	GBR	
66772		PR-MI	20128816-21	06/12/14	GBR	GBR	
66773		PR-MI	20148150-01	12/02/16	GBR	GBR	
66774		PR-MI	20148150-02	12/02/16	GBR	GBR	
66775	*HMS Argyll* 07/17-	PR-MI	20148150-03	12/02/16	GBR	GBR	
66776	*Joanne* 06/17-	PR-MI	20148150-04	12/02/16	GBR	GBR	
66777	*Annette* 06/17-	PR-MI	20148150-05	12/02/16	GBR	GBR	
66778	*Darius Cheskin* 07/17-	PR-MI	20148150-06	12/02/16	GBR	GBR	
66779	*Evening Star* 05/16-	PR-MI	20148150-07	12/02/16	GBR	GBR	
66780	See 66008						
66781	See 66016						
66782	See 66046						
66783	See 66058						
66784	See 66081						
66785	See 66132						
66786	See 66141						
66787	See 66184						
66788	See 66238						
66789	See 66250						
66841	See 66406						
66842	See 66407						
66843	See 66408						
66844	See 66409						
66845	See 66410						
66846	See 66573						
66847	See 66574						
66848	See 66575						
66849	See 66576						
66850	See 66577						
66951		GM-EMD Ca	20028450-01	03/10/04	EVL	FLT	
66952		GM-EMD Ca	20028450-02	19/04/04	EVL	FLT	
66953		GM-EMD Ca	20068922-06	21/06/08	BRL	FLT	
66954		GM-EMD Ca	20068922-07	05/11/08	BRL	FLT	92 70 0066-954FPL
	Exported to Poland as 66954-FPL 01/18						
66955		GM-EMD Ca	20068922-08	05/11/08	BRL	FLT	
66956		GM-EMD Ca	20068922-09	05/11/08	BRL	FLT	
66957	*Stephenson Locomotive Society 1909-2009* 03/09-	GM-EMD Ca	20068922-10	05/11/08	BRL	FLT	

To meet the business growth of GB Railfreight, four further Euro 66s are to transfer to the UK fleet as GBRf Nos. 66790-66793, these will be modified from Euro 66s 20008212-01, 20008212-02, 20018352-03 and 20028352-04, these are scheduled to arrive in the UK in summer 2019.

Notes and key used in above table
1 66048 Involved in runaway accident at Carrbridge Jan-10, recovered and stored, body currently at EMD Longport
2 66734 withdrawn following derailment at Loch Treig, Scotland Jun-12, withdrawn Oct-12 to be broken up on site Sept-13
3 66521 withdrawn following collision at Heck in 05/01, broken up at C F Booths, Rotherham Jun-06
4 Originally operated by Fastline Freight
5 Originally operated by Direct Rail Services
6 Originally operated by Direct Rail Services, then Advenza Freight followed by Colas Freight
7 Replacement loco for crash write-off No. 66521
8 Previously owned by Eversholt and operated by Freightliner
9 Secondary plate read *Ian Lothian* between 19/03/04-23/06/05, *David Gorton* between 24/06/05-22/06/06 *Alan Barnes* added 24/06/06
10 From Mainland Europe fleet (see Euro 66 section for details)

ATL	Angel Trains Leasing	ECR-F	Euro Cargo Rail, France		Division, London, Ontario, Canada
BRL	Beacon Rail Leasing	EVL	Eversholt Leasing	LBG	Lloyds Banking Group
COL	Colas Rail Freight	FLP	Freightliner Poland	PTR	Porterbrook Leasing
DB-C	DB-Cargo	FLT	Freightliner	‡	Painted on name
DBP	DB-Schenker Poland	GBR	GBRf	●	Modified for use by ECR in France
DRS	Direct Rail Services	GM-EMD Ca	General Motors Electro Motive	P	Poland

Above: *Once the Class 66s arrived in the UK a major driver and fitter training programme commenced, with deployment in most areas being rapid. On 6 February 2002, No. 66159 passes Eastleigh, with an automotive train bound for Southampton Docks.* **CJM**

Left Below: *It was not uncommon for Class 66s to be tested on the main line in Canada, using the little used, but main line standard route from London to Stratford. On 18 May 2008, two of the low emissions locos Nos. 66954 and 66953 operated a trial run to Stratford and back. Note the incomplete bodywork and temporary headlights hanging on the front.* **CJM-C**

Below: *In 2000-2002 a daily containerised food train operated on behalf of Safeway, taking products to the far north of Scotland. The containers were off-loaded on a small apron at Georgemas Junction and transported to shops by road. The EWS-operated train worked daily as the 01.00 Mossend to Georgemas Junction. On 28 August 2001, it is seen powered by No. 66109 as it approaches Rogart.* **CJM**

Class 66 Fact File

- Based structurally on the US-designed BR Class 59, the '66' was first ordered by EWS as replacement power under the privatised railway.

- Several follow-on orders placed by Freightliner, GBRf, Fastline and DRS.

- Later built locos fitted with low emissions technology have an extra bodyside door, as drivers are unable to walk passed the cooler group.

- All but two of the DB fleet fitted with combination couplers, the two exceptions being Nos. 66001 and 66002.

- A number of DB and Freightliner locos have been exported to Mainland Europe (see table).

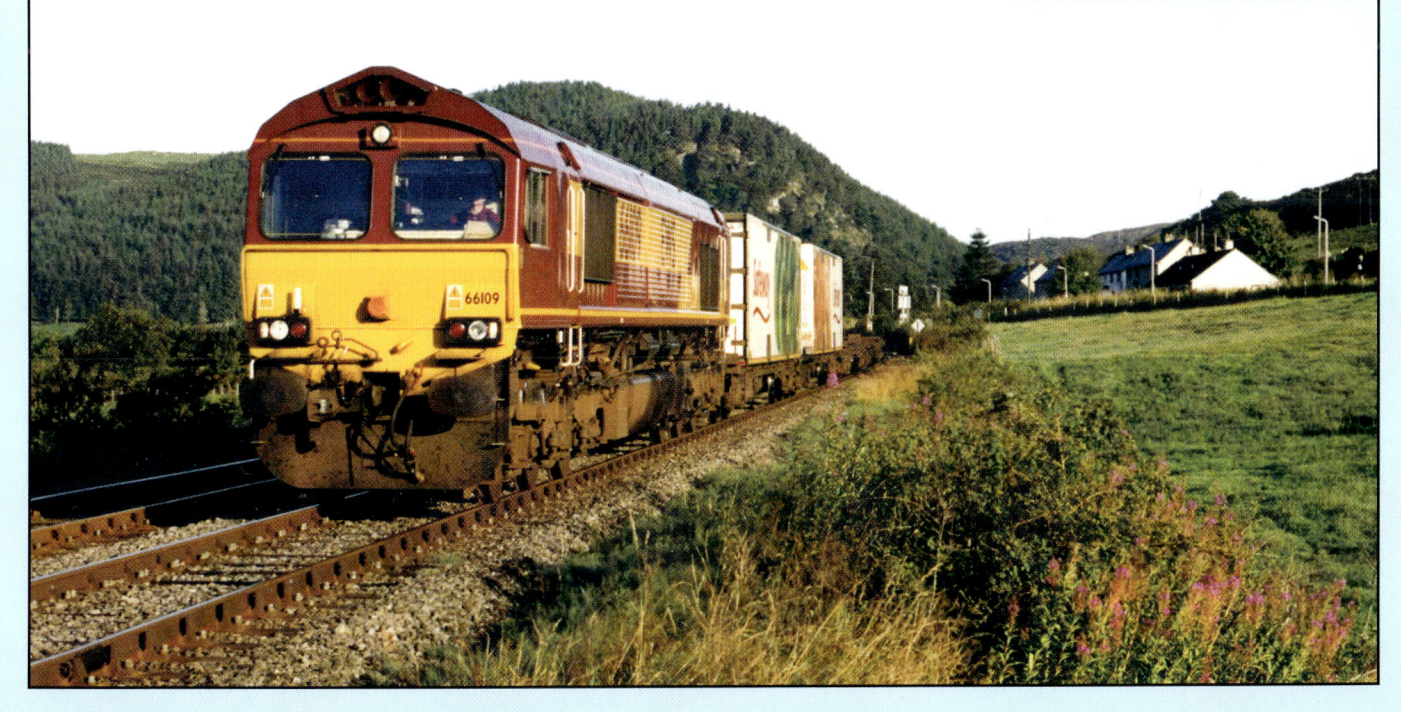

Traction Transition - GM/EMD power in the UK and Ireland

Above: When introduced the EWS Class 66 fleet were placed in charge of a number of high-capacity coal trains, using new wagons, fitted with auto couplers. Today, just a handful of workings remain. On 19 June 2014, No. 66144 passes Barry is South Wales with the 10.50 Aberthaw Power Station to Tower Colliery. **CJM**

Left: Network Rail engineers trains have always been big business for the '66' fleet. Here, No. 66060 passes Woking on 8 March 2010 with the 09.02 Eastleigh to Hoo Junction engineers. **CJM**

Below: While Freightliner operate the majority of container trains, EWS, now DB, handle a number of services. No. 66232, a loco now operating for Euro Cargo Rail in France, departs from Southampton Western Docks on 3 August 2010 with the 09.32 service to Birch Coppice. **CJM**

Traction Transition - GM/EMD power in the UK and Ireland

Above: With the spire of the parish church of St Peter and St Paul dominating the skyline at Kings Sutton, No. 66164 passes by on 4 November 2016 powering the 10.34 Southampton Eastern Docks to Halewood empty Jaguar car train. **CJM**

Right: With its EWS branding removed and a large DB sticker applied to the cab side, No. 66031 passes through Doncaster station on 10 March 2017 in charge of the, 09.36 Wakefield Europort to Felixstowe South container service. **CJM**

Below: Taking the up main through line at Doncaster station on 23 April 2014, No. 66168 powers the daily 09.36 Wakefield Europort to Felixstowe South Terminal. This loco was delivered to the UK on 19 November 1999 and is one of the batch still operating in the UK. Those looking to see DB Class 66s, will find quite a few passing through Doncaster each day. **CJM**

Traction Transition - GM/EMD power in the UK and Ireland

Above: In addition to handling the proportion of UK container traffic, the Freightliner Heavy Haul arm operate a number of block services each day. For many years one such flow was the Hope to Moorswater cement. On 12 April 2008, No. 66614 approaches Aller Junction, Newton Abbot with the westbound service. **CJM**

Left: Sporting the revised Freightliner logo on the front, No. 66594 passes Swindon on 9 April 2018 powering the 09.03 Bristol to Felixstowe North Terminal service. **CJM**

Below: With a number of empty flats in the consist, showing business was not that good, No. 66536 passes Magor in South Wales on 18 December 2017 powering the 09.56 Wentloog (Cardiff) to Southampton, routed by way of Swindon, Reading and Basingstoke. **CJM**

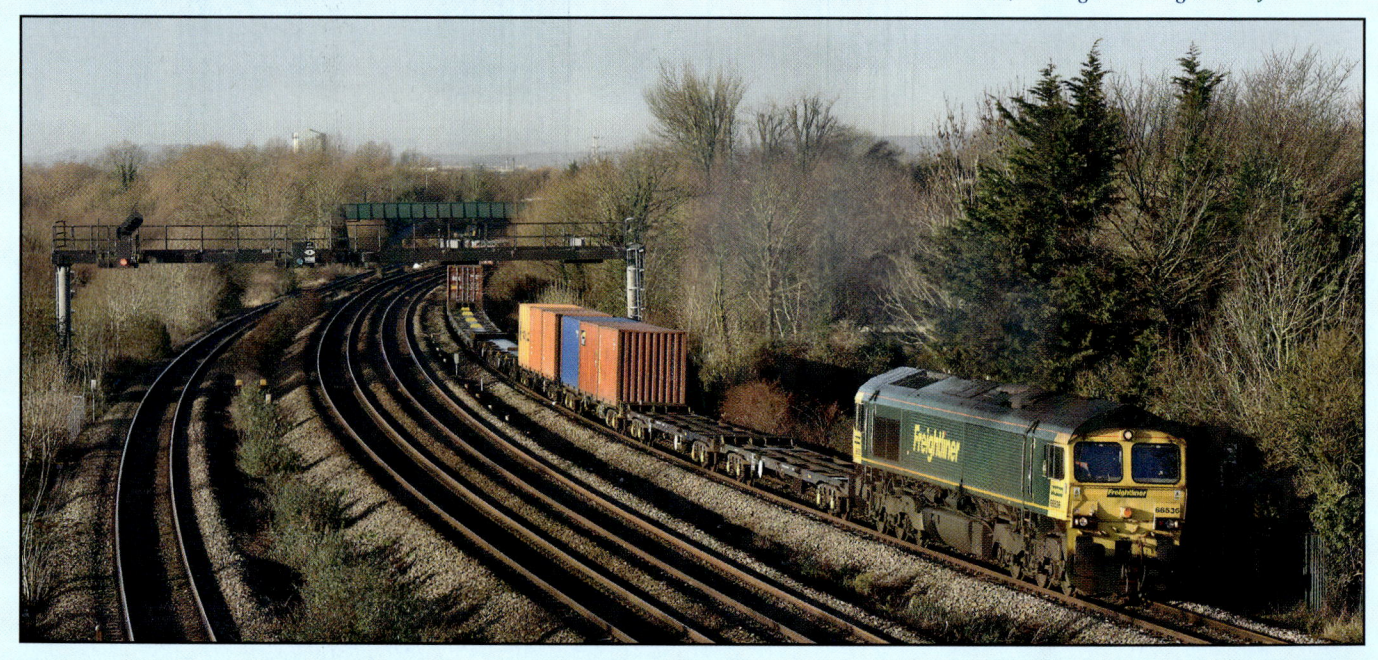

Traction Transition - GM/EMD power in the UK and Ireland

Above: GB Railfreight, now one of the major players in UK freight movement, operates a large number of '66s'. No. 66728 is captured passing Camden Road on 12 May 2017 operating the 10.46 Felixstowe to Hams Hall container service. **CJM**

Right: GBRf have over the years operated some quite unusual trains. One was on 3 January 2005, when No. 66708 with Class 72 No. 73204 as a coupling adaptor hauled 'Hampshire' sets Nos. 205032 and 205028 into preservation on the Dartmoor Railway. The train is seen approaching Exeter Central, running as the 08.25 from Tonbridge. **CJM**

Below: Profile of one of the later built five-door Class 66s No. 66778 **Darius Cheskin***, installed with reduced emissions, upgraded cooler group and smaller fuel tanks to compensate for increased body weight. Built in the Progress Rail plant in Muncie, Indiana in early 2016. The loco is seen at Doncaster on 15 August 2018.* **CJM**

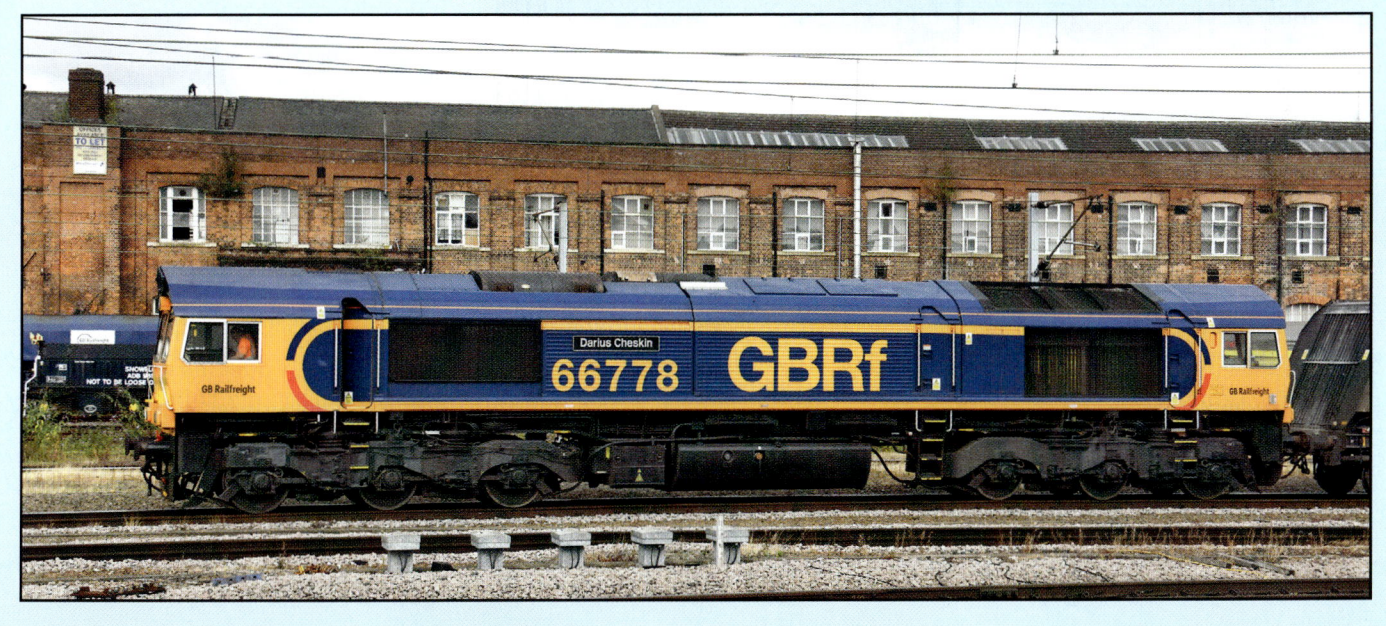

Traction Transition - GM/EMD power in the UK and Ireland 83

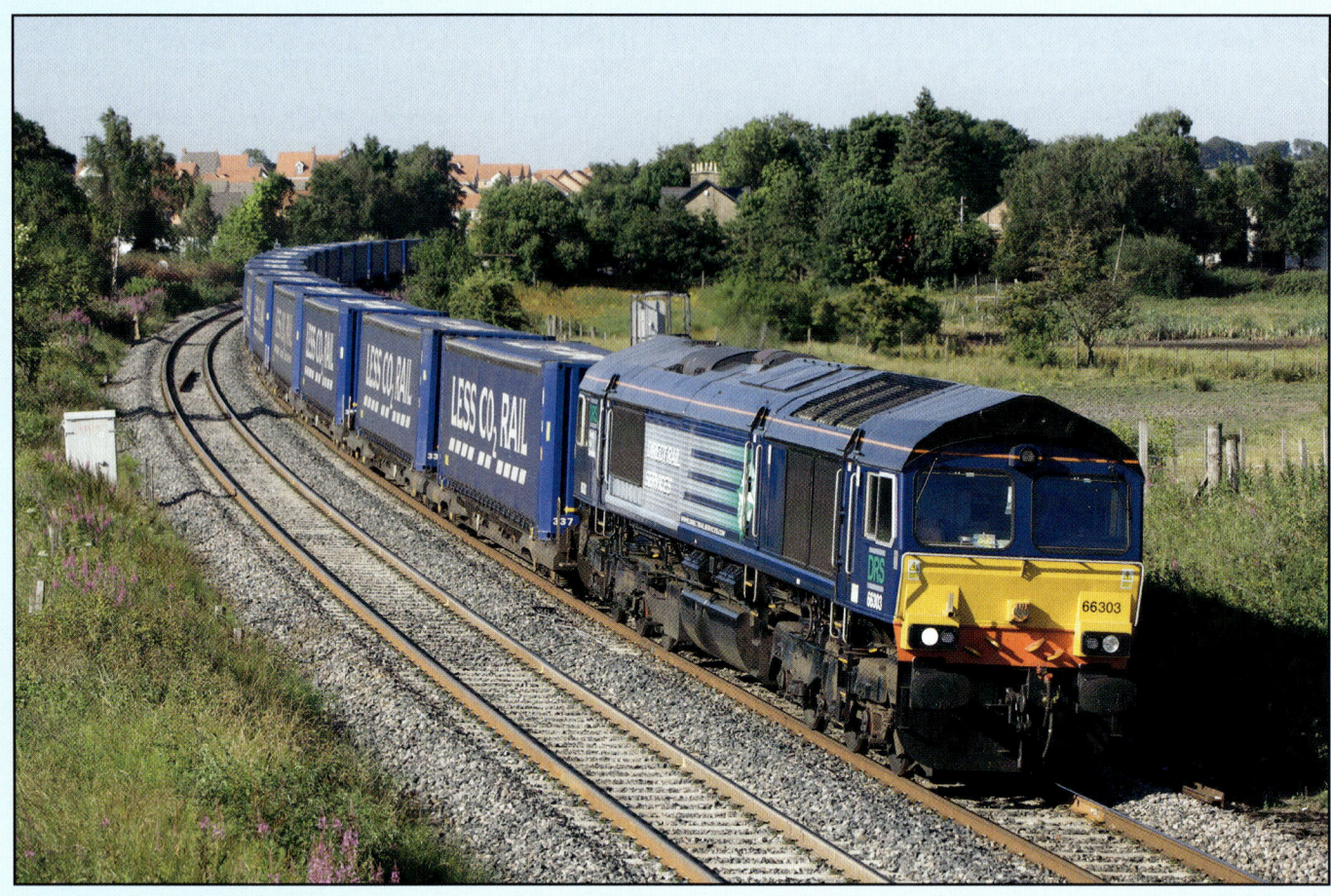

Above: *Carlisle and Crewe-based Direct Rail Services, usually associated with the movement of flask traffic, also operate a number of general freight duties, container trains and engineers duties. Their Class 66 fleet can be found on all types of traffic. Former Fastline Freight Class 66/3 No. 66303 passes Garnqueen, powering train 4D47 the Inverness to Mossend 'Tescoliner' service on 19 July 2013.* **Robin Ralston**

Below: *On 28 December 2017, in lovely low winter sun, with traces of snow on the hills, DRS No. 66431 passes Badgeworth near Cheltenham powering a rake of Tesco intermodal vehicles as train 4V44, the 10.47 Daventry to Wentloog. Various DRS liveries are carried by the DRS fleet, the two main ones are illustrated in this and the above images.* **CJM**

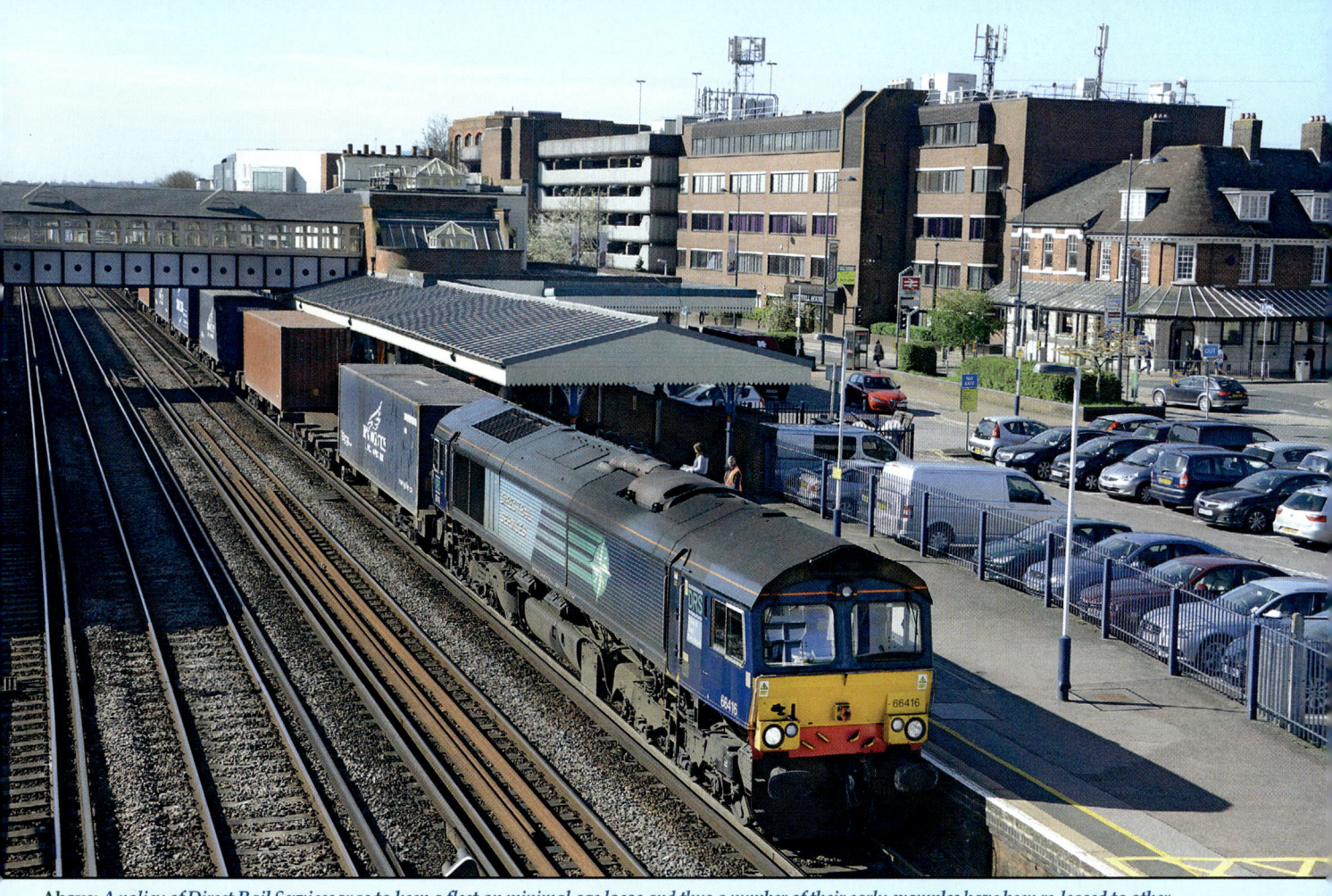

Above: A policy of Direct Rail Services was to keep a fleet on minimal age locos and thus a number of their early examples have been re-leased to other operators, Freightliner taking on a number of locos. On 9 April 2014, No. 66416 pauses at Eastleigh for a crew change while powering the, 09.32 Southampton Maritime Terminal to Ditton service. **CJM**

Below: In 2010 the stand-in loco-hauled set covering some Cardiff-Taunton services was rostered for 'top and tail' Class 57/3s, but their availability was so poor that frequently other locos were used. On 25 June 2010 former DRS No. 66402 (devoid of branding) is seen passing Creech St Michael with a late morning Taunton to Cardiff service. Class 57/3 No. 57308 is coupled on the rear to provide train supply. **Russell Ayre**

Traction Transition - GM/EMD power in the UK and Ireland

Above: *The railway world were stunned in September 2006 when DRS unveiled No. 66411 in Stobart Rail livery, named* **Eddie the Engine***, to mark the launch of a new Stobart/Tesco contract, linking Daventry International Railfreight Terminal (DIRFT) with Grangemouth. Later a second loco was repainted into Stobart colours, No. 66414 which was named* **James the Engine***. On 22 May 2009, No. 66414 is recorded near Greenfaulds powering the 17.14 Grangemouth to Daventry 'Tesco Express'.* **Robin Ralston**

Below: *The 10 early DRS '66/4s' started to go off lease in 2009, four, Nos. 66406-66409 were hired Advenza Freight, part of the Cotswold Rail Group, who attempted to become an open-access operator, picking up one or two freight contracts. The locos, Nos. 66406-409 were transferred in summer 2009, repainted in Advenza livery and renumbered 66841-66845. Advenza Freight and Cotswold went into liquidation on 7 October 2009 and the '66s' reverted to Porterbrook ownership. On 1 September 2009, No. 66841 is seen with an aggregate train at Peak Forest.* **Antony Christie**

86   *Traction Transition - GM/EMD power in the UK and Ireland*

Above: GB Railfreight have over the years branded a number of their Class 66s in special and customer-based liveries. Aggregate Industries who use GBRf to power some of their services saw its corporate colours applied to No. 66711 Sence in Spring 2015, a scheme very similar to that applied to the Class 59/0s. On 17 December 2018, the loco is seen at the head of a bogie aggregate train on the Midland Main Line near Leagrave.
Antony Christie

Right Middle: In September 2016, GBRf repainted No. 66727 into another customer livery, when Maritime Transport blue was applied during a repaint at Arlington Eastleigh Works. The striking colours were supplemented by the application of a cast nameplate **Maritime One**. The loco is not always used on Maritime container traffic, and in this 9 March 2018 view it is seen on aggregate duties at Westbury. **Antony Christie**

Right Below: The last new built Class 66 constructed by Progress Rail, at their plant in Muncie, Indiana, USA was No. 66779 From construction was set to be a celebrity loco, during assembly, Progress Rail fixed a static brass loco bell on the front end, with GBRf contracting Progress Rail to paint the loco in lined BR Brunswick green livery, with large white GBRf bodyside decals. After shipping to the UK under tarps, the loco was 'received' in a special ceremony at the National Railway Museum, York, where it was named **Evening Star**, much in keeping with the last steam loco built for BR, No. 92220 Evening Star. No. 66779 is seen on display at Old Oak Common open day on 2 September 2017. **Antony Christie**

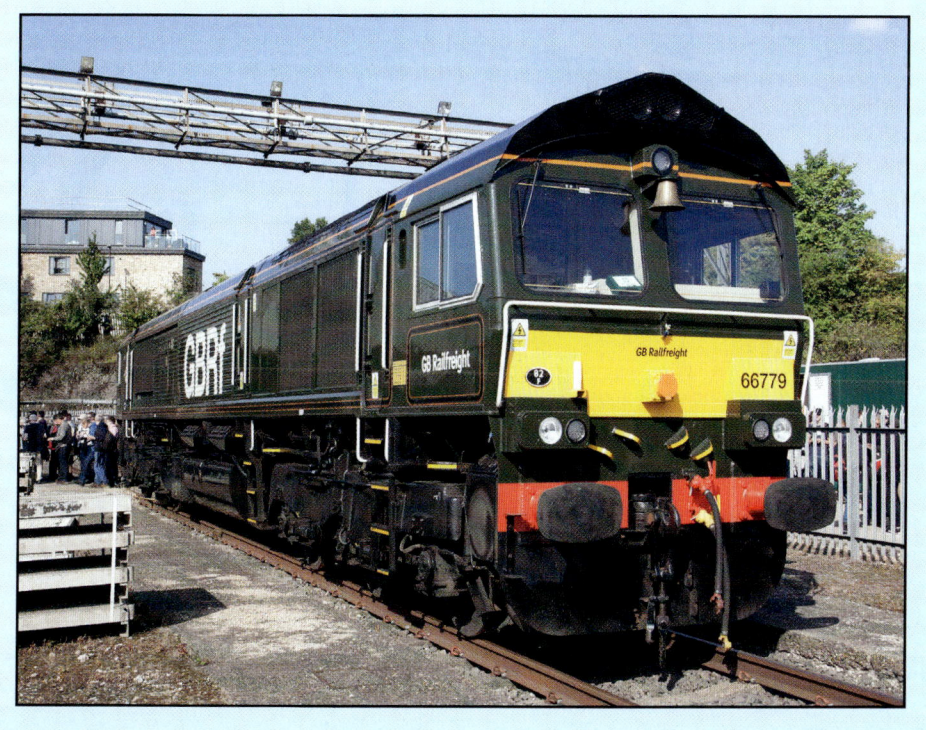

Traction Transition - GM/EMD power in the UK and Ireland

Above: *The EWS operation continued until November 2007, when it was announced that Deutsche Bahn, the German rail operator had purchased the company for £309million. Originally the EWS brand remained, but in January 2009 a slow start was made to introduce the DB Schenker branding and locos started to be repainted in DB red and grey colours. In DB Schenker colours, No. 66118 is seen approaching Lanark Junction on 8 April 2007 with the 10.15 Grangemouth to Daventry service.* **Robin Ralston**

Below: *Repainting of EWS stock into the new DB Schenker colours was undertaken in the paint shop at Toton depot, from where the output was very slow. For a long time, many locos just received DB branding with the EWS letters removed from the bodyside. In immaculate DB Schenker red, No. 66001, one of two locos which have to retain standard draw-gear due to original construction methods, passes Newport (Wales) on 19 June 2014 in charge of the 08.55 Margam to Redcar steel train. This loco is also fitted with extra front end air pipes as it is fitted with LUL style 'trip-cocks' for operation over LUL signalled lines.* **CJM**

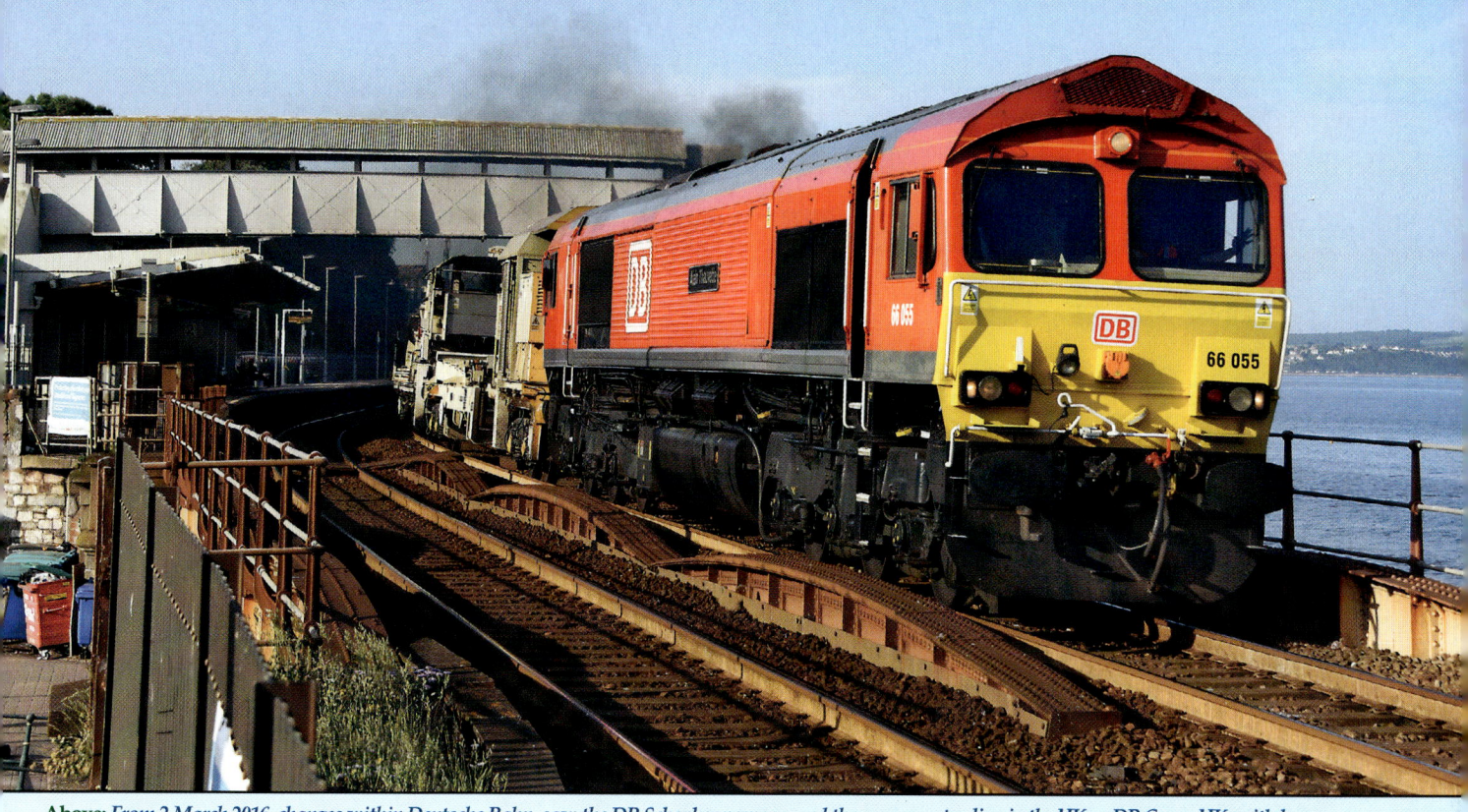

Above: From 2 March 2016, changes within Deutsche Bahn, saw the DB Schenker name go and the company trading in the UK as DB Cargo UK, with locos subsequently repainted carrying a large DB logo. This livery style is shown on No. 66055 **Alan Thauvette** (named after DBs CEO), passing Dawlish with a westbound engineers train on 6 June 2018. This loco sports an additional nose end light and special couplings for use as a Lickey banker. In the period until autumn 2016, EWS/DB locos had historically had cast nameplates applied to their cab sides, this plate is attached to the main hood assembly. **CJM**

Below: By 2019, the number of operational DB Class 66s in the UK was much reduced, with a large number (around 70) working in France for ECR and around 15 operating in Poland. Ten of the original fleet have been sold to GB Railfreight and a large number are out of use at Toton. What future is in store for some locos is unclear. Carrying the red DB-Schenker colours, No. 66097 passes Doncaster on 15 August 2018 with the 15.25 Wakefield Europort to London Gateway. **CJM**

Traction Transition - GM/EMD power in the UK and Ireland

Above: This loco, No. 66747 is one of a batch of five where were originally 'Euro 66s' and obtained by GBRf through Beacon Rail in 2012-2013 to ease a loco shortage. Built as Works No. 20078968-007, this loco was stored in Holland after delivery for a long time, before arriving in the UK in 2012 and modified to UK standards. On 3 September 2018 it is seen passing Longbridge with the 09.20 Clitheroe to Avonmouth cement. **CJM**

Left: One of the five-door low-emission locos, No. 66730 Whitemoor passes Eastleigh on the through road on 10 May 2018 with train 4Y19, the 12.19 Mountfield to Southampton Western Docks loaded gypsum train. **CJM**

Above: In 2013, to mark the 150th anniversary of the London Underground and to celebrate GB Railfreight's partnership with the London Transport Museum, No. 66721 was repainted in a very unusual livery, with a section of the world famous LU map on the bodywork. The map was devised Harry Beck, who's name is also carried by this loco. On 2 June 2016, No. 66721 passes Benhar with an engineering train from Tyne Yard to Mossend. **Robin Ralston**

Above: A stunning locomotive livery and a stunning location. After GBRf won the contract to power the prestigious Royal Scotsman train, a pair of Class 66s Nos. 66743 and 66746 were outshopped in Royal Scotsman livery. When not required for Royal Scotsman duties, the pair operate normal services. On 15 October 2018, No. 66746 passes over the River Clyde at Crawford, powering the 12.16 Carlisle to Millerhill Network Rail service. **Robin Ralston**

Below: Built by Progress Rail at their new factory in Muncie, Indiana in 2014, No. 66771 is recorded passing West Brompton on 29 October 2018 in charge of the 06.41 Peterborough Virtual Quarry to Tonbridge ballast, formed of GBRf-owned high-capacity box wagons. Behind the fence to the right, is the London Underground District Line platforms. **CJM**

Left Upper: *Colas Rail or Colas Rail Freight, depending on the time frame, have operated two fleets of Class 66s. Originally the French-owned company took over former DRS Nos. 66406-66410 in April 2009 and renumbered them as 66841-66845. These five locos branded Colas Rail operated until July 2011, when in an exchange of power the five went to GB Railfreight and were renumbered as 66742-66746. Colas then took on five ex Freightliner locos 66573-66577 and these emerged branded in Colas Rail freight colours and renumbered as 66846-66850. On 29 June 2010, Colas Freight No. 66843 pilots DRS No. 66424 at Wandel on the West Coast Main Line with the 16.06 Coatbridge to Daventry container service.* **Robin Ralston**

Left Middle: *The present fleet of five Colas Class 66/8s carry Colas Rail Freight branding, some are named, with plates centrally mounted on the ribbed bodyside. No. 66849 Wylam Dilly, the original 66576 is seen light loco at Cardiff on 15 November 2018.* **CJM**

Below: *Colas Rail Freight operate a small number of block freight trains as well as operating a large number of infrastructure services. One of their regular freight flows is log traffic from various loading sites to Chirk. On 30 November 2010, No. 66842 fights through a blizzard at Ribblehead on the Settle & Carlisle line with a Carlisle to Chirk loaded timber train.* **Brian Garrett**

92   *Traction Transition - GM/EMD power in the UK and Ireland*

Above: *In July 2007 a new operator emerged, Jarvis, who through its Fastline Freight operation ordered five locos to power coal train for Eon. They arrived between June and November 2008 and based at Roberts Road, Doncaster. The company went into receivership in March 2010 and the locos were sold, passing to lease operator CB Rail who placed them with Carlisle-based DRS. The fleet now carry DRS livery, but retain their 66/3 classification. On 7 January 2010, No. 66304 heads south through Oxford after heavy overnight snow.* **Mark V. Pike**

Below: *After Fastline Freight went into receivership. The five locos were repainted into DRS colours at the ElectroMotive plant at Longport near Stoke-on-Trent. This site is the main ElectroMotive (now progress Rail) facility in the UK and effects a number of specialist repair operations to mainly the UK-based fleets. However, in 2018 a start was made of bringing some of the Euro 66s to the plant to receive attention. On 7 March 2011, Nos. 66302 and 66305 await attention at the Longport facility.* **Cliff Beeton**

Traction Transition - GM/EMD power in the UK and Ireland

Above & Below: *Freightliner, formed in 1995 by a management buy-out was sold to Arcaptia Bank in June 2008. In February 2015 the business was again sold, this time to US short line operator Genesee & Wyoming (G&Y), an operator of many lines in the US and Canada. Still trading as Freightliner, G&Y have started to put their identity on the fleet, with Class 66/4 No. 66413 being the first to carry a stylish version of the corporate orange and black colours. In the above view the loco is seen near Worting Junction on 24 September 2018 with a container train for Southampton. In the image below, taken on 12 September 2018, No. 66413, heads through Horbury, with the empty Dewsbury Blue Circle Cement to Hope Earles Sidings service, formed of PCA hoppers.* **Mark V. Pike / Peter Marsh**

Above: To date, only three Class 66s have been written off due to accident. One, to EWS No. 66048 occurred on 4 January 2010, while powering an Inverness to Grangemouth Stobart train it derailed on the 1:60 grade from Slochd Summit and ran through catch points at the northern end of Carrbridge station. The investigation found it was caused by snow and ice between the wheels and brake blocks and ingestion of snow into the brake system. The loco was recovered and stored at Toton and more recently the body has been stored at ElectroMotive at Longport, where this view was recorded. Painted in black livery. **Cliff Beeton**

Below: Probably the most stunning livery to be applied to a Class 66, was given to GBRf No. 66789, following conversion from ex-EWS Class 66/0 No. 66250 in 2018. Emerging from the paintshop at Arlington Eastleigh in 1980s BR large logo blue, showing how the locos might have looked if purchased during the BR era. It was also named **British Rail 1948-1997**. It is seen stabled at Eastleigh on 10 May 2018. **CJM**

Class 66 Fleet by Operator (04/19)

Operator	Numbers
DB-Cargo UK	66001-007/009/011-015/017-021/023-025/027/030/034/035/037/039-041/043/044/047/050/051/055-057/059-061/063/065-070/074-080/082-112/124-131/133-140/142-145/147-152/154-156/158/160-162/164/165/167-172/174-177/181-183/185-188/192/194/197-200/206/207/221/230/238
DB Cargo (Export)	66010/022/026/028/029/031-033/036/038/042/045/049/052/062/064/071-073/123/146/153/157/159/163/166/173/178-180/189-191/193/195/196/201-205/208-220/222-224/231-237/239-249
Freightliner UK	66413-416/418-420, 66501-520/522-526/528/529/531-534/536-599/66601-607/610/613-623, 66951-953/955-957
Freightliner (Export)	66411/412/417, 66527/530/535/582-584/586/595, 66608/609/611/612/624/625, 66954
Direct Rail Services	66301-66305, 66421-434
Colas Rail Freight	66846-850
GB Railfreight	66701-733/735-789

Traction Transition - GM/EMD power in the UK and Ireland

Traction Transition - GM/EMD power in the UK and Ireland
EMD-Alstom Class 67

The General Motors/Alstom JT-42-HWHS or Class 67s were the first true 125mph (201km/h) dual-cabbed diesel-electric locos to operate in Europe, built in 1999-2000 for UK use with EWS.

30 locos were ordered by English Welsh & Scottish Railway, funded by Angel Trains, after Wisconsin Central purchased the BR railfreight operation in 1996. They were planned as a direct replacement for the Class 47s used on Royal Mail and charter services.

The 3,200hp (2,386kW) locos were ordered from General Motors Electro Motive Division (GM-EMD) as a high-speed version of the Class 66 (see previous section).

In an unusual move, GM sub-contracted assembly to Alstom in Valencia, Spain.

This arrangement was a continuation of an existing partnership involving high-speed passenger/freight traction.

The factory in Valencia, was one of a number of Alstom plants in Spain. It opened in the 1980s as a loco facility. The site was later operated by Vossloh and is now part of Stadler.

EWS sought a 125mph loco - a high-speed version of the Class 66. However, it was clear that this was impracticable. No off-the-shelf design was available. Brush Traction, was asked to quote for diesel version of the Class 89, to GM-EMD design, but nothing materialised. This left only a European high-speed Bo-Bo as option.

The Bo-Bo configuration required a major re-design of the '66' structure. It would also restrict the locos weight, as the UK axle load was firmly set at 22.5 tonnes.

The use of four axles led to a major concern by Railtrack (later Network Rail), that of stresses which could be imposed on the track by a 90-tonne loco travelling at 125mph.

Although the Class 67s were built in Spain, a considerable amount of equipment - including power units, alternators, traction and electrical equipment was supplied from the US and Canada. In fact, most equipment was the same as on a Class 66, the main difference being the fleet was equipped to passenger standards and to a structural design.

The structural assembly of the Class 67, followed traditional loco design, being a load-bearing assembly. This differed from the Class 66, which had a load-bearing platform frame onto which cab and modules were attached.

The Class 67 underframe and body assembly was done at the main Valencia factory. The underframe was formed first, complete with dragboxes. With the aid of jigs, the pre-formed side panels were then installed, assembled in steel plate by an outside contractor and arrived at Alstom in long sections. The cab-ends were fabricated at Alstom and installed on the base frame before the roof section supports were attached.

Loco ends had a large impact absorption 'honeycomb' block, to provide protection in the event of any significant impact. This was required to meet UIC standards.

Once the body structure was assembled, it visited the paint preparation bay, for both inside and external anti-corrosion treatment, followed by primer application. Once complete, the shell was fitted with its fuel tank and transferred to the main shop. Main assembly was carried out using a 'flow line' principal with 12 work stations in two parallel lines, bodyshells slowly progressing down one line and back along the other. This process took around 10-12 weeks and saw all internal items fitted, including the prime mover.

The engine was a GM 12N 710 G3B-EC, these were shipped by rail and sea in containers from GM's La Grange plant in Chicago, USA.

From the main fitting-out bays, the body was united with a pair of bogies; these were assembled at the Alstom factory.

From the assembly shop, finished pre-tested locos were taken to the paint area, where EWS livery was applied. The next phase was test station, where full load-bank, static and dynamic tests were carried out, the latter on a 2,735yd (2.5 km) test track.

In accordance with standard GM practice, the first loco of the build (No. 67001) was the subject of extensive validation tests. These starting in August 1999 and lasted three months. During this time, No. 67002 was completed and transferred to the Alstom dynamic test site at La Sagra, close to the City of Toledo.

With the Spanish gauge being 5ft 5⅝in (1,668mm) testing was a problem. However, a limited section of line on the standard-gauge Madrid-Seville high-speed corridor, allowed testing at up to 125mph (201km/h) to be undertaken.

By mid-September 1999, Nos. 67003 and 67004 were completed and under test at the Valencia factory.

Shipment of locos from Spain to the UK was done by sea, using Jumbo Shipping, the same company which transported the Class 66s to the UK. The '67s' arrived through Newport Docks.

The first Class 67 to arrive in the UK, No. 67003, was off-loaded on 12 October 1999.

Originally, EWS planned on a fleet of 10 locos commissioned and available for traffic by 1 December 1999 - a date Royal Mail were told would see the start of replacement of the troublesome 47s on their trains. However, this was not the case, with the first major delivery to the UK not taking place until February 2000 when six locos arrived. The remaining 23 locos came in a four batches being completed in August 2000.

As the '67s' did not have a full operating certificate for the UK, after No. 67003 had arrived, it was hauled to AEA Technology at the RTC Derby, where bogie rotational, sway, gauge clearance and completion of Railtrack validation tests were conducted. The loco then moved to Toton for testing and training.

Main line running for Railtrack validation was conducted from Old Oak Common, using the GW Berks & Hants route to Exeter and Plymouth for 100 mph (161km/h) operation and via the Didcot-Swindon-Bristol route for 125mph (201km/h) running. While certification was achieved for 125mph (201km/h) operation, the top speed was reduced to 110mph (177km/h) on grounds of reduced maintenance costs.

The Class 67 was designed for fast (Royal Mail) and passenger (charter) traffic. The front end included two RCH (Railway Clearing House) jumpers, enabling operation with Propelling Control Vehicles (PCVs), as well as providing a communication with passenger train staff.

The coupling was a swing-head knuckle/hook unit which consisted of a standard 11-inch US style knuckle coupling on a hinged shank, enabling the knuckle to be swung into use when needed. When the loco was required to couple to conventional stock, the knuckle could be stowed away and the normal hook used.

At the loco's No. 1 end, was the electrical compartment. In the centre of the body was the power unit/alternator group, while the cooler group was at the No. 2 end.

The driving cab was of a completely new design, based on a left-side driving position, incorporating a semi wrap-round desk. A standard GM-EMD power controller group was installed on the driver's right side, with the brake controllers - one for the loco and the other for a train, on the left side. The loco's on-board 'brain', is the EM2000 'Q-Tron' control panel, located on the left inclined panel, while main instrumentation is on the front inclined panel.

When introduced, on a panel to the left of the front windscreen a PACS (Propelling Advisory Control System) display was fitted, showing demands from a remote PCV cab.

Although these locos were introduced into an age in which TPWS (Train Protection & Warning System) and ATP (Automatic Train Protection) were becoming standard, these systems were not ⇨

Left: *The Alstom plant in Valencia employed around 380 staff on a 196,000m² site, which included a covered workshop area of 30,500m². The site included a heavy engineering section where body shells were fabricated from raw steel, a bogie and transmission section and a final assembly shop. In this view taken on 23 September 1999 the raw steel shell for loco No. 67017 taken just after the structure had been removed from the jigs, mounted of three-axle accommodation bogies and awaiting attention in the paint area.* **CJM**

Class:	67
Number range:	67001-67030
Built by:	Alstom/General Motors, Valencia, Spain
GM model:	JT-42-HWHS
Years introduced:	1999-2000
Wheel arrangement:	Bo-Bo
Design speed:	125mph (201km/h)*
Maximum speed:	110mph (177km/h)
Length:	64ft 7in (19.68m)
Height:	12ft 9in (3.88m)
Width:	8ft 9in (2.66m)
Weight:	90 tonnes
Wheelbase:	47ft 3 in (14.40m)
Bogie wheelbase:	9ft 2 in (2.79m)
Bogie pivot centres:	38ft 1in (11.63m)
Wheel diameter (new):	3ft 2in (965mm)
Min curve negotiable:	3.8 chains (75m)
Engine type:	GM 12N-710G3B-EC
Engine output:	3,200hp (2,386kW)
Power at rail:	2,493hp (1,860kW)
Maximum tractive effort:	31,750lb (141kN)
Continuous tractive effort:	20,200 (89.8kN) (with HEP active)
Cylinder bore:	$9^{1}/_{16}$in (230mm)
Cylinder stroke:	11in (279mm)
Traction alternator:	GM-EMD AR9A
Companion alternator:	GM-EMD CA6HEX
Traction motor type:	GM-EMD D43FM
No. of traction motors:	4
Gear ratio:	59:28
Brake type:	Air, Westinghouse PBL3
Brake force:	78 tonnes*
Bogie type:	Alstom high speed
Route availability:	8
Head end power (heating):	Electric - index 66 (in multiple each loco - 48)
Multiple coupling type:	AAR
Fuel tank capacity:	1,201gal (5,460lit)
Lub oil capacity:	202gal (918lit)
Cooling water capacity:	212gal (964lit)
Sanding equipment:	Pneumatic
Note:	

* 67004/007/009/011/030 fitted with cast iron brake blocks for Fort William sleeper and have a top speed of 80mph (129km/h) and a brake force of 68 tonnes

Class 67 Fact File

- Two locos Nos. 67005/006 are dedicated to British Royal Train use and painted in Claret livery.

- Two locos Nos. 67023/027 are now owned by Colas for 100-125mph test train operation.

- Two locos Nos. 67021/024 are painted in Pullman livery and are dedicated to the Belmond British (VSOE) Pullman.

Top: *The primer painted body shell of No. 67012 is seen just after arrival from the pre-paint area on works stands awaiting the first stage of fitting out on 23 September 1999.* **CJM**

Middle: *During the period of construction of the 67s, around 12 locos were under assembly at the same time, with the main assembly taking around 10-12 weeks to complete. No. 67007 is seen at one of the main assembly work stations, where components arrived on a 'just-in-time' basis.* **CJM**

Left: *The body shell of No. 67019 is seen mounted in the main formation jig, which holds together the frame, sides, cab ends and roof to enable welding into the complete frame. Behind No. 67019 a frame is seen in a manipulator, while on the right is a raw frame section, note the recess to accommodate the base of the prime mover.* **CJM**

Traction Transition - GM/EMD power in the UK and Ireland

Class 67 Fleet List

Number	Works No.	Name	Original Owner	Date Delivered	Delivery Ship	Date off-Loaded	Current Operator
67001	968742-01	Night Mail (21/7/00 – c07/04)	Angel Trains	20 Feb 2000	MV Arktis Meridian	21 Feb 2000	DBC
67002	968742-02	Special Delivery (8/8/00 – c09/11)	Angel Trains	20 Feb 2000	MV Arktis Meridian	21 Feb 2000	DBC
67003	968742-03		Angel Trains	6 Oct 1999	MV Fret Langueodo	12 Oct 1999	DBC
67004	968742-04	Post Haste (9/9/00 – c07/04) Cairn Gorm (03/15-11/17)	Angel Trains	20 Feb 2000	MV Arktis Meridian	20 Feb 2000	DBC
67005	968742-05	Queen's Messenger (6/12/00)	Angel Trains	20 Feb 2000	MV Arktis Meridian	22 Feb 2000	DBC
67006	968742-06	Royal Sovereign (25/2/05)	Angel Trains	9 Mar 2000	MV Jumbo Spirit	11 Mar 2000	DBC
67007	968742-07		Angel Trains	20 Feb 2000	MV Arktis Meridian	21 Feb 2000	DBC
67008	968742-08		Angel Trains	20 Feb 2000	MV Arktis Meridian	22 Feb 2000	DBC
67009	968742-09		Angel Trains	9 Mar 2000	MV Jumbo Spirit	10 Mar 2000	DBC
67010	968742-10	Unicorn (7/7/01 – 02/10)	Angel Trains	9 Mar 2000	MV Jumbo Spirit	10 Mar 2000	DBC
67011	968742-11		Angel Trains	9 Mar 2000	MV Jumbo Spirit	10 Mar 2000	DBC
67012	968742-12	A Shropshire Lad (3/7/08-06/15)	Angel Trains	9 Mar 2000	MV Jumbo Spirit	10 Mar 2000	DBC
67013	968742-13	Dyfrbont Pontcysylite (9/7/08-10/14)	Angel Trains	9 Mar 2000	MV Jumbo Spirit	10 Mar 2000	DBC
67014	968742-14	Thomas Telford (15/7/08-05/15)	Angel Trains	9 Mar 2000	MV Jumbo Spirit	10 Mar 2000	DBC
67015	968742-15	David J. Lloyd (16/5/08-06/15)	Angel Trains	9 Mar 2000	MV Jumbo Spirit	9 Mar 2000	DBC
67016	968742-16		Angel Trains	9 Mar 2000	MV Jumbo Spirit	9 Mar 2000	DBC
67017	968742-17	Arrow - (30/1/02)	Angel Trains	9 Mar 2000	MV Jumbo Spirit	9 Mar 2000	DBC
67018	968742-18	Rapid - (31/1/02 – c12/09) Keith Heller (15/1/10)	Angel Trains	9 Mar 2000	MV Jumbo Spirit	10 Mar 2000	DBC
67019	968742-19		Angel Trains	17 Apr 2000	MV Stella Prima	18 Apr 2000	DBC
67020	968742-20		Angel Trains	17 Apr 2000	MV Stella Prima	18 Apr 2000	DBC
67021	968742-21		Angel Trains	17 Apr 2000	MV Stella Prima	18 Apr 2000	DBC
67022	968742-22		Angel Trains	17 Apr 2000	MV Stella Prima	18 Apr 2000	DBC
67023§	968742-23	Stella (06/17)	Angel Trains	23 May 2000	MV Fairload	28 Apr 2000	COL
67024	968742-24		Angel Trains	23 May 2000	MV Fairload	28 Apr 2000	DBC
67025	968742-25	Western Star (28/9/01)	Angel Trains	23 May 2000	MV Fairload	28 Apr 2000	DBC
67026	968742-26	Diamond Jubilee (03/12)	Angel Trains	23 May 2000	MV Fairload	28 Apr 2000	DBC
67027§	968742-27	Rising Star (5/9/02-02/14) Charlotte (06/17)	Angel Trains	4 Aug 2000	MV Fairload	10 Aug 2000	COL
67028	968742-28		Angel Trains	4 Aug 2000	MV Fairload	10 Aug 2000	DBC
67029	968742-29	Royal Diamond (12/10/07)	Angel Trains	4 Aug 2000	MV Fairload	10 Aug 2000	DBC
67030	968742-30		Angel Trains	4 Aug 2000	MV Fairload	10 Aug 2000	DBC

§ Sold to Colas Rail Freight 06/17.   DBC - Deutsche Bahn Cargo, COL - Colas Rail Freight

installed from new, but were retro fitted.

The General Motors 12N 710 G3B EC engine set to deliver 3,200hp (2,386kW) was identical to the Class 66. Of this, 2,494hp (1,860kW) was available for traction. Coupled to the power unit was a GM AR9AC traction alternator unit. Traction motors of the GM D43 were fitted, these are frame-mounted.

Westinghouse supplied the brake equipment, the '67s' were the first main line diesel loco to have disc brake equipment.

By late 2000 the change from older power to Class 67s was nearing completion. At the same time more trains were formed with PCVs to allow limited push-pull working, especially into and out of the Princess Royal, Royal Mail 'Hub' at Willesden.

The original introductory plan for the class had to be trimmed, Railtrack would not authorise their use on all routes without speed restrictions. Eventually the fleet was authorised to operate on the core business routes.

In 2002-2003 the fleet settled down to Royal Mail and charter use. However, the fleet looked doomed in mid-2003 after Royal Mail announced it was withdrawing from the movement of mail by rail, following a breakdown in discussions with EWS.

Royal Mail said the price was 'way too high' to justify continuation of the contract. EWS were not prepared to lower its profit on the contract and thus Royal Mail started the controversial change from rail to road and air transport for Royal Mail traffic from the end of 2003. The final Travelling Post Office trains operated on 9 January 2004 and by mid-year all remaining mail trains were withdrawn.

This fundamental change and the main reason for the '67s' saw 75% of the fleets duties lost and EWS started to deploy the fleet on general freight traffic, especially the longer distance high speed services.

In the summer of 2004 Virgin Trains entered into a deal with EWS to provide four locos each peak weekend to power North West/East to Paignton relief passenger trains. These trains proved popular with enthusiasts and photographers, but were never filled due to early starts in both directions which did not suit passenger needs.

In the autumn of 2004 some Class 67s were deployed on the annual Rail Head Treatment Trains (RHTT) services.

Another beneficiary of the Royal Mail withdrawal was the East Coast Main Line (ECML), then operated by Great North Eastern Railway, who negotiated deployment of five Class 67s at 'Thunderbirds' at their prime locations to rescue Class 91 and Mk4 sets or HST sets if needed, this work continues today, but will soon end with the full deployment of Class 800 and 801 stock.

Following many years of Class 47s being

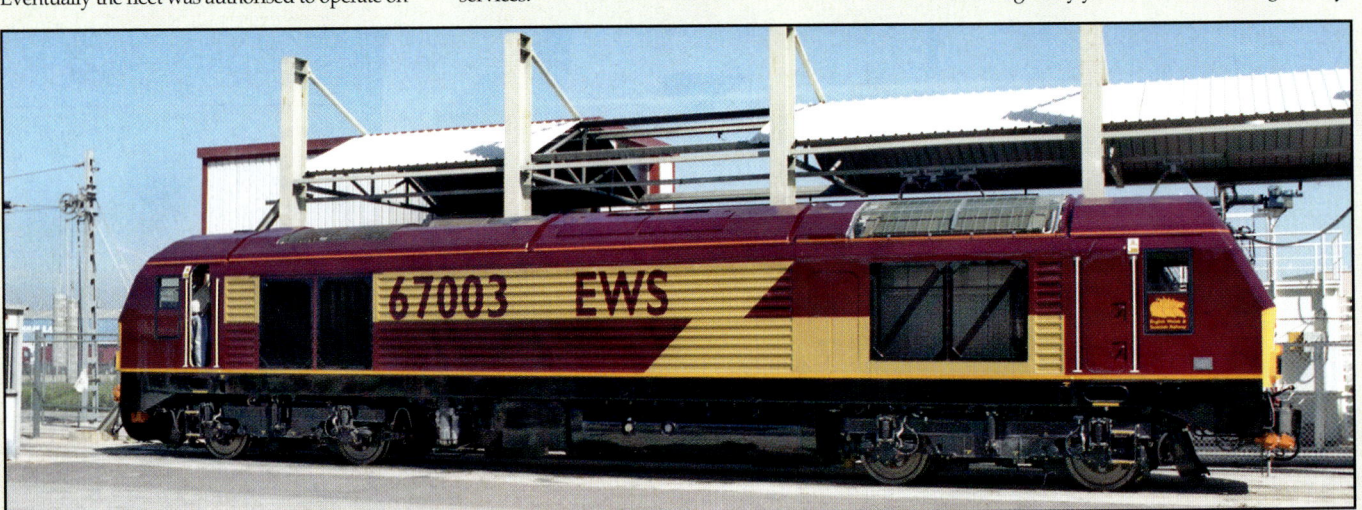

responsible for powering the Royal Trains, Class 67s took over. In late 2003, two locos Nos. 67005 and 67006 were dedicated to Royal Train use. When not needed they would operate in the core fleet. In February 2004 No. 67005 was repainted in Royal Claret at Toton depot and named *Queen's Messenger*. The second loco No. 67006 was repainted into Royal Claret in January 2005.

In 2004, EWS decided to introduce a US style Management Train, formed of three Mk3 passenger carriages, a modified Mk3 DVT and a Class 67, essentially to transport the hob-knobs of EWS around the UK. For this, Class 67 No. 67029 was modified to operate with the DVT, and painted in silver livery. When not needed for Management Train operation the loco was worked as part of the core fleet.

From October 2007, No. 67029 became the official Royal Train standby loco when it was named *Royal Diamond* by Her Majesty The Queen.

In 2004-05, the '67s' took over the diesel legs of the ScotRail Sleeper services on the Inverness and Aberdeen routes, and from 2006 commenced operation on the West Highland Sleeper to Fort William. Over the West Highland route the '67s' were heavily restricted due to their high axle load and many speed restrictions were imposed. On this route major brake block problems were identified with normal blocks often being worn out after just one trip! To address this, cast iron blocks were fitted to a dedicated pool, Nos. 67004, 67007, 67009, 67011 and 67030 they were also fitted with Radio Electronic Token Block (RETB) for West Highland use. The cast iron brake blocks while increasing wear required a lower maximum speed of 80mph (130km/h).

In 2007 Open Access operator Wrexham & Shropshire announced plans to launch a loco hauled service between Marylebone and Wrexham. Formed of Mk3 stock, it was powered by hired-in Class 67s. EWS set-aside Nos. 67012-015 for these duties and installed modified fire detection equipment allowing the locos to trail a train with no staff member on board.

Further passenger work came the way of the Class 67s for First Group both in Scotland and the West of England. In Scotland a shortage of DMUs saw a Class 67 hauled service introduced on the Fife Circle from December 2008, this was increased to two trains from December 2009.

On Great Western an acute shortage of DMUs saw a Cardiff to Taunton duty transfer to Class 67s 'top and tailing' EWS Mk2s from December 2008, from December 2009 a second duty was introduced including a Cardiff to Paignton and return train. The Paignton roster was withdrawn in October 2010 and the Taunton to Cardiff service ended in November 2010.

From 2009, the fleet were operated by DB Schenker, with their operations remaining the same. Today the fleet are under control of DB Cargo.

In 2019 the fleet sees little work, apart from occasional charter services. Until introduction of new Mk5 stock on Caledonian sleeper services, the '67s' have hung on to some sleeper work. In Wales two locos operate on a daily Holyhead to Cardiff and a North Wales passenger service for Transport for Wales (TfW). Some increase in this operation might be on the cards as TfW are taking on redundant Mk4s to be powered by '67s'.

Spare capacity in 2017 saw DB offer some Class 67s for sale, two locos Nos. 67023 and 67027 being sold to Colas Rail Freight for operation at up to 125mph on Network Rail test trains. In 2018 these locos were sold to lease company Beacon Rail and leased back to Colas Rail Freight.

In 2018 Belmond Pullman, a long term and good customer to DB had a pair of Class 67s Nos. 67021 and 67024 repainted in Pullman livery and dedicated to power the British Pullman train.

The long term future for the remaining locos is not good, apart from plodding around on the odd freight train. Perhaps a sale to another operator might be on the cards. ■

Top: *Performing the work for which the fleet was ordered, powering a Royal Mail parcels service. Taking the Plymouth line at Aller Junction on 15 July 2002, No. 67019 leads the 09.32 Bristol Barton Hill to Plymouth vans.* **CJM**

Left: *After completion and a final coat of EWS maroon and gold livery, the locos spent some time at the works test facility, where static and dynamic testing was possible, including several runs on a short dual-gauge test track No. 67003 is seen being put through its paces on 23 September 1999.* **CJM**

Right: *The other main reason for introducing the fleet was to operate charter passenger work, but with private companies providing locos and some passenger TOCs offering traction, their use was limited. On 2 June 2005, No. 67019 heads for Paignton at Aller Junction, powering the 08.01 Longbridge to Paignton, carrying staff from Rover on a day trip to Torbay.* **CJM**

Traction Transition - GM/EMD power in the UK and Ireland

Above: In the summer of 2004, with spare capacity in the '67' roster, Virgin Trains contracted EWS to provide four locos on peak summer Saturdays to power North West/East to Paignton relief passenger trains. These proved popular with haulage enthusiasts and photographers, but did not run in either direction at a time suitable to the holiday trade. On a wonderful sunny day, No. 67026 passes Horse Cove, Dawlish on 4 September 2004 with the 07.08 York to Paignton. **CJM**

Below: When designed, the Class 67s were fitted with equipment to allow operation with the new Class 325 'Railnet' EMUs, these dual-voltage sets were recently introduced and could be used as electric multiple units working for 25kV AC overhead, 750V DC third or as hauled stock. The '67's were fitted with a PACS (Propelling Advisory Control System) display, so the operator in the remote cab could issue power/brake demands to the driver of the 67. The pioneer of the fleet No. 67001 passes Milford Junction on 25 August 2000 with an 'up' Royal Mail working formed of two Class 325s. **John Whiteley**

Above: *An acute shortage of DMUs on Great Western saw a Cardiff to Taunton duty worked by 'top & tail' Class 67s with four Mk2s from December 2008. A year later a second duty was introduced with a Cardiff to Paignton. On 4 January 2010, Nos. 67017 and 67016 flank four Mk2s at Beam Bridge, Whiteball with a Cardiff to Paignton service.* **Russell Ayre**

Right: *On 15 April 2010, Nos. 67022 and 67017 'top and tail' four air conditioned Mk2s through Cogload Junction, east of Taunton, operating a First Great Western Cardiff Central to Taunton service. These trains have always been subject to some unusual power, after a period of DMU operation of Classes 150, 153, 158, 165 and 166, from early 2019, some short form 2+4 'Castle' HST sets have been introduced, again to cover for a shortage of multiple unit stock.* **Brian Garrett**

In 2004 the '67s' took over the diesel legs of the then ScotRail Sleeper services on the Inverness and Aberdeen routes and from 2006 this extended to the West Highland route to Fort William. Due to brake issues on the graded route a small batch were fitted with cast-iron brake pads. Modified loco No. 67009 is shown passing Achallader near Bridge of Orchy on 1 April 2013 with the Edinburgh-Fort William service. **Jamie Squibbs**

Above: Under privatisation, the operation of the Royal Train fell to EWS, now DB Cargo to provide motive power and train crew. To power the service two of the new Class 67s, Nos. 67005 and 67006 were painted in matching Royal Claret livery. When not required to power the Royal Train, the pair assume a normal place in the fleet roster. On 11 September 2009, Nos. 67005 and 67006 flank Royal stock Nos. 2921, 2922, 2923, 2916, 2917, 2915, 2920 along the Sea Wall at Dawlish forming the 09.33 Newton Abbot to Exeter 'Royal Train' carrying the Prince of Wales. **CJM**

Below: Another Class 67 often associated with the Royal Train is No. 67026, which was repainted in silver with Union flag branding to mark the Queens Diamond Jubilee. The loco is also named **Diamond Jubilee**. On 16 August 2012. The loco is seen near Eastwood in the Calder Valley, with empty Royal Train stock bound for the trains home at Wolverton Works after dropping off its passengers at Burnley. **John Whiteley**

With capacity in the fleet, the East Coast main line commenced using Class 67s as 'Thunderbirds' in GNER days, which has continued through various operators until the present time. The locos are used to rescue failed trains or provide diesel haulage over non electrified routes in the case of diversions. Royal No. 67006 pilots a Mk4 set with DVT No. 92220 leading near Haltwhistle on 6 October 2018 forming the diverted 11.00 King's Cross to Edinburgh. **Jamie Squibbs**

Right: EWS/DB control, try whenever possible to allocate the 'special' locos including the Royal locos to VIP and high-profile charter trains whenever possible. On 26 April 2014 a visit of the VSOE Pullman to the South West. During the weekend stay it operated a Plymouth to Taunton and return 'luncheon' priced at £250 per person. Powered by 'Royal' No. 67006 and 67024 in multiple, the train emerges from Whiteball Tunnel at Marlands. **Brian Garrett**

Below: In March 2018 a rough sea knocked down several sections of the steel fence between the King's Walk and the railway at Dawlish, closing the path, and providing a gap to photograph trains until it was repaired. The down 'Royal' passes along the sea wall at Dawlish on 27 March 2018 forming train 1Z70, the 23.38 Windsor & Eton Riverside to Plymouth, transporting the Queen to Plymouth Dockyard for the decommissioning of HMS Ocean. The train is formed of No. 67006 coaches 2921, 2903, 2904, 2922, 2923, 2916, 2917, 2915, 2920 and No. 67005 on the rear. **CJM**

Traction Transition - GM/EMD power in the UK and Ireland 103

Above: *In 2007 Open Access operator Wrexham & Shropshire launched a loco-hauled service between London Marylebone and Wrexham. Formed of Mk3 stock, powered by hired-in Class 67s. EWS allocated Nos. 67012-67015 for these duties, installed modified fire detection equipment and repainted them in two-tone grey livery. After Wrexham & Shropshire closed down, the loco and stock formations were taken over by Chiltern Railways to operate a Marylebone to Birmingham 'express' service. No. 67014 propels the 12.17 from London Marylebone to Wrexham over Neasden Junction on 8 October 2009.* **Antony Guppy**

Below: *Originally EWS, then DB-Schenker now DB Cargo are the selected provider of motive power and train crew to operate the VSOE, operated by Belmond. Recently a pair of dedicated, Pullman-liveried locos have been provided, but for a long time any available loco was used. On 24 September 2017, the VSOE is seen pass Westwell, south of Charing forming the 11.15 London Victoria to Ashford. Motive power is provided by one of the original Wrexham and Shropshire locos No. 67014.* **Jamie Squibbs**

Due to their higher maximum speed, it is not uncommon to find Class 67s powering Network Rail infrastructure testing trains. On 21 March 2015, former Wrexham & Shropshire No. 67012 and 67027 'top and tail' two NR test cars at Selside on the Settle and Carlisle route with a Derby to Heaton move. **John Whiteley**

Right: *On 3 May 2010, DB 'Executive' liveried No. 67029, painted and modified to operate the EWS Management Train is working in the 'top and tail' mode with No. 67022 passing Dawlish, forming the stand-in 08.00 Cardiff to Paignton service.* **CJM**

Below: *After EWS was sold to DB-Schenker, a small start was made to apply red/grey DB-Schenker colours to some '67s'. Repainted No. 67027 passes Dryclough Junction near Halifax on 6 July 2014 hauling the DB Management DVT No. 82146 and ex-Virgin Trains Mk3s on a special 10.36 Leeds to Hebden Bridge for the Tour de France.* **John Whiteley**

Above: *After a period of using Class 57s on the Arriva Trains Wales Holyhead-Crewe business train, EWS hired Class 67s for the duty and repainted three (67001-67003) in Arriva turquoise. Looking very smart with a matching train, No. 67002 passes Ponthir near Newport on 10 April 2012 with the afternoon Cardiff to Holyhead service.* **Jamie Squibbs**

Left: *The three Arriva Trains Wales dedicated Class 67s were frequently supplemented by other Class 67s and in more recent times no effort has been made to keep the locos on the service. Under the new Transport for Wales franchise, DB Cargo have been told that they will still require Class 67s to power the express services, which from late 2019 early 2020 will be formed of Mk4 stock. On 19 June 2014, No. 67001 is seen at Newport.* **CJM**

Above: *In the UK we seldom see more than two locos at the helm of trains. However, on 5 November 2012, this amazing line up was captured at Barrow-on-Trent, when Nos. 67026, 67029, 66047, 66063 and 60065 led the daily Bescot to Toton engineers train. Only the front loco was reported working, the others were just getting a lift back to their home depot.* **Jamie Squibbs**

Left Below: *After the new TOC Caledonian Sleepers took over the operation of the Scottish sleeper services, initially Class 67s continued to be used until GBRf took over the provision of traction. At the start of the new service in March 2015, EWS repainted No. 67004 in the new teal Caledonian Sleeper colours, applied operator branding and the cast nameplate* **Cairn Gorm.** *The loco is seen at Fort William on 31 March 2015.* **Antony Christie**

Below: *In January 2010, No. 67018 was repainted at Toton depot into DB Schenker red and grey colours, complete with a Canadian maple leaf on the side. The cast name* **Keith Heller** *was applied and the loco was unveiled at the National Railway Museum. The naming and livery embellishment was in honour of the Canadian-born former EWS and DB Schenker UK chairman. On 23 May 2010, No. 67018 leads the Victoria to Folkestone West leg of a VSOE working, in the deep cutting between Hollingbourne and Harrietsham.* **Brian Stephenson**

Traction Transition - GM/EMD power in the UK and Ireland

Above: *In 2017, capacity existed for two Class 67s to be sold, both, Nos. 67023 and 67027 were quickly snapped up by Colas Rail freight, to power higher-speed Network Railway infrastructure monitoring trains, especially when the New Measurement Train was out of service, enabling post 100mph running. The locos were overhauled at Toton and repainted into Colas orange and yellow house colours and both were named. On 29 June 2018, Nos. 67023 and 67027 'top and tail' four Network Rail test vehicles at Powderham, Devon, while forming train 1Q18, the 06.06 Reading Triangle to Paignton via Penzance. (Inset) cast nameplate and bodyside branding.* **Both: CJM**

Below: *Led by No. 67027 Charlotte, a 'stand-in' New Measurement Train is seen at Teignmouth on 3 June 2017, during a reversal move on a Reading to Paignton via Penzance and Teignmouth service.* **CJM**

Below: *Looking across the River Teign from Ringmoor and Shaldon to the area just west of Teignmouth boat yard towards Bishopsteignton, some pleasing views of trains skirting the rive can be obtained, especially when they are in a bright livery. On 29 June 2018, 67023, test cars Nos. 975091, 72631, 977997, 9481 and 67027 head west towards Bishopsteignton with train 1Q18, the 06.06 Reading Triangle to Paignton via Penzance, following its turn at Teignmouth.* **CJM**

Traction Transition - GM/EMD power in the UK and Ireland
The Euro '66s'

General Motors/EMD had operated in Mainland Europe for a number of years, with in several countries, including Denmark, Hungary and Sweden. It was therefore no surprise that following their huge success in entering the UK market, that the same model, with some modifications, could be offered to Mainland European customers.

In 1999, GM attempted to sell its JT42-CWR model to various operators. The first to sign up was private German operator Häfen und Güterverkehr Köln (HGK) who required two locos to power container trains between Germany and the Port of Rotterdam. GM were delighted that they had broken back into the lucrative European market and with agreement of EWS took two part assembled locos off the EWS production line (Nos. 66154/155) and used these as the first two Euro 66s. The locos were slightly modified from the production UK model, especially in terms of cab layout, drawgear and air pipes. The pair were finished in HGK red and numbered DE61 and DE62.

This pair were shipped from the London plant in Canada via Halifax in mid-August 1999 to Rotterdam, from where they were taken to the NedTrains workshops at Tilburg.

The Tilburg site quickly become the main focus of Euro 66 commissioning with the majority being got ready for work at the site.

HGK and General Motors agreed to jointly take the Euro 66 project forward, by seeking operational approval for use in Germany, Holland and Belgium. This turned out to be a drawn out affair.

After the first two locos arrived, orders started to be placed, in May 2000 TGOJ of Sweden ordered a pair of locos. These were heavily modified for Arctic conditions as low as possibly -40c.

In an interesting twist to frame/body allocations at Diesel Division, London, the TGOJ locos took the shells originally allocated to Freightliner Nos. 66519 and 66520.

At the start of 2001, General Motors had completed UK orders for Class 66s for EWS, Freightliner and GB Railfreight and at the ceremony held in London, Canada to hand over the GB Railfreight locos, GM announced that the full time 66 production line in London would cease, but the product would remain in the product portfolio and be built on an 'as required' basis.

Speculative building of locos was something new to the UK and European market, but common in the US. So, in early 2001 UK-based Porterbrook Leasing announced a speculative order for 10 Euro 66s. These would remain Porterbrook property and hired on a 'spot hire' basis to any open access operator who required power. At around the same time, no stranger to the GM product range, Heavy Haul Power International (HHPI), owned by Richard Painter (the Son of Ken Painter who was the Rail Director at Foster Yeoman and the operator of No. 59003 in Germany and Eastern Europe) placed an order for three Euro 66s, funded by a GM subsidiary GMAC Leasing.

General Motors/EMD were firmly on the path for European operation, the company opened an office in Russelsheim, near Frankfurt.

From then on orders came thick and fast and full details of these can be found in the complex table within this section. Some of the lease owners have been reluctant to provide operator information and some even say they do or have not owned specific locos. However the list is based on the Diesel Division production schedule and updated to include as many movements and change of owner as can be proven.

A huge number of owner changes have been recorded for the Euro locos.

In early 2002 the start of the mass introduction of Class 66s in Mainland Europe commenced with Porterbrook locos going on lease to various operators

The biggest single order for Euro Class 66s came in 2006 when EWS signed a contract for the building of 60 locos for its Mainland European operation Euro Cargo Rail (ECR). These locos commenced assembly in the London plant in Canada in autumn 2007 and were delivered throughout 2008 with the final locos being finished in 2009. Many of these locos after delivery found little work and all but a handful have been sold to other operators, with a large number going to the parent company DB.

No further 'Euro 66s' will be built, but some have been modified and shipped to the UK to operate with GB Railfreight. This is likely to be repeated in the years ahead.

In addition to the true Euro 66s, a significant number of EWS and Freightliner UK Class 66s have been modified for European use and shipped to France or Poland for further operation. These are detailed in the Class 66 section of this publication. ■

Below: *One of the early Euro 66s was works No. 20008254-02, allocated the delivery number of PB02, owned by Porterbrook Leasing, and originally hired to ShortLines of Rotterdam. It was later sold to CB Rail, then to Ascendos Rail Leasing of Luxembourg and is currently owned by Beacon Rail, it was last seen running as No. DE676 and has the international identity of 92 80 1266 004-1 D-RHC. On 20 November 2006, No. PB02 is seen passing Tilburg in very wet conditions, powering an eastbound intermodal service.* **CJM**

Right Above: *Assembly of the Euro 66s was carried out at the Diesel Division plant in London, Ontario and many were built alongside UK locos. To meet European specification the cabs were of a different style and headlights were revised, depending on the operator. Locos to operate in arctic conditions were specially weather proofed. After locos were complete, some dynamic testing was conducted on the test track. On 13 November 2004, two Mitsui Rail Capital Leasing locos, built to works Nos. 20038561-003 and 20038561-004, which carried identity EM3 and EM4 at the time are seen on the test track. Today, these locos are owned by Beacon Rail. 20038561-003 is now numbered 90 80 1266 040-5 and is in use with Freightliner Poland, while 20038561-004 was last reported working for Rotterdam Rail Feeding.* **CJM**

Right Middle: *Built in August 2003 HSBC order 20038513-001 and 20038513-002 (Euro Rail Shuttle 6607 and 6607 are seen on the test track. The loco nearest the camera ERS6607 was sold to Beacon Rail in March 2009 and is currently working for Freightliner in Poland as 92 80 1266 026-4. The rear loco ERS6606 was again sold to Beacon Rail in March 2009 and was subsequently transferred to the UK in October 2013 and now operates for GB Railfreight as No. 66750.* **CJM**

Below: *In early 2009, thee locos were built to order 20078941, these were built for Veolia Cargo in the Netherlands. The three were complete in May 2009 and shipped to Europe where they were immediately stored. In June 2011 they were sold to French-based Akiem Rail. Thus as far as can be ascertained, these three locos never operated with this branding No. 77501 is seen on the Diesel Division test track on 4 May 2009.* **CJM**

Traction Transition - GM/EMD power in the UK and Ireland

Euro 66 Fleet List

GM/EMCC Works No.	Date Built	Original Owner	History	Identity	Notes
998101-01	08/99	GM/Opal Leasing	Häfen und Güterverkehr Köln (HGK) Sold to HGK 06/2000, renumber Registered as 06/12 To RheinCargo GmbH as 92 80 1266 061-1 D-RHC	9902 DE61 92 80 1266 061-1 D-HGK	Also carried No. DE61 EBA No. EBA 00L13C 002
998101-02	08/99	GM/Opal Leasing	Häfen und Güterverkehr Köln (HGK) Sold to HGK 03/2001, renumber Registered as 06/12 to RheinCargo GmbH as 92 80 1266 062-9 D-RHC	9901 DE62 92 80 1266-062-9 D-HGK	Also carried No. DE62 EBA No. EBA 00L13C 001
20008212-01	07/00	HSBC Rail	Trafikaktiebolaget Grängesbergs- Oxelösunds Järnväg, Sweden (TGOJ) Sold to Beacon Rail as Hire to TGOJ 01/01/11 hire to Green Cargo Mid-2012 hire to Rushrail, Sweden 12/16 hire to Hector Rail, Sweden as Exported to UK 03/19 for GBRf renumber 66790	T66-713 92 74 0066 713-9 S-BRLL T66-713	
20008212-02	07/00	HSBC Rail	Trafikaktiebolaget Grängesbergs- Oxelösunds Järnväg, Sweden (TGOJ) Sold to Beacon Rail as 01/01/11 hire to Green Cargo, Sweden Mid-11 hire to CFL Cargo Denmark, renumber Mod for Denmark, Sweden and Norway 11/13 hire to Cargolink, Norway as 04/17 hire to Captrain, Denmark as Exported to UK mid 2019 for GBRf renumber 66791	T66-714 92 74 0066 714-7 S-BRLL T66K 714 T66K 714 T66K 714	Named: *Kruthornet*
20008254-01	07/01	Porterbrook Leasing	ShortLines, Rotterdam (31/01/02) Rail4Chem, Benelux (11/10/04) 11/04 sold to CB Rail Leasing, Luxembourg 01/07 registered 12/09 hire to Veolia Cargo, Breda NL 04/10 to Ascendos Rail Leasing, Luxembourg 04/10 hire to Rurtalbahn Cargo (RTB) 06/16 sold to Beacon Rail, Luxembourg 09/16 hire to Rurtalbahn Cargo (RTB)	PB01 PB01 92 80 1266 003-3 D-CBRL PB01 PB01 V264 92 80 1266 003-3 D-RTBC PB01 V264 92 80 1266 003-3 D-RTBC	EBA No. EBA 00L13C 003
20008254-02	07/01	Porterbrook Leasing	ShortLines, Rotterdam (01/02) Azfet Container Transport System (ACTS) Rail4Chem, Benelux (11/10/04) Sold to CB Rail Leasing, Luxembourg Hire to Rail4Chem, Benelux 03/09 hire to SNCF Fret, Belgium 03/10 hire to Crossrail, Belgium Registered as 04/10 to Ascendos Rail Leasing, Luxembourg as 07/11 hire to HGK 08/12 hire to RheinCargo 06/16 sold to Beacon Rail, Luxembourg	PB02 PB02 PB02 PB02 PB02 PB02 92 88 0266 004-5 D-CBRL PB02 92 80 1266 004-1 D-HGK DE676 and 92 80 1266 004-1 D-RHC PB02	EBA No. EBA 00L13C 004
20008254-03	07/01	GM/GMAC Leasing	Heavy Haul Power International (from 22/02/02) Sold to CB Rail Leasing, Luxembourg (02/05) Tested 02/06 in Romania by CFR Cailor Ferate Romane 01/07 registered 04/10 sold to Ascendos Rail Leasing, Luxembourg 06/10 hire to Rurtalbahn Cargo (RTB) 01/11 hire to Crossrail, Belgium 06/11 hire to Eisenbahngesellschaft Potsdam (EGP) 02/13 hire to Lappwaldbahn, Weferlingen, Germany 08/13 hire to RheinCargo 02/16 hire to HHPI 06/16 sold to Beacon Rail Leasing, Luxembourg	29001 92 80 1266 005-8 92 80 1266 005-8 V265 92 80 1266 005-8 D-RTB 29001 29001 92 80 1266 005-8 D-EGP 29001 92 80 1266 005-8 D-LWB DE687 / 92 80 1266 005-8 D-RHC 29001 / 92 80 1266 005-8 D-HHPI	Named: *Robert J G Savage* EBA No. EBA 00L13C 005
20008254-04	08/01	GM/GMAC Leasing	Heavy Haul Power International (28/03/02) ShortLines, Rotterdam (03-04/03) Sold to CB Rail 02/05 Hire to Heavy Haul Power International Sold to Ascendos Rail, Lugembourg Registered Hire to HGK as 03/10 hire to Crossrail 06/11 hire to Eisenbahngesellschaft, Fresden 04/13 hire to HHPI 09/14 hire to Crossrail Sold to Beacon Rail, Luxembourg 10/16 hire to Railtraxx, Belgium 06/17 hire to HHPI as	29002 29002 92 80 1266 006-6 DE54 / 92 80 1266 006-6 D-HGK 29002 29002 / 92 80 1266 006-6 D-ITL 29002 / 92 80 1266 006-6 D-HHPI 29002 / 92 80 1266 006-6 D-XRAIL 29002 / 92 80 1266 006-6 D-RTX 29002	Named: *Hans Cermak* EBA No. EBA 00L13C 006 Named: *Hans Cermak*
20008254-05	09/01	Porterbrook Leasing	04/02 Dillen & Le Jeune Cargo Rly (02/02/02) Sub lease to ACTS (05/11/04) Sold to CB Rail (16/11/04) Hire to Dillen & Le Jeune Cargo Rly 06/08 hire to Crossrail, Belgium Registered 04/10 sold to Ascendos Rail, Luxembourg Issued re-number Fitted for ETCS level 2, Germany, Belgium, Nethelands 06/16 sold to Beacon Rail, Luxembourg	PB03 PB03 PB03 PB03 92 80 1266 018-1 D-XRAIL PB03 92 80 1266 007-4 D-XRAIL PB03	EBA No. EBA 00L13C 007

20008254-06	09/01	Porterbrook Leasing	06/02 Häfen und Güterverkehr Köln (HGK)	PB04 then DE63
			Sold to CB Rail 16/11/04	
			Häfen und Güterverkehr Köln (HGK)	DE63
			Registered	92 80 1266 063-7 D-HGK
				EBA No. EBA 00L13C 008
			04/10 sold to Ascendos Rail, Luxembourg	
			08/12 hire to RheinCargo	DE63 / 92 80 1266 063-7 D-RHC
			04/15 hire to SNCB,	PB04 / 92 80 1266 063-7 D-BLX
			06/16 sold to Beacon Rail, Luxembourg	
			09/16 hire to Crossrail	PB04
			10/16 to B Logistics	PB04
			04/17 to Lineas Group	PB04
20008254-07	09/01	Porterbrook Leasing	Rail4Chem, Essen (25/05/02)	PB05
			11/04 sold to CB Rail	PN05 EBA No. EBA 00L13C 009
			Registered	92 80 1266 009-0 S-CBRL
			01/06 hire Rail4Chem, Essen	PB05
			12/09 to Veolia Cargo, Netherlands	PB05
			01/10 to SNCF, Belgium	6609 / 92 80 1266 009-0 D-SFB
			04/10 sold to Ascendos Rail, Luxembourg	PB05
			05/10 hire to Captrain Belgium	6609 / 92 80 1266 009-0 D-CTB
			06/16 sold to Beacon Rail, Luxembourg	PB05
20008254-08	09/01	Porterbrook Leasing	Häfen und Güterverkehr Köln (HGK) (12/07/02)	PB06 then DE64
			Sold to CB Rail 16/11/04	PB06 EBA No. EBA 00L13C 010
			Registered	92 80 1266 064-5 D-HGK carried DE64
			04/10 sold to Ascendos Rail, Luxembourg	PB06
			Hire to RheinCargo as	DE64 / 92 80 1266 064-5 D-RHC
			05/14 hire to Rotterdam Rail Feeding	PB06 / 92 80 1266 064-5 D-RRF
			06/16 sold to Beacon Rail Luxembourg	PB06
			2017 hire to HHPI	PB06
20008254-09	09/01	Porterbrook Leasing	European Rail Shuttle (02/09/02)	PB07 then 6601
			Sold to CB Rail 16/11/04	EBA No. EBA 00L13C 011
			European Rail Shuttle	6601 Named: *Blue Arrow*
			12/08 hire to SNCF Belgium	6601
			Registered	92 88 0266 001-1 B-SFB
			06/10 sold to Ascendos Rail, Luxembourg	PB07
			05/10 hire to Captrain Belgium	6601 / 92 88 0266 001-1 B-CTB
			06/16 sold to Beacon Rail, Luxembourg	PB07 Allocated UK No. 66999
20008254-10	09/01	Porterbrook Leasing	European Rail Shuttle (28/09/02)	PB08 then 6602
			Sold to CB Rail 16/11/04	EBA No. EBA 00L13C 012
			European Rail Shuttle	6602 Named: *Blue Bullet*
			12/08 hire to SNCF, Belgium	6602
			Registered	92 88 0266 002-9 B-SFB
			04/10 sold to Ascendos Rail, Luxembourg	PB08
			05/10 hire to Captrain, Belgium	6602 / 92 88 0266 002-9 B-CTB
			--/14 hire to HHPI	PB08 / 92 88 0266 002-9 B-HHPI
			--/15 hire to Crossrail, Belgium	PB08 / 92 88 0266 002-9 B-XRAIL
			11/15 hire to Captrain, Belgium	6602 / 92 88 0266 002-9 B-CTB
			06/16 sold to Beacon Rail, Luxembourg	PB08
			10/17 hire to Freightliner Poland, Warszawa	PB08
			11/17 hire to Freightliner, Germany	PB08
20008254-11	02/02	Porterbrook Leasing	European Rail Shuttle (30/09/02)	PB09 then 6603
			Sold to CB Rail (16/11/04)	EBA No. EBA 00L13C 013
			European Rail Shuttle	6603 Named: *Blue Catapult*
			11/04 sold to CB Rail, Luxembourg	PB09
			12/08 hire to SNCF, Belgium	6603
			Registered	92 88 0266 003-7 B-SFB
			04/10 sold to Scendos Rail, Luxembourg	PB09
			05/10 hire to Captrain, Belgium	6603 / 92 88 0266 003-7 B-CTB
			06/16 sold to Beacon Rail, Luxembourg	PB09
20008254-12	02/02	Porterbrook Leasing	European Rail Shuttle (02/09/02)	PB10 then 6604
			Sold to CB Rail (16/11/04)	EBA No. EBA 00L13C 014
			European Rail Shuttle	6604 Named: *Blue Dart*
			--/09 hire to Deutsche Gleisbau Material Transport, Leipzig	6604
			Registered	92 80 1266 014-0 D-DGMT
			--/10 hire to Captrain, Belgium	6608
			04/10 sold to Ascendos Rail, Luxembourg	PB10
			01/11 hire to Rurtalbahn	V266 / 92 80 1266 014-0 D-RTB
			06/16 sold to Beacon Rail, Luxembourg	PB10
20008254-13	03/02	GM/GMAC Leasing	Heavy Haul Power International	29003 Named: *Rhoda Painter*
			03/02 hire to Rail4Chem	EBA No. EBA 00L13C 015
			Heavy Haul Power International	29003 Named: *Rhoda Painter*
20018352-01	11/02	HSBC Rail	11/02 CargoNet, Norway	66 401, Di9-01
			03/09 sold to Beacon Rail	66401
			Registered	92 76 0309 401-6 N-CN
			Hire to CargoNet Norway	
			Modified for Sweden and Norway operations	
			Renumbered	T66 401 / 92 74 0066 401-1 S-BRLL
			2015 hire to Rushrail, Sweden	T66 401
20018352-02	11/02	HSBC Rail	CargoNet, Norway	66 402, Di9-02
			03/09 sold to Beacon Rail	66 402
			Registered	92 76 0309 402-4 N-CN
			Hire to CargoNet, Norway	
			Modified for Sweden and Norway operations	
			Renumbered	T66 402 / 92 74 0066 402-9 S-BRLL
			2015 hire to Rushrail, Sweden	T66 402
			12/16 hire to Hector Rail, Sweden	T66 402

20018352-03	11/02	HSBC Rail	CargoNet, Norway	66 403, Di9-03
			03/09 sold to Beacon Rail	66 403
			Registered	92 76 0309 403-2 N-CN
			03/09 hire to CargoNet, Norway	
			Modified for Sweden and Norway operations	
			2015 hire to Cargolink, Norway	T66 403
			Exported to UK 03/19 for GBRf renumber 66792	
20018352-04	11/02	HSBC Rail	CargoNet, Norway	66 404, Di9-04
			03/09 sold to Beacon Rail	66 404
			Registered	92 76 0309 404-0 N-CN
			03/09 hire to CargoNet, Norway	
			Modified for Sweden and Norway operations	
			Renumbered	T66 404
			2015 hire to Cargolink, Norway	T66 404
			Exported to UK 03/19 for GBRf renumber 66793	
20018352-05	11/02	HSBC Rail	CargoNet, Norway	66 405, Di9-05
			03/09 sold to Beacon Rail	66 405
			Registered	92 76 0309 405-7 N-CN
			03/09 hire to CargoNet, Norway	
			Modified for Sweden and Norway operations	
			Renumbered	T66 405
			2015 hire to Rushrail, Sweden	T66 405
			12/16 hire to Hector Rail, Sweden	T66 405
20018352-06	11/02	HSBC Rail	CargoNet, Norway	66 406, Di9-06
			03/09 sold to Beacon Rail	66 406
			Registered	92 76 0309 406-5 N-CN
			03/09 hire to CargoNet, Norway	
			Modified for Sweden and Norway operations	
			Renumbered	T66 406 / 92 74 0066 406-0 S-BRLL
			2015 hire to Rushrail, Sweden	T66 406
			12/16 hire to Hector Rail, Sweden	T66 406
20018360-01	05/02	Porterbrook Leasing	European Rail Shuttle (05/11/02)	PB11
			Sold to CB Rail 16/11/04	6605 EBA No. EBA 00L13C 016
			European Rail Shuttle Railways	6605 Named: *Blue Escabalur*
			09/09 hire to SNCF, Belgium	6605
			Registered	92 80 1266 016-5 D-SFB
			03/10 hire to CrossRail, Belgium	DE6605
			04/10 sold to Ascondos Rail, Luxembourg	PB11
			Hire to Captrain, Belgium	6605 / 92 80 1266 016-5 D-CTB
			02/16 fitted with ETCS	
			07/16 sold to Beacon Rail, Luxembourg	PB11
20018360-02	06/02	Porterbrook Leasing	Dillen & Le Jeune Cargo Rly (09/12/02)	PB12
			Sold to CB Rail 16/11/04	PB12 EBA No. EBA 00L13C 017
			08/15 hire to European Rail Shuttle	
			06/08 hire to CrossRail, Belgium	PB12
			Registered	92 80 1266 017-3 D-XRAIL named *Marleed*
			06/16 sold to Beacon Rail Luxembourg	PB12
20018360-03	06/02	Porterbrook Leasing	Häfen und Güterverkehr Köln (HGK)	PB13 then DE65
			Sold to CB Rail 16/11/04	PB13 EBA No. EBA 00L13C 065
			01/06 Häfen und Güterverkehr Köln (HGK)	DE65
			06/08 hire to CrossRail, Belgium	PB13
			Registered	92 80 1266 018-1 D-XRAIL. nameed Ilse
			04/10 sold to Ascendos Rail, Luxembourg	PB13
			06/16 sold to Beacon Rail, Luxembourg	PB13
20018360-04	07/02	Porterbrook Leasing	Dillen & Le Jeune Cargo (09/12/02)	PB14
			Sold to CB Rail 16/11/04	PB14 EBA No. EBA 00L13C 018
			06/08 hire to CrossRail, Belgium	PB14
			Registered	92 80 1266 065-2 D-XRAIL
			Sold to Ascendos Rail, Luxembourg	PB14
			Modified for for DB, SNCB, NS plus ETCS Level 2	
			17/6/16 sold to Beacon Rail	PB14 Allocated UK No. 66998
20018360-05	07/02	Porterbrook Leasing	Häfen und Güterverkehr Köln (HGK)	PB15 then DE66
			Sold to CB Rail 16/11/04	PB15 EBA No. EBA 00L13C 019
			01/06 Häfen und Güterverkehr Belgium (HGK)	PB15
			04/08 hire to CrossRail Belgium	PB15
			Registered	92 80 1266 066-0 D-XRAIL
			Sold to Ascendos Rail, Luxembourg	PB15
			04/13 hire to Rotterdam Rail Feeding	PB15
			17/6/16 sold to Beacon Rail, Luxembourg	PB15
20018360-06	07/02	Porterbrook Leasing	Häfen und Güterverkehr Köln (HGK)	PB16 then DE67
			Sold to CB Rail 16/11/04	PB16 EBA No. EBA 00L13C 067
			European Rail Shuttle (07/12/05)	6613
			Registered	92 80 1266 067-6 D-CBRL
			11/07 hire to Veolia Cargo, Netherlands	6613
			10/09 hire to Nordbayerische Eisenbahngesellschaft, Germany	266 067-6
			03/10 hire to Rurtalbahn Germany RTB	V263
			Registered	92 80 1266 067-8 D-RTB
			03/10 sold to Ascendos Rail, Luxembourg	PB16
			05/10 hire to Captrain, Belgium	6607
			04/11 hire to Osthannoversche Eisenbahnen, Germany	PB16 / 92 80 1266 067-8 D-OHE
			11/11 hire to CFL Cargo, Germany	PB16
			07/12 hire to HGK Germany	DE67 / 92 80 1266 067-8 D-HGK
			17/6/16 sold to Beacon Rail, Luxembourg	PB16

20018360-07	07/02	Porterbrook Leasing	ShortLines, Rotterdam (09/01/03)	PB17	
			Hire to Rail4Chem, Belgium (11/10/04)	PB17	
			Sold to CB Rail 16/11/04	PB17	EBA No. EBA 00L13C 021
			Rail4Chem, Benelux	PB17	
			12/09 hire to Veolia Cargo, NL	PB017	
			01/10 hire to Captrain Netherlands	PB017	
			06/04/10 sold to Ascendos Rail, Luxembourg	PB17	
			02/11 hire to RTB Cargo, Germany	V267	
			Registered	92 80 1266 021-6 D-RTB	
			17/6/16 sold to Beacon Rail, Luxembourg	PB17	
			09/16 hire to RTB Cargo	V267 / 92 80 1266 021-5 D-RTBC	
20018360-08	04/03	Porterbrook Leasing	European Rail Shuttle 08/03	PB18	
			Hire ShortLines, Rotterdam (09/03)	PB18	
			Hire Dillen & Le Jeune Cargo Rly (05/12/03)	PB18	
			Sold to CB Rail 16/11/04		EBA No. EBA 00L13C 022
			06/08 hire to Crossrail	PB18	
			04/10 sold to Ascendos Rail, Luxembourg	PB18	
			hire to Eisenbahngesellschaft, Germany	PB18	
			Registered	92 80 1266 022-3 D-ITL	
			03/13 hire to Captrain, Belgium	PB18	
			04/13 hire to Captrain, Germany as	92 80 1266 02203 D-CTD	
			06/15 hire to RTB Cargo as	V271 / 92 80 1266 022-3 D-RTBC	
			17/6/16 sold to Beacon Rail, Luxembourg	V271 92 80 1266 022-3 D-RTBC	
20018360-09	04/02	Porterbrook Leasing	Heavy Haul Power International (08/03)	PB19	
			Hire ShortLines, Rotterdam (09/03)	PB19	
			Hire European Rail Shuttle (09/03)	PB19	
			Hire Dillen & Le Jeune Cargo Rly (10/03)	PB19	
			Sold to CB Rail 16/11/04	PB19	EBA No. EBA 00L13C 023
			Hire Dillen & Le Jeune Cargo Railway	PB19	
			Eichholz Verkehr & Logistik, Germany (01/03/05)	PB19	
			06/08 hire to Crossrail, Belgium	PB19	
			06/04/10 sold to Ascendos Rail, Luxembourg	PB19	
			08/11 hire to HGK, Germany	DE678	
			Registered	92 80 1266 023-1 D-HGK	
			08/12 hire to RheinCargo, Germany	DE678 / 92 80 1266 023-1 D-RHC	
			17/06/16 sold to Beacon Rail, Luxembourg	PB19	
20018360-10	03/02	Porterbrook Leasing	European Rail Shuttle (08/03)	PB20	
			Hire Dillen & Le Jeune Cargo Rly (07/12/03)	PB20	
			Sold to CB Rail 16/11/04	PB20	EBA No. EBA 00L13C 024
			06/08 hire to Crossrail, Belgium	PB20	
			06/04/10 sold to Ascendos Rail, Luxembourg	PB20	
			hire to Railtraxx, Belgium	PB20	
			Registered	92 80 1266 024-9 D-RTX	
			17/06/16 sold to Beacon Rail, Luxembourg	PB20	
			Renumbered	266 024-9 / 92 80 1266 024-9 D-RTX	
20028453-01	03/03	HSBC Rail	Häfen und Güterverkehr Köln (HGK)	DE668 (Originally No. DE168)	
			01/07 Registered	92 80 1266 068-6 D-HGK	
					EBA No. EBA 00L13C 668
			03/09 sold to Beacon Rail, UK	DE668	
			03/09 hire to HGK, Germany	DE668	named *Klaus Meschede*
			08/12 hire to RheinCargo, Germany	DE668 / 92 80 1266 068-6 D-RHC	
20028453-02	03/03	HSBC Rail	Häfen und Güterverkehr Köln (HGK)	DE669 (Originally No. DE169)	
					EBA No. EBA 00L13C 669
			Registered	92 80 1266 069-4 D-HGK	
			03/09 sold to Beacon Rail, UK	DE669	
			08/12 hire to RheinCargo	DE669 / 92 80 1266 069-4 D-RHC	
20028453-03	04/03	HSBC Rail	Häfen und Güterverkehr Köln (HGK)	DE670 (Originally No. DE170)	
					EBA No. EBA 00L13C 670
			Registered	92 80 1266 070-2 D	
			03/09 sold to Beacon Rail, UK		
			Hire to Häfen und Güterverkehr Köln (HGK)	92 80 1266 070-2 D	
			08/12 hire to Rhein Cargo	DE670 / 92 80 1266 070-2 D-RHC	
20028453-04	04/03	HSBC Rail	Häfen und Güterverkehr Köln (HGK)	DE671 (Originally No. DE171)	
					EBA No. EBA 00L13C 671
			Registered	92 80 1266 071-0 D-HGK	
			03/09 sold to Beacon Rail, UK	DE671	
			Lease to Häfen und Güterverkehr Köln (HGK)		
			08/12 hire to Rhein Cargo	DE671 / 92 80 1266 071-0 D-RHC	
20028453-05	04/03	HSBC Rail	Häfen und Güterverkehr Köln (HGK)	DE672 (Originally No. DE172)	
					EBA No. EBA 00L13C 672
			Registered	92 80 1266 072-8 D-HGK	
			03/09 sold to Beacon Rail, UK	DE672	
			Hire to Häfen und Güterverkehr Köln (HGK)		
			08/12 hire to Rhein Cargo	DE672 / 92 80 1266 072-8 D-RHC	
20038513-01	08/03	HSBC Rail	European Rail Shuttle (ERS) (24/12/03)	6606	EBA No. EBA 00L13C 025
			03/09 sold to Beacon Rail		
			Registered	92 80 1266 025-6 D-BRLL	
			04/09 Hire to Freightliner Poland		
			01/10 Hire to Crossrail Benelux as	DE6606	
			-/13 Hired to RushRail, Sweden	T664025	
			10/13 To UK for use by GB Railfreight	66750	
20038513-02	08/03	HSBC Rail	European Rail Shuttle (ERS) (19/12/03)	6607	EBA No. EBA 00L13C 026
			03/09 sold to Beacon Rail	6607	
			Registered	92 80 1266 026-4 D-BRLL	
			04/09 Hire to Freightliner Poland	6607	
			01/10 Hire to Crossrail Benelux	DE6607	

			-/12 Hire to Lappwaldahn, Weferlingen (LWB)	DE6607
			Registered	92 80 1266 026-4 D-LWB
			03/16 renumbered	92 80 1266 026-4 D-BRLL
			Hired to Railtraxx, Beligum	92 80 1266 026-4 D-BRLL
			05/16 hired to HHPI, Germany	DE6607
			05/17 hired to Freightliner Poland	513-02
20038513-03	08/03	HSBC Rail	European Rail Shuttle (ERS) (19/12/03)	6608 EBA No. EBA 00L13C 027
			03/09 sold to Beacon Rail	
			Registered	92 80 1266 027-2 D-BRLL
			Hire to HHPI, Germany	29004
20038513-04	08/03	HSBC Rail	European Rail Shuttle (ERS) (19/12/03)	6609 EBA No. EBA 00L13C 028
			03/09 sold to Beacon Rail	
			Registered	92 80 1266 028-0 D-BRLL
			01/10 Hired to HHPI, Germany	29006
			08/13 to UK for use by GB Railfreight	66751
20038513-05	08/03	HSBC Rail	European Rail Shuttle (ERS) (24/12/03)	6610 EBA No. EBA 00L13C 029
				Named: *10 Years ERS 1994-2004*
			03/09 sold to Beacon Rail	
			Registered	92 80 1266 029-8
			02/10 Hired to HHPI, Germany	29005
20038513-06	03/04	GM/EMD	Spot hire loco	ER6
			02/05 sold to Mitsui Rail Capital Europe	EBA No. EBA 00L13C 033
			Hire Dillen & Le Jeune Cargo Railway (DLC)	ER6 / MRCE 513-6 / DE6301
			2007 sold to KB Lease, Belgium	
			Registered	92 80 1266033-0 D-XRAIL
			Hire to Crossrail Benelux	DE6301
20038513-07	03/04	GM/EMD	Spot hire loco	ER7
			Sold to Mitsui Rail Capital Europe	EBA No. EBA 00L13C 034
			Hire Dillen & Le Jeune Cargo Railway (DLC)	ER7 / MRCE 513-7 / DE6302
			2007 sold to KB Lease, Belgium	
			Registered	92 80 1266034-8 D-XRAIL
			Hire to Crossrail Benelux	DE6302
20038513-08	03/04	GM/EMD	Spot hire loco	ER8
			Sold to Mitsui Rail Capital Europe	MRCE 513-8 EBA No. EBA 00L13C 035
			Hire Mitteldeutsche Eisenbahn GmbH (11/04)	398
			Hire Rail4Chem, Benelux (03/12/04)	ER8
			02/05 Hire Häfen und Güterverkehr Köln (HGK)	DE54
			Hire European Rail Shuttle (ERS) (21/06/05)	6612
			Registered	92 80 1266 035-5 D-DISPO
			-/09 hire to HTRS, Rotterdam	513-8
			06/12 hire to Rotterdam Rail Feeding	513-8
			06/13 hire to Railtraxx, Beligum	266 035-5
			09/15 Sold to Beacon Rail	513-8
20038513-09	03/04	GM/EMD	Spot hire loco	ER9
			Sold to Mitsui Rail Capital Europe	
			Hire Azfet Container Transport System (ACTS)	ER9 / MRCE 513-9
			Hire European Rail Shuttle (ERS) (25/05/06)	MRCE 513-9
			Hire Rail4Chem, Benelux (25/08/06)	MRCE 513-9 EBA No. EBA 00L13C 036
			Hire European Rail Shuttle (ERS) (30/09/06)	MRCE 513-9
			Registered	92 80 1266 036-3 D-DISPO
			Hire to ACTS	513-9
			07/11 hire to Osthannoversche Eisenbahn, Germany	513-9
			-/11 hire to CFL Cargo, Germany	513-9
			01/13 hire to Häfen und Güterverkehr Köln (HGK)	DE679
			02/13 hire to CTL Logistics, Germany	513-9
			05/13 hire to HTRS, Netherlands	513-9
			06/13 hire to Locon, Netherlands	513-9
			08/13 hire to ETF, France	513-9
			07/15 sold to Beacon Rail	92 80 1266 036-3 D-BRLL
			-/16 hire to CTL Logistics	513-9
20038513-10	03/04	GM/EMD	Spot hire loco	ER10
			Sold to Mitsui Rail Capital Europe	
			Hire Rail4Chem, Benelux (08/02/05)	ER10 / MRCE 513-10
			03/05 hire Azfet Container Transport System (ACTS)	ER10
			Hire Dillen & Le Jeune Cargo Railway (DLC)	DE6303 EBA No. EBA 00L13C 037
			Registered	92 80 1266 037-1 D-DISPO
			06/08 hire to Crossrail, Beligum	DE6303
			10/10 hire to ERSR, Netherlands	513-10
			11/11 hire to RTB Cargo, Germany	V268
			08/12 hire to RheinCargo, Germany	DE675
			01/13 hire to RheinCargo, Germany	DE679
			03/15 hire to HHPI, Germany	513-10
			Sold to Beacon Rail	513-10 / 92 80 1266 037-1 D-BRLL
			04/16 hire to RheinCargo	DE279
			03/17 hire to B Logistics, Belgium	513-10
			04/17 hire to Lineas Group, Belgium	513-10
20038545-01	11/03	GM/EMD	Spot hire loco	EC1
			Sold to Deutsche Lease	EBA No. EBA 00L13C 030
			Hire Rail4Chem, Benelux (21/07/04)	66 020
			12/07 renumbered	6602
			12/09 hire to Veolia Cargo, Netherlands	6602
			-/10 hire to Captrain, Netherlands	6602
			Registered	92 80 1266 030-6
			-/11 hired to Captrain, Germany	92 80 1266 030-6
			-/12 operated by Regiobahn Bitterfeld, Berlin	6602
			-/13 operated by Eisenbahngesellschaft, Dresden	6602

20038545-02	11/03	Porterbrook	Spot hire loco	EC2
			08/04 Hire Railion, Nederland	RN 266 452-2 EBA No. EBA 00L13C 031
			11/04 sold to CB Rail	266 452-2
			02/09 lease to DB Schenker, Netherlands	266 452-2
			11/09 hired to Fret SNCF, Belgium	6602
			Registered	92 80 1266 031-4
			Sold to Ascendos Rail Leasing, Luxembourg	RL001
			05/10 lease to Captrain, Belgium	6606
			-/12 hire to CFL Cargo, Denmark	RL001
			01/13 hire to HTRS, Netherlands	RL001
			07/13 hire to Captrain, Belgium	RL001
			10/13 hire Railtraxx, Belgium	RL001
			Renumbered	266 013-4
			Sold to Beacon Rail, Luxembourg	RL001
20038545-03	11/03	Porterbrook	Spot hire loco	EC3
			Railion, Nederland (26/08/04)	266 453-0 EBA No. EBA 00L13C 032
			11/04 sold to CB Rail	
			Registered	92 80 1266 032-2
			02/09 lease to DB Schenker, Netherlands	266 453-0
			Sold to Ascendos Rail, Luxembourg	RL002
			-/10 hire to CFL, Denmark	255-453-0
			-/12 hire to Railtraxx, Belgium	RL002
			03/13 hire to HHPI, Germany	29006
			06/14 hire to Lappwaldbahn, Germany	RL002
			01/15 hire to Rurtanbahn Cargo, Germany	V270
			06/16 sold to Beacon Rail, Luxembourg	RL002
			09/16 hire to Rurtanbahn Cargo, Germany	V270
			-/17 hire to HHPI, Germany	RL002
20038561-01	11/04	GM/EMD	Spot hire loco	EM1
			Sold to Mitsui Rail Capital Europe	
			03/05 hire to Häfen und Güterverkehr Köln (HGK)	DE673 / MRCE 561-01
			Registered	92 80 1266 038-9 EBA No. EBA 00L13C 038
			-/11 hire to TXL Logistics, Germany	561-1
			-/12 hire to CFL Logistics, Germany	561-1
			08/14 hire to Freightliner Poland	561-1
			07/15 sold to Beacon Rail	561-1
			-/16 hire to Rotterdam Rail Feeding	561-01
			11/16 hire to HHPI, Germany	561-01
20038561-02	11/04	GM/EMD	Spot hire loco	EM2
			04/05 sold to Mitsui Rail Capital Europe	
			Hire to Häfen und Güterverkehr Köln (HGK)	DE674 / MRCE 561-02
			Registered as 92 80 1266 039-7	EBA No. EBA 00L13C 039
			-/11 hire to Freightliner, Poland	66012 / 92 51 3650 015-2
			06/13 hire to HTRS, Netherlands	561-2
			08/13 hire to ETF, France	561-2
			07/16 sold to Beacon Rail	561-2 / 92 80 1266 039-7
			05/16 hire to Freightliner Poland	66012
20038561-03	11/04	GM/EMD	Spot hire loco	EM3
			Sold to Mitsui Rail Capital Europe	
			Hire to OstHavelländische Eisenbahn (OHE)	561-03
			06/05 hire European Rail Shuttle (ERS)	6611 EBA No. EBA 00L13C 040
			Registered	92 80 1266 040-5 D-DISPO
			01/13 hire to Häfen und Güterverkehr Köln (HGK)	
			01/13 hire to RheinCargo	
			08/13 hire to ETF, France	561-3
			08/15 sold to Beacon Rail	561-3 / 92 80 1266 040-5 D-BRLL
			07/16 hire to Rotterdam Rail Feeding	561-03
			06/18 hire to Freightland, Poland	561-03
20038561-04	11/04	GM/EMD	Spot hire loco	EM4
			Sold to Mitsui Rail Capital Europe	
			06/05 hire Dillen & Le Jeune Cargo Railway (DLC)	DE6304 / MRCE 561-04
			Hire Rail4Chem, Benelux	DE6304
			09/05 hire to Dillen & Le Jeune Cargo Railway (DLC)	DE6304 EBA No. EBA 00L13C 041
			Registered	92 80 1266 041-3
			06/08 hire to Crossrail, Belgium	DE6304
			10/08 hire to ACTS, Netherlands	561-4
			11/09 hire to ESR, Netherlands	561-4
			12/09 hire to Rurtalbahn, Germany	V262
			02/12 hire to ESR Netherlands	561-4
			01/13 hire to Häfen und Güterverkehr Köln (HGK)	DE55
			01/13 hire to RheinCargo, Germany	DE55
			08/13 hire to ETF, France	561-4
			09/15 sold to Beacon Rail	561-4 / 92 80 1266 041-3 D-BRLL
			06/16 hire to Rotterdam Rail Feeding	561-04
20038561-05	11/04	GM/EMD	Spot hire loco	EM5
			07/05 sold to Mitsui Rail Capital	
			07/05 hire Häfen und Güterverkehr Köln (HGK)	561-05
			Hire Connex Cargo/Veolia Transport	561-05
			07/05 Hire to RegioBahn, Bitterfeld, Berlin	561-05
			05/06 Hire to Dortmunder Eisenbahn	561-05 EBA No. EBA 00L13C 042
			06/06 hire to Veolia Cargo	
			Registered	92 80 1266 042-1 F-DSPO
			07/10 hire to ATCS, Netherlands	561-5
			03/11 hire to HTRS, Netherlands	
			07/11 hire to ERSR, Netherlands	561-5
			01/13 hire to Häfen und Güterverkehr Köln (HGK)	DE680

Traction Transition - GM/EMD power in the UK and Ireland

			01/13 hire to RheinCargo, Germany	DE680
			09/15 hire to HHPI, Germany	561-5
			07/15 sold to Beacon Rail	561-5
			01/17 hire to Rotterdam Rail Feeding	561-5
20048653-01	01/06	Mitsui Rail Capital	Mitsui Rail Capital Europe	8653-01 / EMCC No. JT1
			01/07 hire Veolia Transport	8653-01 EBA No. EBA 05D21K 001
			Registered	92 80 1266 111-4 D DISPO
			01/07 hire to Veolia Cargo, Netherlands	
			01/10 hire to Captrain, Netherlands	
			08/10 hire to Häfen und Güterverkehr Köln (HGK)	DE675
			08/12 hire to RheinCargo, Germany	DE675
			01/14 hire to Häfen und Güterverkehr Köln (HGK)	DE675
			05/15 sold to Beacon Rail	8653-01 / 92 80 1266 111-4 D-BRLL
			05/17 hire to Rotterdam Rail Feeding	8653-01
			08/17 hire to VTG Rail Logistics, Germany	8653-01
			09/17 hire to Retack, Hamburg	8653-01
			06/18 hire to Rotterdam Rail Feeding	653-01
20048653-02	01/06	Mitsui Rail Capital	Tested in Switzerland 02-06-2006	MRCE 653-02 / EMCC No. JT2
			At NedTrain Tilburg 14/2/06-04/12/06	6615 EBA No. EBA 05D21K 002
			12/06 hire European Rail Shuttle (ERS)	6615 Named: *Kayden*
			Registered	92 80 1266 112-2 D-DISPO
			04/10 hire to ACTS, Netherlands	653-2
			10/10 hire to ERSR, Netherlands	6615
			05/11 hire Rail Transport Services, Germany	653-2
			01/13 hire to Häfen und Güterverkehr Köln (HGK)	DE681
			01/13 hire to RheinCargo, Germany	DE681
			01/15 hire to ETF, France	653-02
			09/15 sold to Beacon Rail	653-02
			03/16 hire to Lappwaldbahn, Germany	653-02
			06/16 hire to HSL Logistics, Germany	653-2
			08/16 operated by HSL Logitics, Belgium	653-2
			10/16 hired to Railtraxx, Belgium	653-2
			03/17 hired to Lineas Group, Belgium	653-2
			10/17 operated by Crossrail, Belgium	653-2
20048653-03	01/06	Mitsui Rail Capital	At NedTrain Tilburg 14/2/06-05/12/06	MRCE 653-03 / EMCC No. JT3
			12/06 hire European Rail Shuttle (ERS)	6614 EBA No. EBA 05D21K 003
			Registered	92 80 1266 113-0 D-DISPO
			10/09 hire to ERSR, Netherlands	6614 Named: *Lauryn*
			07/10 hire to Rail Transport Services, Germany	653-03
			05/12 hire to Eisenbahngesellschaft, Germany	653-03
			01/13 hire to RheinCargo, Germany	DE682
			06/15 sold to Beacon Rail	653-03
			04/17 hire to Railtraxx, Belgium	653-03
			04/17 hire Rotterdam Rail Feeding	653-03
			09/17 hire to HSL Logestics, Germany	653-03
			02/18 operated by Lineas Group, Belgium	653-03
20048653-04	01/06	Mitsui Rail Capital	ETCS test loco, used on Betuweroute	653-04 / EMCC No. JT4
				EBA No. EBA 05D21K 004
			06/07 hire Azfet Container Transport System (ACTS)	653-04
			Registered	92 80 1266 114-8 D-DISPO
			10/09 hire ERSR, Netherlands	JT-4
			11/09 hire to Azfet Container Transport System (ACTS)	653-4
			06/10 hire to ERSR, Netherlands	JT-4
			07/10 hire Rurtalbahn, Germany	653-4
			09/10 hire to Odin Logistics, Germany	653-4
			01/13 hire to RheinCargo, Germany	DE653
			05/15 sold to Beacon Rail	653-04 92 80 1266 114-8 D-BRLL
			06/17 hire to Railtraxx, Belgium	653-04
			08/17 hire HSL Logistics, Germany	653-04
			06/18 hire to VTG Rail Logistics, Germany	653-04
			07/18 operated by Retrack, Germany	653-04
20048653-05	01/06	Mitsui Rail Capital	Hire Rurtalbahn, Germany	MRCE 653-05 / EMCC No. JT5
			10/06 hire Häfen und Güterverkehr Köln (HGK)	DE55 EBA No. EBA 05D21K 005
			Registered	92 80 1266 115-8 D-DISPO
			04/07 Trainsport AG, Belgium	653-05
			12/11 hire to HTRS, Netherlands	653-05
			02/14 hire to Rotterdam Rail Feeding	653-05
			05/15 sold to Beacon Rail	653-05
			01/16 hire to Captrain, Netherlands	653-05
			03/16 hire to Freightliner Poland	653-05
20048653-06	02/06	Mitsui Rail Capital	At NedTrain Tilburg 13/4/06-06/12/06	653-06 / EMCC No. JT6
			12/06 hire European Rail Shuttle (ERS)	6616 EBA No. EBA 05D21K 006
			Registered	92 80 1266 116-3
			Destroyed in collision on 24/09/09 at Barendrecht	
20048653-07	02/06	Mitsui Rail Capital	At NedTrain Tilburg 13/4/06-07/12/06	653-07 / EMCC No. JT7
			12/06 European Rail Shuttle (ERS)	6617 EBA No. EBA 05D21K 007
			Registered	92 80 1266 117-1 D-DISPO
			08/13 hire to Häfen und Güterverkehr Köln (HGK)	DE685
			08/13 hire to RheinCargo, Germany	DE685
			05/15 sold to Beacon Rail	653-07
			09/16 hire to HSL Logistics, Germany	653-07
			05/18 hire to Lineas, Belgium, HSL Logistics	653-07
20048653-08	02/06	Mitsui Rail Capital	11/06 hire Rail4Chem, Benelux	653-08 / EMCC No. JT8 Named: *Wessel*
				EBA No. EBA 05D21K 008
			Registered	92 80 1266 118-9
			12/09 hire to Veolia Cargo, Netherlands	653-08

			06/10 hire to Captrain, Netherlands	653-08
			01/13 hire to Häfen und Güterverkehr Köln (HGK)	DE686
			08/13 hire to RheinCargo, Germany	DE686
			06/15 hire to Railtraxx, Belgium	266 118-9
			09/15 sold to Beacon Rail	653-08
			05/18 hire to Railtraxx, Belgium as 266 118-9	
20048653-09	02/06	Mitsui Rail Capital	At NedTrain, Tilburg 11/06 - 03/07	653-09 / EMCC No. JT9
			03/07 hire Dillen & Le Jeune Cargo Railway (DLC)	DE6305 EBA No. EBA 05D21K 009
			Registered	92 80 1266 119-7
			08/08 hire to Osthannoversche Eisenbarhan, Germany	653-09
			05/12 hire to HTRS, Netherlands	653-09
			06/12 hire to Rail Transport Services, Germany	653-09
			08/13 hire to ETF, France	653-09
			05/15 hire to Freightliner Poland	653-09
			07/15 sold to Beacon Rail	653-09 / 92 80 1266 119-7
20048653-10	02/06	Mitsui Rail Capital	NedTrain, Tilburg, ETMS cab signal testing	MRCE 653-10 (EMCC No. JT10)
			Registered	92 80 1266 120-5 EBA No. EBA 05D21K 010
			02/10 hire to Veolia Cargo, Netherlands	653-0
			07/10 hire to Captrain, Netherlands	653-10
			11/10 hire to Freightliner, Poland	653-10
			01/13 hire Häfen und Güterverkehr Köln (HGK)	DE684
			01/13 hire to RheinCargo, Germany	DE684
			07/15 sold to Beacon Rail	653-10
			05/16 hire to Freightliner, Poland	653-10
			08/16 hire to RheinCargo, Germany	DE684
			02/17 hire to Rotterdam Rail Feeding	653-10
			06/18 hire to Crossrail, Belgium	653-10
20058725-01	11/06	CB Rail	As EMCC Demonstrator	EMCC No. EU01 Delivered in Green livery
			12/07 hire to Railion	266 107-2
			Registered	92 80 1266 107-2 D-DB
			02/09 hire to DB Schenker, Netherlands	
			03/10 hire to Railpool, Germany	92 80 1266 107-2 D-RPOOL
			03/10 operated by Eichholz, Germany	266-107-2
			05/11 hire to Häfen und Güterverkehr Köln (HGK)	DE677
			01/13 Sold to Macquaire European Rail, Luxembourg	266 107-2 01/13
			06/13 hire to Crossrail, Belgium	DE6313
			10/14 hire to Eisenbahngesellschaft, Germany	266 107-2
20058725-02	11/06	Angel Trains	08/07 Hire to Freightliner Poland	66001 / EMDD No. EU02
			Registered as	92 51 3650 000-4 PL-FPL
			01/10 sold to Alpha Trains 01/10	
20058725-03	11/06	Angel Trains	08/07 Hire to Freightliner Poland	66002 / EMDD No. EU03
			Registered	92 51 3650 001-2 PL-FPL
			01/10 sold to Alpha Trains	
20058725-04	11/06	Angel Trains	08/07 Hire to Freightliner Poland	66003 / EMDD No. EU04
			Registered	92 51 3650 002-0 PL-FPL
			01/10 sold to Alpha Trains	
20058725-05	11/06	Angel Trains	08/07 Hire to Freightliner Poland	66004 / EMDD No. EU05
			Registered	92 51 3650 003-8 PL-FPL
			01/10 sold to Alpha Trains	
20058725-06	11/06	CB Rail	09/07 Hire to Rail4Chem	CB1000 / EMDD No. EU06
			Registered	92 80 1266 105-6 D-RCHEM
			12/09 hire to Veolia Cargo, Netherlands	CB1000
			01/10 hire to Captrain, Netherlands	CB1000 / 92 80 1266 105-6 D-CTD
			01/13 sold to Macquaire European Rail, Luxembourg	CB1000
20058725-07	11/06	CB Rail	08/07 Hire to Rail4Chem	CB1001 / EMDD No. EU07
			Registered	92 80 1266 106-4 D-RCHEM
			07/08 hire to Veolia Cargo, Germany	CB1001
			08/08 hire to Regiobahn Bitterfeld, Germany	CB1001
			09/08 hire to rail4Chem	CB1001
			12/09 hire to Veolia Cargo, Netherlands	CB1001
			04/10 hire to Captrain, Netherlands	CB1001
			02/12 hire by Eisenbahngesellschaft, Germany	CB1001
			01/13 sold to Macquarie European Rail, Luxemburg	CB1001
20058725-08	11/06	KBC Lease	10/07 Hire to Dillen & Le Jeune Cargo Railway (DLC)	DE6306 / EMDD No. EU08
			Registered	92 80 1266 101-9 D-DLC
			04/08 Hire to Crossrail, Belgium	DE6306
20058725-09	11/06	KBC Lease	10/07 Hire to Dillen & Le Jeune Cargo Railway (DLC)	DE6307 / EMDD No. EU09
			Registered	92 80 1266 102-3
			06/08 Hire to Crossrail	DE6307
20058725-10	11/06	KBC Lease	08/07 Hire to Dillen & Le Jeune Cargo Railway (DLC)	DE6308 / EMDD No. EU10
			Registered	92 80 1266 103-1
			06/08 Hire to Crossrail	DE6308
20058725-11	11/06	KBC Lease	08/07 Hire to Dillen & Le Jeune Cargo Railway (DLC)	EU11 / DE6309
			Registered	92 80 1266 104-9
			06/08 Hire to Crossrail, Belgium	DE6309
20058725-12	11/06	Angel Trains	10/07 hire to Freightliner Poland	66005 / EMDD No. EU12
			Registered	92 51 3650 004-6 PL-FPL
			01/10 sold to Alpha Trains, Belgium	
20058725-13	11/06	Angel Trains	10/07 hire to Freightliner Poland	66006 / EMDD No. EU13
			Registered	92 51 3650 005-3 PL-FPL
			01/10 sold to Alpha Trains, Belgium	
20058725-14	11/06	Angel Trains	03/08 hire to Freightliner Poland	66007 / EMDD No. EU14
			Registered	92 51 3650 006-1 PL-FPL
			01/10 sold to Alpha Trains, Belgium	
20068864-01	09/07	ECR	Euro Cargo Rail, Paris	77001
			Registered	92 87 0077 001-1 F-ECR
			12/15 sold to DB-Schenker	077 001-1

20068864-02	09/07	ECR	Euro Cargo Rail, Paris Registered 12/15 sold to DB Schenker	77002 92 87 0077 002-9 F-ECR 077 002-9
20068864-03	09/07	ECR	Euro Cargo Rail, Paris Registered 02/16 hire to DB-S, Netherlands	77003 92 87 0077 003-7 F-ECR 77003
20068864-04	09/07	ECR	Euro Cargo Rail, Paris Registered 01/16 sold to DB Schenker	77004 92 87 0077 004-5 F-ECR 077 004-5
20068864-05	09/07	ECR	Euro Cargo Rail, Paris Registered 06/10 hire to DB-S, Germany	77005 92 87 0077 005-2 F-ECR 247 005-2
20068864-06	10/07	ECR	Euro Cargo Rail, Paris Registered 10/14 hire to DB-S, Netherlands	77006 92 87 0077 006-0 F-ECR 77006
20068864-07	10/07	ECR	Euro Cargo Rail, Paris Registered 04/10 hire to DB Schenker, Germany 03/13 sold to DB-Schenker, Germany	77007 92 87 0077 007-6 F-ECR 247 007-8 247 007-8
20068864-08	10/07	ECR	Euro Cargo Rail, Paris Registered 03/16 sold to DB-Schenker, Germany	77008 92 87 0077 008-6 F-ECR 077 008-6 03/16
20068864-09	10/07	ECR	Euro Cargo Rail, Paris Registered	77009 2 87 0077 009-4 F-ECR
20068864-10	2008	ECR	Euro Cargo Rail, Paris Registered 10/15 sold to DB-Schenker, Germany	77010 92 87 0077 010-2 F-ECR 077 010-2
20068864-11	2008	ECR	Euro Cargo Rail, Paris Registered 10/10 hire to DB-S, Germany 03/13 sold to DB-Schenker, Germany	77011 92 87 0077 011-0 F-ECR 247 011-0 247 011-0 / 92 80 1266 411-8 D-DB
20068864-12	2008	ECR	Euro Cargo Rail, Paris Registered 01/15 hire to Mitteldeutsche Eisenbahn (MEG) 07/15 sold to DB-Schenker, Germany 03/16 working for DB-S, Germany 03/18 renumbered	77012 92 87 0077 012-8 F-ECR 401 401 / 92 87 1266 012-8 F-MEG 077 012-8 321 / 92 87 0077 012-8 D-MEG
20068864-13	2008	ECR	Euro Cargo Rail, Paris Registered	77013 92 87 0077 013-6 F-ECR
20068864-14	2008	ECR	Euro Cargo Rail, Paris Registered 01/16 sold to DB-Schenker	77014 92 87 0077 014-4 F-ECR 077 014-4 01/16
20068864-15	2008	ECR	Euro Cargo Rail, Paris Registered -/09 hired to DB-S, Netherlands	77015 92 87 0077 015-1 F-ECR 77015
20068864-16	2010	ECR	Euro Cargo Rail, Paris Registered -/10 Hire to DB-Schenker, Germany 06/13 sold to DB-Schenker	77016 92 87 0077-016-9 F-ECR 247 016-9 / 92 80 1266 416-7 247 016-9 / 92 80 1266 416-7 D-DB
20068864-17	2008	ECR	Euro Cargo Rail, Paris Registered	77017 92 87 0077 017-7 F-ECR
20068864-18	2008	ECR	Euro Cargo Rail, Paris Registered 09/14 hire to DB-Schenker, Netherlands 07/16 sold to DB-Schenker, Germany	77018 92 87 0077 018-5 F-ECR 77018 077 018-5
20068864-19	2008	ECR	Euro Cargo Rail, Paris Registered	77019 92 87 0077 019-3 F-ECR
20068864-20	2008	ECR	Euro Cargo Rail, Paris Registered -/10 hire to DB-Schenker, Germany 09/13 sold to DB-Schenker	77020 92 87 0077 020-1 F-ECR 247 020-1 / 92 80 1266 420-9 247 020-1 / 92 80 1266 420-9
20068864-21	2008	ECR	Euro Cargo Rail, Paris Registered	77021 92 87 0077 021-9 F-ECR
20068864-22	2008	ECR	Euro Cargo Rail, Paris Registered 12/15 sold to DB-Schenker	77022 92 87 0077 022-7 F-ECR 077 022-7 / 92 87 0077 022-7 F-DB
20068864-23	2008	ECR	Euro Cargo Rail, Paris Registered 09/15 hire to DB-Schenker, Netherlands 03/16 hire to Mitteldeutsche Eisenbahn, Germany 12/15 sold to DB-Schenker, Germany	77023 2 87 0077 023-5 77023 077 023-5 077 023-5 / 92 87 0077 023-5 F-MEG
20068864-24	2008	ECR	Euro Cargo Rail, Paris Registered 12/13 sold to DB-Schenker, Germany	77024 92 87 0077 024-3 F-ECR 077 024-3 / 92 87 0077 024-3 F-DB
20068864-25	2008	ECR	Euro Cargo Rail Registered -/10 hire to DB-Schenker, Germany 02/15 hire to DB-Schenker, Netherlands 03/16 sold to DB-Cargo	77025 92 87 0077 025-0 F-ECR 247 025-0 / 92 80 1266 425-8 D-DB 77025 077 025-0 / 92 87 0077 025-0 F-DB
20068864-26	2008	ECR	Euro Cargo Rail, Paris Registered -/10 hire to DB-Schenker, Germany 05/13 sold to DB-Schenker, Germany	77026 92 87 0077 026-8 F-ECR 247 025-8 / 92 80 1266 426-6 D-DB 247 025-8 / 92 80 1266 426-6 D-DB
20068864-27	2008	ECR	Euro Cargo Rail, Paris Registered 04/16 sold to DB-Schenker, Germany	77027 92 87 0077 027-6 F-ECR 077 027-6 / 92 87 0077 027-6 F-DB

20068864-28	2008	ECR	Euro Cargo Rail, Paris Registered 04/16 sold to DB-Schenker	77028 92 87 0077 028-4 F-ECR 077 028-4 / 92 87 0077 028-4 F-DB
20068864-29	2008	ECR	Euro Cargo Rail, Paris Registered -/10 hire to DB-Schenker, Germany 05/13 sold to DB Schenker	77029 92 87 0077 029-2 F-ECR 247 029-2 / 92 80 1266 429-0 D-DB 247 029-2 / 92 80 1266 429-0 D-DB
20068864-30	2008	ECR	Euro Cargo Rail, Paris Registered 12/15 sold to DB Schenker, Germany	77030 92 87 0077 030-0 F-ECR 077 030-0 / 92 87 0077 030-0 F-DB
20068864-31	2008	ECR	Euro Cargo Rail, Paris Registered -/10 hire to DB-Schenker, Germany 09/13 sold to DB-Schenker, Germany	77031 92 87 0077 031-6 F-ECR 247 031-8 / 92 80 1266 431-6 D-DB 247 031-8 / 92 80 1266 431-6 D-DB
20068864-32	2008	ECR	Euro Cargo Rail, Paris Registered 04/16 sold to DB-Cargo, Germany	77032 92 87 0077 032-6 F-ECR 077 032-6 / 92 87 0077 032-6 F-DB
20068864-33	2008	ECR	Euro Cargo Rail, Paris Registered 04/16 sold to DB-Cargo, Germany	77033 92 87 0077 033-4 F-ECR 077 033-4 / 92 87 0077 032-6 F-DB
20068864-34	2008	ECR	Euro Cargo Rail, Paris Registered 09/10 hire to Mitteldeutsche Eisenbahn, Germany 11/10 hire to DB-Schenker, Germany 09/13 sold to DB-Schenker, Germany	77034 92 87 0077 034-2 F-ECR 247 034-2 247 034-2 / 92 80 1266 434-0 D-DB 247 034-2 / 92 80 1266 434-0 D-DB
20068864-35	2008	ECR	Euro Cargo Rail, Paris Registered 09/10 hire to DB-Schenker, Germany 03/16 sold to DB-Cargo, Germany	7035 92 87 0077 035-9 F-ECR 247 035-9 / 92 80 1266 435-7 D-DB 247 035-9 / 92 80 1266 435-7 D-DB
20068864-36	2008	ECR	Euro Cargo Rail, Paris Registered 09/15 hire to DB-Schenker, Netherlands 12/15 sold to DB-Schenker, Germany	77036 92 87 0077 036-7 F-ECR 77036 077 036-7 / 92 87 0077 036-7 F-DB)
20068864-37	2008	ECR	Euro Cargo Rail, Paris Registered	77037 92 87 0077 037-5 F-ECR
20068864-38	2008	ECR	Euro Cargo Rail, Paris Registered 09/10 hire to DB-Schenker, Germany 12/13 sold to DB-Schenker, Germany	77038 92 87 0077 038-3 F-ECR 247 038-3 / 92 80 1266 438-1 D-DB 247 038-3 / 92 80 1266 438-1 D-DB
20068864-39	2008	ECR	Euro Cargo Rail, Paris Registered 09/10 hire to DB-Schenker, Germany 12/13 sold to DB-Schenker, Germany	77039 92 87 0077 039-1 F-ECR 247 039-1 / 92 80 1266 439-9 D-DB 247 039-1 / 92 80 1266 439-9 D-DB
20068864-40	2008	ECR	Euro Cargo Rail, Paris Registered 09/16 sold to DB-Cargo, Germany	77040 92 87 0077 040-9 F-ECR 077 040-9 / 92 87 0077 040-9 F-DB
20068864-41	2008	ECR	Euro Cargo Rail, Paris Registered 09/10 hire to DB-Schenker, Germany 12/13 sold to DB-Cargo, Germany	77041 92 87 0077 041-7 F-ECR 247 041-7 / 92 80 1266 441-5 D-DB 247 041-7 / 92 80 1266 441-5 D-DB
20068864-42	2008	ECR	Euro Cargo Rail, Paris Registered 09/10 hire to DB-Schenker, Germany 08/10 hired to Mitteldeutsche Eisenbahn, Germany 12/13 sold to DB-Schenker, Germany Hired to Mitteldeutsche Eisenbahn, Germany 03/16 renumbered	77042 92 87 0077 042-5 F-ECR 247 042-5 / 92 80 1266 442-3 D-DB 247 042-5 / 92 80 1266 442-3 D-DB 247 042-5 / 92 80 1266 442-3 D-DB 247 042-5 / 92 80 1266 442-3 D-DB 266 442-3 / 92 80 1266 442-3 D-DB
20068864-043	2008	ECR	Euro Cargo Rail, Paris Registered 09/10 hire to DB-Schenker, Germany 12/13 sold to DB-Cargo, Germany	77043 92 87 0077 043-3 F-ECR 247 043-3 / 92 80 1266 443-1 D-DB 247 043-3 / 92 80 1266 443-1 D-DB
20068864-044	2008	ECR	Euro Cargo Rail, Paris Registered 09/10 hire to DB-Schenker, Germany 12/13 sold to DB-Cargo, Germany	77044 92 87 0077 044-1 F-ECR 247 044-3 / 92 80 1266 444-9 D-DB 247 044-3 / 92 80 1266 444-9 D-DB
20068864-045	2008	ECR	Euro Cargo Rail, Paris Registered 09/10 hire to DB-Schenker, Germany 12/13 sold to DB-Schenker, Germany	77045 92 87 0077 045-8 F-ECR 247 045-8 / 92 80 1266 445-6 D-DB 247 045-8 / 92 80 1266 445-6 D-DB
20068864-046	2009	ECR	Euro Cargo Rail, Paris Registered 09/10 hire to DB-Schenker, Germany 12/13 sold to DB-Cargo, Germany	77046 92 87 0077 046-6 F-ECR 247 046-6 / 92 80 1266 446-4 D-DB 247 046-6 / 92 80 1266 446-4 D-DB
20068864-047	2009	ECR	Euro Cargo Rail, Paris Registered 09/10 hire to DB-Schenker, Germany 12/13 sold to DB-Schenker, Germany	77047 92 87 0077 047-4 F-ECR 247 047-4 / 92 80 1266 447-2 D-DB 247 047-4 / 92 80 1266 447-2 D-DB
20068864-048	2009	ECR	Euro Cargo Rail, Paris Registered 09/10 hire to DB-Schenker, Germany 12/13 sold to DB-Cargo, Germany	77048 92 87 0077 048-2 F-ECR 247 048-2 / 92 80 1266 448-0 D-DB 247 048-2 / 92 80 1266 448-0 D-DB
20068864-049	2009	ECR	Euro Cargo Rail, Paris Registered 09/10 hire to DB-Schenker, Germany 12/13 sold to DB-Cargo, Germany	77049 92 87 0077 049-0 F-ECR 247 049-0 / 92 80 1266 449-8 D-DB 247 049-0 / 92 80 1266 449-8 D-DB
20068864-050	2009	ECR	Euro Cargo Rail, Paris Registered	77050 92 87 0077 050-8 F-ECR

			09/10 hire to DB-Schenker, Germany	247 050-8 / 92 80 1266 450-6 D-DB
			12/13 sold to DB-Cargo, Germany	247 050-8 / 92 80 1266 450-6 D-DB
20068864-051	2009	ECR	Euro Cargo Rail, Paris	77051
			Registered	92 87 0077 051-6 F-ECR
			09/10 hire to DB-Schenker, Germany	247 051-6 / 92 80 1266 451-4 D-DB
			12/13 sold to DB-Cargo, Germany 12/13	247 051-6 / 92 80 1266 451-4 D-DB
20068864-052	2009	ECR	Euro Cargo Rail, Paris	77052
			Registered	92 87 0077 052-4 F-ECR
			09/10 hire to DB-Schenker, Germany	247 052-4 / 92 80 1266 452-2 D-DB
			09/16 sold to DB-Cargo, Germany	247 052-4 / 92 80 1266 452-2 D-DB
20068864-053	2009	ECR	Euro Cargo Rail, Paris	77053
			Registered	92 87 0077 053-2 F-ECR
			09/10 hire to DB-Schenker, Germany	247 053-2 / 92 80 1266 453-0 D-DB
			12/13 sold to DB-Cargo, Germany	247 053-2 / 92 80 1266 453-0 D-DB
20068864-054	2009	ECR	Euro Cargo Rail, Paris	77054
			Registered	92 87 0077 054-0 F-ECR
			09/10 hire to DB-Schenker, Germany	247 054-0 / 92 80 1266 454-8 D-DB
			12/13 sold to DB-Cargo, Germany	247 054-0 / 92 80 1266 454-8 D-DB
20068864-055	2009	ECR	Euro Cargo Rail, Paris	77055
			Registered	92 87 0077 055-5 F-ECR
			09/10 hire to DB-Schenker, Germany	247 055-7 / 92 80 1266 455-5 D-DB
			12/13 sold to DB-Cargo, Germany	247 055-7 / 92 80 1266 455-5 D-DB
20068864-056	2009	ECR	Euro Cargo Rail, Paris	77056
			Registered	92 87 0077 056-5 F-ECR
			09/10 hire to DB-Schenker, Germany	247 056-5 / 92 80 1266 456-3 D-DB
			12/13 sold to DB-Cargo, Germany	247 056-5 / 92 80 1266 456-3 D-DB
20068864-057	2009	ECR	Euro Cargo Rail, Paris	77057
			Registered	92 87 0077 057-3 F-ECR
			07/10 hire to RBH Logistics, Germany	247 057-3 / 92 80 1266 457-1 D-DB
			02/11 hire to DB-Schenker, Germany	247 057-3 / 92 80 1266 457-1 D-DB
			03/16 sold to DB-Cargo, Germany	247 057-3 / 92 80 1266 457-1 D-DB
20068864-058	2009	ECR	Euro Cargo Rail, Paris	77058
			Registered	92 87 0077 058-1 F-ECR
			09/10 hire to DB-Schenker, Germany	247 058-1 / 92 80 1266 458-9 D-DB
			12/16 sold to DB-Cargo, Germany	247 058-1 / 92 80 1266 458-9 D-DB
20068864-059	2009	ECR	Euro Cargo Rail, Paris	77059
			Registered	92 87 0077 059-9 F-ECR
			09/10 hire to DB-Schenker, Germany	247 059-9 / 92 80 1266 459-7 D-DB
			03/16 sold to DB-Cargo, Germany	247 059-5 / 92 80 1266 459-7 D-DB
20068864-060	2009	ECR	Euro Cargo Rail, Paris	77060
			Registered	92 87 0077 060-7 F-ECR
			09/10 hire to DB-Schenker, Germany	247 060-7 / 92 80 1266 460-5 D-DB
			12/13 sold to DB-Cargo, Germany	247 060-7 / 92 80 1266 460-5 D-DB
20078920-001	2008	Crossrail	Built for Crossrail	DE6310
			To Akiem, France	77504
			Registered	92 87 0077 504-4 F AKIEM
20078920-002	2008	Crossrail	Built for Crossrail	DE6311
			To Akiem, France	77505
			Registered	92 87 0077 505-1 F AKIEM
20078920-003	2008	Crossrail	Built for Crossrail	DE6312
			To Akiem, France	77506
			Registered	92 87 0077 506-9 F AKIEM
20078920-004	2008	Crossrail	Built for Crossrail	DE6313
			To Akiem, France	77507
			Registered	92 87 0077 507-7 F AKIEM
20078941-001	2009	Veolia Cargo	Registered	77501 / 92 87 0077 501-0 F-VC
			Stored	
			06/11 to Akiem, France	77501 / 92 77 0077501-0 F-AKIEM
20078941-002	2009	Veolia Cargo	Registered	77502 / 92 87 0077 502-8 F-VC
			Stored	
			06/11 to Akiem, France	77502 / 92 77 0077502-8 F-AKIEM
20078941-003	2009	Veolia Cargo	Registered	77503 / 92 87 0077 503-6 F-VC
			Stored	
			06/11 to Akiem, France	77503 / 92 77 0077503-6 F-AKIEM
20078963-001	2009	ENR	Delivered to Egyptian National Railways	2124
20078963-002	2009	ENR	Delivered to Egyptian National Railways	2125
20078963-003	2009	ENR	Delivered to Egyptian National Railways	2126
20078963-004	2009	ENR	Delivered to Egyptian National Railways	2127
20078963-005	2009	ENR	Delivered to Egyptian National Railways	2128
20078963-006	2009	ENR	Delivered to Egyptian National Railways	2129
20078963-007	2009	ENR	Delivered to Egyptian National Railways	2130
20078963-008	2009	ENR	Delivered to Egyptian National Railways	2131
20078963-009	2009	ENR	Delivered to Egyptian National Railways	2132
20078963-010	2009	ENR	Delivered to Egyptian National Railways	2133
20078963-011	2009	ENR	Delivered to Egyptian National Railways	2134
20078963-012	2009	ENR	Delivered to Egyptian National Railways	2135
20078963-013	2009	ENR	Delivered to Egyptian National Railways	2136
20078963-014	2009	ENR	Delivered to Egyptian National Railways	2137
20078963-015	2009	ENR	Delivered to Egyptian National Railways	2138
20078963-016	2009	ENR	Delivered to Egyptian National Railways	2139
20078963-017	2009	ENR	Delivered to Egyptian National Railways	2140
20078963-018	2009	ENR	Delivered to Egyptian National Railways	2141
20078963-019	2009	ENR	Delivered to Egyptian National Railways	2142
20078963-020	2009	ENR	Delivered to Egyptian National Railways	2143
20078963-021	2009	ENR	Delivered to Egyptian National Railways	2144
20078963-022	2009	ENR	Delivered to Egyptian National Railways	2145
20078963-023	2009	ENR	Delivered to Egyptian National Railways	2146

20078963-024	2009	ENR	Delivered to Egyptian National Railways	2147
20078963-025	2009	ENR	Delivered to Egyptian National Railways	2148
20078963-026	2009	ENR	Delivered to Egyptian National Railways	2149
20078963-027	2009	ENR	Delivered to Egyptian National Railways	2150
20078963-028	2009	ENR	Delivered to Egyptian National Railways	2151
20078963-029	2009	ENR	Delivered to Egyptian National Railways	2152
20078963-030	2009	ENR	Delivered to Egyptian National Railways	2153
20078963-031	2009	ENR	Delivered to Egyptian National Railways	2154
20078963-032	2009	ENR	Delivered to Egyptian National Railways	2155
20078963-033	2009	ENR	Delivered to Egyptian National Railways	2156
20078963-034	2009	ENR	Delivered to Egyptian National Railways	2157
20078963-035	2009	ENR	Delivered to Egyptian National Railways	2158
20078963-036	2009	ENR	Delivered to Egyptian National Railways	2159
20078963-037	2009	ENR	Delivered to Egyptian National Railways	2160
20078963-038	2009	ENR	Delivered to Egyptian National Railways	2161
20078963-039	2009	ENR	Delivered to Egyptian National Railways	2162
20078963-040	2009	ENR	Delivered to Egyptian National Railways	2163
20088096-001	2009	ENR	Delivered to Egyptian National Railways	2164 (AAST2) (originally driver trainer)
20078968-001	2008	Fortis Lease	Registered 09/11 lease to Crossrail, Belgium	92 80 1266 280-7 D XRAIL named *Griet* DE6310
20078968-002	2008	Fortis Lease	Registered 09/11 lease to Crossrail, Belgium	92 80 1266 281-5 D XRAIL named *Hana* DE6311
20078968-003	2008	Fortis Lease	Registered 09/11 lease to Crossrail, Belgium	92 80 1266 282-3 D XRAIL named *Alix* DE6312
20078968-004	2008	Fortis Lease	Registered Stored at Jan de Rijk forwarding 2011-2012 -/12 sold to Beacon Rail -/12 Hire to GB Railfreight as	92 80 1266 283-1 D XRAIL Planned as DE6313 66748
20078968-005	2008	Fortis Lease	Registered 09/11 lease to Crossrail, Belgium	92 80 1266 284-9 D XRAIL named *Hanna* DE6314
20078968-006	2008	Fortis Lease	Registered Stored at Jan de Rijk forwarding 2011-2012 -/12 sold to Beacon Rail -/12 Hire to GB Railfreight as	92 80 1266 285-6 D XRAIL Planned as DE6315 66749
20078968-007	2008	Fortis Lease	Registered Stored at Jan de Rijk forwarding 2011-2012 -/12 sold to Beacon Rail -/12 Hire to GB Railfreight as	92 80 1266 286-4 D XRAIL Planned as DE6316 66747
20088076-001	2009		Stored 2009-2011, NedTrain, Rotterdam 06/11 sold to Beacon Rail Registered 06/11 hire to HHPI, Germany	92 80 1266 461-3 92 80 1266 461-3 D-HHPI 29001 named *Hans Cermak*
20088076-002	2009		Stored 2009-2011, NedTrain, Rotterdam 06/11 sold to Société d'Exploitation du Transgabonais, (SETRAG) Libreville, Gabon	 CC401
20088076-003	2009		Stored 2009-2011, NedTrain, Rotterdam 06/11 sold to Société d'Exploitation du Transgabonais, (SETRAG) Libreville, Gabon	 CC402
20088076-004	2009		Stored 2009-2011, NedTrain, Rotterdam 06/11 sold to Beacon Rail Registered 06/11 hire to HHPI, Germany	92 80 1266 464-7 92 80 1266 464-7 D-HHPI 29002 named *Robert J. G. Savage*
20108460-001	2011		Société d'Exploitation du Transgabonais (SETRAG), Libreville, Gabon	 CC403
20108460-002	2011		Société d'Exploitation du Transgabonais (SETRAG), Libreville, Gabon	 CC404
20108460-003	2011		Société d'Exploitation du Transgabonais (SETRAG), Libreville, Gabon	 CC405
20108460-004	2011		Société d'Exploitation du Transgabonais (SETRAG), Libreville, Gabon	 CC406

Right: *Mitsui Rail Capital Europe No. MRCE 653-08, built as works number 20048653-008, painted in all-over MRCE black livery off-set by operator Rail4Chem branding passes Lage Zwaluwe station in Holland on 14 June 2007 powering a short containerised freight. This loco is one of the batch of 'five door' locos indicating that the walkway space in the between cab area has been taken up by improved exhaust emissions equipment. This loco operated for a number of different companies and is now owned by Beacon Rail it is registered as No. 92 80 1266 118-9 and when seen in late 2018 was carrying the identity 266 118-9.* **CJM**

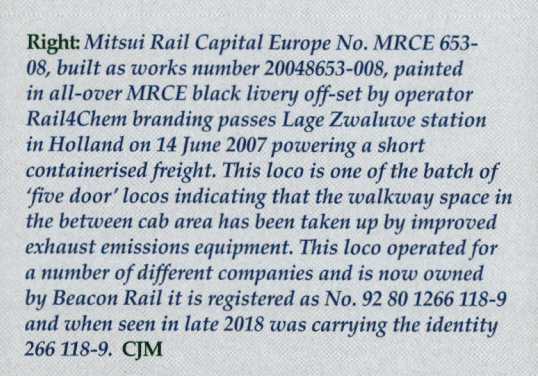

Above: *The 60 Euro Cargo Rail (ECR) 770xx series locos were constructed to order 20068864 in 2008-2009. On 22 February 2009, No. 92 87 0077044-1 is seen being shunted over Oxford Road at Diesel Division, London, Canada awaiting collection for export.* **CJM**

Left: *After using Class 59 No. 59003 in Germany, Heavy Haul Power International ordered its own fleet of Euro 66s. Painted in the red and blue of the short lived Yeoman-DB operation, HHPI No. 29003 is seen on the EMD test track on 9 March 2002. Built as works No. 20008254-013 this loco was leased by GM/GMAC Leasing. Once in Germany the loco was named Rhoda Painter.* **CJM**

Below: *The export trains, transferring new Class 66s to the port for export was always impressive, with two small GEXR short line locos hauling 12-16 locos. On 22 February 2009, GEXR4019 and RLK2211 pass St Marys, Ontario, en route from Diesel Division to Toronto, formed of Egyptian Nos. 2129, 2141, 2130, 2124, 2125, 2133, 2128, 2136, 2135, 2131, 2127, 2132, 2126, 2140, 2139, and ECR No. 77044.* **CJM**

Above: *Originally built for Euro Rail shuttle as ERS 6602 (20008254-010) this loco later went to CB Rail and is part of the Beacon Rail portfolio. It is currently registered as 92 88 -266003-7 and in use with Captrain. It is seen stabled in Antwerpen Noord Yard on the 12 August 2018.* **Howard Lewsey**

Right: *Painted in Heavy Haul Power International dark blue livery, HHPI 29002 passes Bremen Hbf with a coal train on 6 September 2016. Built to order 20008254-004 this loco originally worked for HHPI, it was then owned by CB Rail Leasing, Ascendos Rail and currently with Beacon Rail. It has worked for various operators but is currently back with HHPI.* **Howard Lewsey**

77501, how it is today, see the image at the bottom of page 111. 77501 is seen in the yard at Haubourdin, on the outskirts of Lille on 12 November 2017. This loco owned by Akiam Rail is operated by SNCF subsidiary Voies Ferrées Locales et Industrielles (VFLI). **Howard Lewsey**

Above: *Painted in its as built all-over grey livery, works No. 20038561-005 was a spot hire loco by GM and originally carried the identity EM5. It was later sold to Mitsui Rail Capital who positioned it with many different operators. It was registered as 92 80 1266 042-1. It is currently owned by Beacon Rail and operated by Rotterdam Rail Feeding. On 29 September 2016 it is seen Hamburg Harburg with a self discharge train.*
Howard Lewsey

Left Middle: *Built as works No. 2004853-003 this loco was originally with Mitsui Rail Capital Europe and had operated with a number of companies. It was sold to Beacon Rail Leasing in June 2015. It is registered as 92 80 1266-113-0 and is currently with Lineas Group. It is seen at Spontin ready to work a train to Ciney. The loco displays the livery of HSL Belgium and was photographed on 11 August 2018.* **Howard Lewsey**

Left Below: *Painted in the stunning colours of the Genesee & Wyoming (G&Y) North American short line operator, No. 561-03 is seen at Bernburg Works on 3 December 2018. This loco is owned by Beacon Rail and leased to Rotterdam Rail Feeding and in late 2018 went to Poland to operate for G&Y subsidiary Freightliner Poland. This loco was built to works number 20038561-003 and was a GM hire loco, originally identified as EM3, it later went to Mitsui Rail Capital Europe and registered as 92 80 1266 040-5.* **Howard Lewsey**

126   *Traction Transition - GM/EMD power in the UK and Ireland*

Above: *Another loco which carries a running number derived from its original works number is 513-10, which is works number 20038513-10. This loco was introduced as a GM spot-hire machine and soon sold to Mitsui Rail Capitol, Europe. Registered as 92 80 1266 037-1 the loco operated for many different rail businesses. It was later sold to Beacon Rail and from late in 2017 has been operated by Lineas Group in Belgium. No. 513-10 stands in Antwerpen Noord Yard on 22 August 2017.* **Howard Lewsey**

Below: *How the Euro 66 story all began, The very first Euro 66 built to works No. 998101-01, for Häfen und Güterverkehr Köln (HGK). The loco was originally owned by GM/Opal Lasing and eventually sold to HGK. It was numbered 9902 and subsequently DE61. It was given euro registration 92 80 1266 061-1 and in June 2012 it was sold to RheinCargo. Fresh from overhaul, DE61 stands outside its home depot of Brühl Vochem on 4 February 2018.* **Howard Lewsey**

Above: *Originally funded by HSBC Rail this loco 20008212-002 is one of a pair built for Trafikaktiebolaget Grängesbergs-Oxelösunds Järnväg (TGOJ) in Sweden. It was later transferred to Beacon Rail ownership and registered as 92 74 0066 714-7 and most recently has been operated by Captrain in Denmark. The loco carrying mid blue and the identity T66K714 is seen stabled at Padborg on the German/Danish border on 27 May 2018. This loco is set to return to the UK in mid 2019 and operate as No. 66791 with GB Railfreight. Note the front standback area, wing mirror design and large snowploughs.*
Howard Lewsey

Below: *Another loco with front end standback areas is No. T66402. On 11 September 2015 the loco waits for the signal to head into Borlänge central station in Sweden. This loco was originally funded by HSBC Rail as works number 20018352-002 and was delivered to CargoNet in Norway. In March 2009 it was sold to Beacon Rail. Its registration is 92 76 0309 402-4 with CargoNet. It later operated under the Rush-Rail banner and from December 2016 with Hector Rail, Sweden.*
Howard Lewsey

Above: *Euro 66 line up, captured at Montzen near Aachen on 1 October 2017 we see (from left to right) HSL No. 653-07, RailTraxx No. 266 118, Crossrail No. PB03 and Beacon Rail No. PB14, this loco ventured to the UK at ElectroMotive, Longport in early 2019 for overhaul.*
Howard Lewsey

Right: *Built as Works No. 20078920-002 in 2008 for CrossRail, this loco is now owned by Akiem. It is registered as 92 87 0077 505-1, and also carries the CrossRail No. DE6311. It is seen stabled in Antwerpen Noord Yard on 12 August 2018.*
Howard Lewsey

Below: *Displaying a stunning gold HSL livery No. 653-07 is seen stabled in Montzen on 1 October 2017. Built to works No. 20048653-007 for Mitsui Rail Capitol this loco was later registered as 92 80 1266 117-1 and is now on the Beacon Rail hire roster.* **Howard Lewsey**

Traction Transition - GM/EMD power in the UK and Ireland

Left Above: *Euro Cargo Rail No. 77010 shares depot space at Saarbrücken on the French/German border on 22 November 2018, along side UK Class 66 No. 66071 now working for ECR in France. The depot at Saarbrücken carries out repairs to all types of Class 66.* **Howard Lewsey**

Left Middle: *The DB UK Class 66s exported to Poland have received major modification and none are likely to return to the UK. Sporting revised light clusters and extra roof equipment, No. 66227 is seen stabled in Ruda Sláska yard near Katowice, Poland on the 7 February 2016.* **Howard Lewsey**

Below: *The 41 Class 66 design locos built for Egyptian National Railways (ENR) to order number 20078963, incorporated a front end based of that of the Class 59/0s, with a standard twin headlight group in the middle of the front end. Draw gear and buffing was slightly different, with a loco-train jumper connection is located on the nose end on the drivers side. The locos are fitted with cab end window bars for added safety of the cab area against impact. The locos are finished in two-tone blue and carry their running numbers in both Egyptian and standard form. On 5 March 2019, No. 2134 is seen at Qalyub station with a local service from Cairo Ramses. 40 locos of the fleet were built for normal service, with the last, No. 2164, built to order 20088096 constructed as a training locomotive.* **Howard Lewsey**

130 Traction Transition - GM/EMD power in the UK and Ireland